THE
VIETNAM
WAR

*In American Stories,
Songs, and Poems*

BOOKS BY H. BRUCE FRANKLIN

The Wake of the Gods: Melville's Mythology

Future Perfect: American Science Fiction of the 19th Century

Who Should Run the Universities (with John A. Howard)

From the Movement: Toward Revolution

Herman Melville's Mardi (edition)

Herman Melville's The Confidence Man (edition)

Back Where You Came From

The Scarlet Letter *and Hawthorne's Critical Writings* (edition)

The Essential Stalin (edition)

Prison Literature in America: The Victim as Criminal and Artist

Countdown to Midnight

American Prisoners and Ex-Prisoners: An Annotated Bibliography

Robert A. Heinlein: America as Science Fiction

Vietnam and America: A Documented History (with Marvin Gettleman, Jane Franklin, and Marilyn Young)

War Stars: The Superweapon and the American Imagination

M.I.A. Or Mythmaking in America

THE
VIETNAM
WAR

In American Stories, Songs, and Poems

Edited by H. Bruce Franklin

BEDFORD BOOKS *of* **ST. MARTIN'S PRESS**   **BOSTON**

For Jane

For Bedford Books
President and Publisher: Charles H. Christensen
General Manager and Associate Publisher: Joan E. Feinberg
Managing Editor: Elizabeth M. Schaaf
Developmental Editor: Stephen A. Scipione
Editorial Assistant: Mark Reimold
Production Editor: John Amburg
Production Assistant: Karen S. Baart
Copyeditor: Nancy Bell Scott
Text Design: John Amburg
Cover Design: Hannus Design Associates

Library of Congress Catalog Card Number: 95-76723

Manufactured in the United States of America.

0   9   8   7   6
f   e   d   c   b   a

For information, write: St. Martin's Press, Inc.
175 Fifth Avenue, New York, NY 10010

Editorial Offices: Bedford Books *of* St. Martin's Press
75 Arlington Street, Boston, MA 02116

ISBN: 0–312–11552–0

Acknowledgments
    Appleman, Philip, "Peace with Honor." Copyright © 1976 by Philip Appleman. From Philip Appleman, *Open Doorways* (W. W. Norton, 1976). Reprinted by permission of the author.

    Acknowledgments and copyrights are continued at the back of the book on pages 340–43, which constitute an extension of the copyright page. It is a violation of the law to reproduce these selections by any means whatsoever without the written permission of the copyright holder.

Preface

This book is based on the belief that knowing the American stories, songs, and poems generated by the Vietnam War is essential for comprehending American history, literature, and culture since the early 1960s. With that assumption central, this volume has been designed not only for history and literature courses but also for anyone interested in recent American historical and cultural experience. Because I also believe that the writing induced by the war includes some of the finest and most distinctive achievements of contemporary American literature, I have tried to select stories and poems that exemplify the qualities and range of this writing from the 1960s through the mid-1990s.

The short stories and poems were created by forty-two authors; most of these men and women engaged directly with the war as soldiers, antiwar activists, nurses, journalists, and relief workers. Among the awards received by these authors are the Pulitzer Prize for fiction, the Pulitzer Prize for poetry, the National Book Award for fiction, two of the highest prizes presented by the Academy of American Poets, the O'Henry Award for short fiction, several Pushcart prizes for fiction and poetry, and the Hugo, Nebula, and World Fantasy top fiction awards.

This anthology includes a total of eighty-four stories, songs, and poems. The sixteen stories are grouped by themes that provide contexts for thinking about the war and American culture. The five songs are arranged chronologically, each representing a major response in popular culture from the wartime years to the present. The sixty-three poems are presented alphabetically by author, an arrangement emphasizing the relation between poetry and individual experience.

The general introduction explores the history of this literature, and relates it to other genres, such as the novel, drama, film, and autobiography. Introductions to each genre and to each group of stories offer both cultural history and interpretation. The biographical headnote introducing each author provides an essential link between the writer's experience and the literature. The chronology and glossary serve to make the complexities of Vietnamese history and the obscurity of the war's terminology clearer and more accessible. For those wishing to explore this literature further, I have included an annotated bibliography of relevant bibliographies, anthologies, histories, and criticism.

I am grateful to a number of people at Bedford Books, especially Chuck Christensen for zealously encouraging and guiding this project, to Steve Scipione for his wonderful help in shaping the book, to John Amburg, Karen Baart, and Nancy Bell Scott for exemplary editing, to Donna Dennison for extra labors on cover design, and to Joan Feinberg and Elizabeth Schaaf for advice. Bill Ehrhart, Virginia Creedon, and Lynda Van Devanter all generously helped secure permissions. I am deeply indebted to the following scholars for many invaluable suggestions and critiques: Philip Beidler, Michael Bibby, David Buck, Michael Ferber, Vince Gotera, John Hellmann, David Hunt, Philip Jason, Susan Jeffords, Blake McNulty, John Carlos Rowe, Lorrie Smith, David Willson, and Marilyn Young.

As always, I owe the most to Jane Morgan Franklin, who has given more to this book than can possibly be acknowledged.

Contents

Preface *v*

Introduction *1*

STORIES _____ 9

Inside the War 14

Michael Paul McCusker *The Old Man* 16

Larry Rottmann *Thi Bong Dzu* 18

David Huddle *The Interrogation of the Prisoner Bung by Mister Hawkins and Sergeant Tree* 25

George Davis   *Ben*   34

Tom Mayer   *Kafka for President*   41

Tim O'Brien   *The Man I Killed*   64

Against the War   70

Ward Just   *The Congressman Who Loved*
                Flaubert   76

Mary Hazzard   *From* Idle and Disorderly Persons   96

Wayne Karlin   *Moratorium*   107

The Vietnam War and American
Science Fiction   116

Kate Wilhelm   *The Village*   123

Karen Joy Fowler   *The Lake Was Full of Artificial*
                       Things   133

Aftermaths   146

Ronald Anthony Cross   *The Heavenly Blue*
                           Answer   148

Stephanie Vaughn   *Kid MacArthur*   159

Lewis Shiner   *The War at Home*   178

Robert Olen Butler   *A Good Scent from a Strange*
                         Mountain   181

Wayne Karlin   *The Last VC*   194

SONGS _____ 201

Country Joe McDonald   *I-Feel-Like-I'm-Fixin'-to-*
                       Die Rag   209
Barry Sadler with Robin Moore   *The Ballad of the*
                                Green Berets   211
Crosby, Stills, Nash and Young/Neil Young   *Ohio*   213
Creedence Clearwater Revival/John Fogerty   *Fortunate*
                                            Son   215
Bruce Springsteen   *Born in the U.S.A.*   217

POEMS _____ 219

Larry Rottmann   *A Porter on the Trail*   223
Philip Appleman   *Peace with Honor*   225
John Balaban   *After Our War*   228
               Along the Mekong   229
               In Celebration of Spring   231
               News Update   232
               For Mrs. Cam, Whose Name Means
               "Printed Silk"   233
               Mau Than   234
Jan Barry   *In the Footsteps of Genghis Khan*   237
            Thap Ba   238
Lady Borton   *A Boom, A Billow*   240
Ron Carter   *Vietnam Dream*   242

Horace Coleman *OK Corral East / Brothers in the
                Nam*   243

                *The Adrenaline Junkie and
                "The Daily Emergency"*   244

Frank A. Cross, Jr. *Gliding Baskets*   247

                Rice Will Grow Again   248

W. D. Ehrhart *Guerrilla War*   250

                Making the Children Behave   251

                *To Those Who Have Gone Home
                Tired*   251

                The Invasion of Grenada   252

                For Mrs. Na   253

                Guns   253

Joan A. Furey *Camouflage*   255

Sharon Grant *The Best Act in Pleiku, No One Under
                18 Admitted*   257

Steve Hassett *And What Would You Do, Ma*   258

                Christmas   258

June Jordan *To My Sister, Ethel Ennis, Who Sang
                "The Star-Spangled Banner" at
                the Second Inauguration of Richard
                Milhous Nixon, January 20, 1973*   260

Penny Kettlewell *The Coffee Room Soldier*   263

Yusef Komunyakaa *Prisoners*   264

                The Dead at Quang Tri   266

Denise Levertov *From* Staying Alive: *Prologue:
                An Interim (i & ii)*   267

                The Pilots   268

                Fragrance of Life, Odor of Death   270

	A Poem at Christmas, 1972, during the Terror-Bombing of North Vietnam	270
Gerald McCarthy	*From* War Story	272
	Finding the Way Back	274
	The Sound of Guns	275
Marilyn M. McMahon	*In This Land*	277
	Wounds of War	279
	July 20, 1969 . . . an Introduction in 3 Voices	281
	Dying with Grace	283
	Confession	285
	Knowing	287
Janice Mirikitani	*Loving from Vietnam to Zimbabwe*	290
Richard M. Mishler	*Ceremony*	294
Basil T. Paquet	*Morning—A Death*	296
Pedro Pietri	*Para la Madre de Angel Luna*	298
Stan Platke	*Bury the Body, Bury the Thought*	301
Dale Ritterbusch	*Search and Destroy*	302
	At the Crash Site of a B-52: January 1994	303
Larry Rottmann	*APO 96225*	305
	For Cissy Shellabarger, R.N., Wherever You Are	306
	What Kind of War?	306
	Thanks, Guys	307
	The Bones of an American M.I.A. Speak to the Members of the Joint Casualty Resolution Team	308

Luis Omar Salinas   *Death in Vietnam*   310

Lynda Van Devanter   *TV Wars—First Blood Part II*   311
                                  For Molly   311

Bruce Weigl   *Surrounding Blues on the Way Down*   313
                        Burning Shit at An Khe   314
                        Him, on the Bicycle   316
                        Song of Napalm   317
                        Snowy Egret   318
                        Dialectical Materialism   319

Glossary   321

**Bibliographies and Secondary Sources on Vietnam War
Literature**   324

Chronology   328

THE VIETNAM WAR

In American Stories, Songs, and Poems

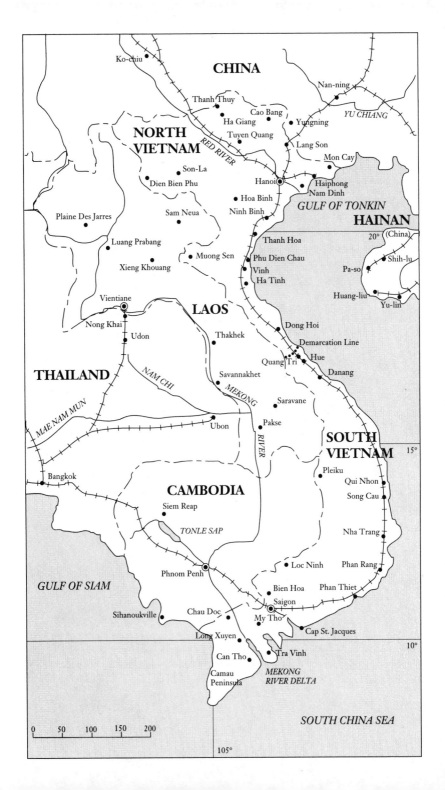

Introduction

Vietnam. Just mention the word in a group of Americans and feel the emotional temperature rise. For what is called "the Vietnam War" is one of the most controversial single events in the history of the United States. Is there any aspect of the conflict that is not itself the subject of conflict?

Discord still seethes about whether it was a "noble cause" (the words of President Ronald Reagan), a genocidal exercise in imperialism (the view of its most vehement opponents), or just a "quagmire" of "mistakes" (the centrist position). One's stance on such fundamental issues determines and is determined by one's answers to such seemingly simple questions as these: When did the Vietnam War begin? Who were the opposing sides? When did it end? Who won? Why?

Even calling it "the Vietnam War" is questionable. The war was fought also in Laos and Cambodia, with devastating consequences for those nations and effects that still reverberate in American politics and culture. The so-called "secret wars" in Laos and Cambodia are a basis for much ongoing public distrust of Washington, focused sharply by the POW/MIA (prisoner-of-war/missing-in-action) lobby, which draws its main arguments from the fate of fliers missing in Laos, not Vietnam. American popular culture still memorializes the Ohio students killed while protesting the 1970 U.S. invasion of Cambodia, as discussed in relation to the song "Ohio" here anthologized. "The Indochina War," although a more accurate term, is not quite inclusive enough. For example, George Davis, an author included in this volume, is a combat veteran who flew all his missions from one of the five U.S. Air Force bases in Thailand, a nation not included in "Indochina" (which itself is a European colonial category).

Many Americans compound these problematics by calling the war simply "Vietnam," as though that nation itself were merely an event in American history. Yet this usage also suggests that "Vietnam" has attained multifaceted symbolic meaning for America. After all, we don't refer to the Mexican-American War as "Mexico," the war with Spain as "Spain," or the War of 1812 as "England."

Whatever "Vietnam" or "the Vietnam War" does mean for America is revealed most directly and explicitly by the vast and astonishing body of literature, film, and music generated by the war and its aftermath. The immense output of Vietnam War literature shows no signs of dwindling, and the recognition of its value has been steadily increasing. The authors represented in this volume have won scores of prestigious awards for Vietnam-related works, including the 1974 Prize from the Academy of American Poets, the 1979 National Book Award for fiction, the 1979 Prize from the Academy of American Poets, the 1986 O. Henry Award for short fiction, the 1993 Pulitzer Prize for fiction, and the 1994 Pulitzer Prize for poetry.

Both the production and recognition of this literature surely owe much to the unresolved and conflicted perceptions of the war, its lessons, and its effects. American literature about the Vietnam War is not a luxury but a necessity, something we vitally need for the present and future. As readers of this volume will see, one of the distinguishing features of this literature is its intense purposefulness, flowing from its sense of discovery, usually through painful experience, of insights far too valuable to be lost or forgotten.

As a literature of experience, discovery, insight, and purpose, these stories, songs, and poems run counter to some high fashions in contemporary literary theory and practice. One of the most knowledgeable critics of Vietnam literature, Philip Beidler (himself a Vietnam veteran), has argued that its "impassioned intensity" and "profound experiential authority" suggest how the nation's literature could escape from the barren desert of texts that are mainly about themselves and that are largely unreadable except by a literary coterie.[1] Indeed, Vietnam War literature directly challenges the notion that "great" literature is too complex and ambiguous either to carry any social message or to be accessible to an audience of common people.

The Vietnam War actually had a major impact on the teaching and criticism of literature years before most of the works in this volume were published. Issues related to the war plunged the 1968 convention of the Modern Language Association (MLA)—the world's largest organization of teachers of literature and language—into a series of heated meetings, demonstrations, and confrontations, leading to a sit-in by hundreds of professors while hundreds of New York City riot police waited for the association's president to give them the signal to attack. By the time the convention was over, the MLA had officially condemned the Vietnam War and elected to succeed to its presidency the antiwar leader whose arrest had sparked the demonstration.

In the wake of the convention, fierce debates erupted throughout the MLA and the profession, focusing more and more on the relations among politics, literature, and teaching. Soon the lines were clearly drawn for battles that were to rage throughout the 1970s, 1980s, and 1990s about the literary "canon," the criteria used to define "great" literature, the ethnic and gender composition of literature departments, multiculturalism, and the relations between "high" and "mass" culture and between critical theory and social power. These events profoundly changed my own views of literature, liberating them from the elitist college training I had received in the 1950s and leading me eventually into conceptualizing and creating the volume that you are reading. In fact, the critical criteria used in selecting the works in this collection are themselves products of the Vietnam War.

The war's effects on the academic conceptualization and teaching of literature are far less conspicuous than its effects on popular culture. Virtually no aspect of social life—including styles of dress and language, politics and race relations, gender and generational relationships, images of the past and future—was left unchanged. Many works in this collection explore these metamorphoses. It is of course impossible to determine how directly or how much the war contributed to all the differences between "pre-Vietnam" and "post-Vietnam" American culture. However, two sections of this book are devoted to realms of popular culture quite directly and dramatically transformed by the war: science fiction and popular music. Each genre influences and is influenced by the wider culture, and each became the site of major battles in the cultural war over the war.

Then there are movies. The Vietnam War plays an overt role in more than one hundred and fifty Hollywood feature films, and some of these films today exert an overwhelming influence on how Americans, especially young Americans, imagine the war.

Until U.S. combat officially ceased in 1973, almost every American feature film about Vietnam promulgated images boosting U.S. intervention. During the French Indochina war, Hollywood portrayed Vietnam mainly as an exotic locale for exciting adventures, as in *Rogue's Regiment* (1948), *Saigon* (1948), and *A Yank in Indochina* (1952). In the early stages of covert U.S. military activity, the main function of feature movies was prowar propaganda. For example, *China Gate* (1957) opened with a voice-over proclaiming that the French had taught the Vietnamese "the love of God and love of fellow man," "advanced their way of living," and turned Vietnam into a "thriving nation" now threatened by Moscow's puppet, Ho Chi Minh; the movie then dramatized the adventures of heroic American soldiers of fortune fighting to repel the communists.[2]

In the critical 1958–1963 period, while Washington was moving from merely supporting its client regime in Saigon toward extensive military intervention, Hollywood turned for raw material to the two novels most central to the emerging cultural conflict. The 1958 film version of *The Quiet American* transformed Graham Greene's 1955 novel, which had excoriated American machinations in Vietnam, into a cartoonish polemic against communism and a celebration of idealistic American interventionism. Like the spectacular 1958 best-seller it brought to the screen, *The Ugly American* (1963) helped build the belief system to support the "winning hearts and minds" approach to Vietnam.

During the years of heaviest U.S. fighting in Vietnam—1964 through 1972—only about five American feature films even attempted to show this combat. Just one of these, the immensely popular *The Green Berets* (1968), was a major release; based on Robin Moore's 1965 best-seller and made with considerable help from the Pentagon, it starred John Wayne in a reimaging of the Vietnam War as a John Wayne western combined with elements of World War II combat movies. Accompanying the movie was the Barry Sadler hit "The Ballad of the Green Berets," included and discussed in the songs section of this book.

From the mid-1970s on, however, Hollywood has been zealously imaging and reimaging the Vietnam War and its aftermath. The Vietnam veteran soon became the central figure in these movies, usually shown as psychologically maimed, and often conducting bloody rampages, as in *Welcome Home, Soldier Boys* (1972), *Taxi Driver* (1976), *Black Sunday* (1977), *Rolling Thunder* (1977), and *First Blood* (1982). Vietnam veterans were action heroes in many films, ranging through the black militants in *Gordon's War* (1973), the counterculture protagonist of the three Billy Jack movies (1971, 1974, 1977), and Chuck Norris's right-wing martial artist in *Good Guys Wear Black* (1979) and *A Force of One* (1979). By the 1980s, the Vietnam vet-action hero formula had become a staple of such TV series as *Miami Vice* and *Magnum, P.I.*

In 1978, the cultural war over the war shaped at least five major movies: *Coming Home* and *The Deer Hunter*, which each dramatized Vietnam veterans as the main victims of the war but from very different points of view; *Who'll Stop the Rain*, an adaptation of *Dog Soldiers*, Robert Stone's savage vision of post-Vietnam America; and *The Boys in Company C* and *Go Tell the Spartans*, perhaps the first fairly realistic dramatizations of the war in feature films. (The fact that over a decade had to pass before Daniel Ford's 1967 novel *Incident at Muc Wa* was brought to the screen as *Go Tell the Spartans* reveals Hollywood's reluctance to display the realities of the war during the combat.) In 1979 came *Apocalypse Now*, which, as John Hellmann has argued, projected the Vietnam War as a bitter amalgam of the American hardboiled detective movie and Joseph Conrad's *Heart of Darkness*.[3]

In the early and mid-1980s, the story of the Vietnam War became more and more a tale of American victimization at the hands of the Vietnamese, as foreshadowed by *The Deer Hunter*. This theme became dominant in the form of the POW/MIA myth, expressed most influentially in the POW/MIA rescue movies, including *Uncommon Valor* (1983), *Missing in Action* (1984), *Rambo: First Blood Part II* (1985), *Missing in Action 2* (1985), *P.O.W.: The Escape* (1986), and *Operation Nam* (1987).

In the late 1980s and 1990s have come some of the bleakest visions of the war, including *Full Metal Jacket* (1987), *Casualties of War* (1989), and *Jacob's Ladder* (1990), which dramatizes post-Vietnam America as a surrealistic nightmare being experienced by an American soldier dying in Vietnam. Some films from these years erase the Vietnamese entirely from the story of the war. For example, *Forrest Gump*, given the Academy Award for the Best Picture of 1994, projects Vietnam as merely a shadowy jungle that shoots at American soldiers. But the focal cinematic work of this period is the trilogy directed by Vietnam veteran Oliver Stone: *Platoon* (1986), where surface realism is used to suggest mythic dimensions for the experience of the American grunts; *Born on the Fourth of July* (1989), an adaptation of the uncompromising autobiography by paralyzed antiwar veteran Ron Kovic; and *Heaven and Earth* (1993), one of the rare Hollywood attempts to look at the war from a Vietnamese point of view.

Many of the stories and poems collected here refer or allude to these Hollywood versions of the war and their effects. The history of written fiction about the war, in fact, is inextricably intertwined with movies, as will be seen in the introduction to this book's section on stories.

That section is organized thematically, because the stories and their introductions establish the main themes of the volume, while also providing context and background for the songs and poems. The songs are in chronological order, for they are representative of the evolution of the conflict over the war within popular music. Because a number of the poets have multiple selections, written over an extended period and dealing with varied themes, the poetry section is organized alphabetically by author. After each work, the date of first publication (in substantially its present form) or performance is noted in parentheses.

These stories, songs, and poems derive their meaning, their value, and their power from history and from the experience of individual human beings, including their authors, as part of this history. Therefore the biographical sketches of these authors need to be read as integral to their works.

In fact, the great bulk of American Vietnam War literature has consisted of autobiographical nonfiction—by combatants, journalists, nurses, antiwar activists, prisoners of war, family members, and other participants. None of these is included because their power does not come through effectively in excerpts, and because many of the most important memoirs are readily available in paperback editions. Furthermore, one underlying purpose of this volume is to display the kinds of "truth" and "reality" projected in literature of the fictive imagination.

Although I selected stories and poems based only on what seemed to me their literary excellence and value to contemporary readers, I ended up with a disproportionate number of works by Vietnam veterans in the strictest sense—that is, those who served in the U.S. military forces in Vietnam. Of the fifteen authors of short stories, seven are by this kind of Vietnam veteran. Two of the others were war correspondents, one of whom still carries grenade fragments in his body. Another is the mother of a Vietnam veteran. Of the twenty-seven poets, nineteen, including five nurses, are veterans of the U.S. military in Vietnam. Two of the other poets are civilian veterans, each with years of experience in Vietnam during the war.

These selections thus reflect one truly precious consequence of the Vietnam War: the literature created by its veterans. The fiction by Vietnam veterans discussed or reprinted in this volume represents only a small sample of their immense collective achievement. Even more extraordinary—indeed, virtually unprecedented as a cultural phenomenon—is the body of poetry by Vietnam veterans.

Yet, in a larger sense, all people old enough to remember living through the Vietnam War in America are also veterans, especially those who, like some of the other writers in this volume, devoted much of their lives to opposing the war. And in a still larger sense, every American old enough to be reading this book is a veteran of the Vietnam War, because, as many of these stories, songs, and poems show, the war goes on in—and for—America.

Notes

1. Philip D. Beidler, *Re-Writing America: Vietnam Authors in Their Generation* (Athens: University of Georgia Press, 1991), 2.

2. See Rick Berg, "Losing Vietnam" in *From Hanoi to Hollywood: The Vietnam War in American Film*, edited by Linda Dittmar and Gene Michaud (New Brunswick: Rutgers University Press, 1990), 51–53. This collection of essays and comprehensive filmography is the best single source on Vietnam movies.

3. John Hellmann, *American Myth and the Legacy of Vietnam* (New York: Columbia University Press, 1986), 188–202.

When did the Vietnam War begin? When President Lyndon Johnson began massive bombing of North Vietnam and openly dispatched two battalions of U.S. Marines in February and March 1965? In early November 1963, when the assassination of President Ngo Dinh Diem left no civilian government in Saigon for the sixteen thousand U.S. combat "advisers" to support? When President John F. Kennedy committed U.S. Special Forces and began large-scale chemical defoliation shortly after assuming office in 1961? When President Dwight Eisenhower's administration installed Ngo Dinh Diem in the Imperial Palace and began covert warfare in 1954? Or when the United States provided most of the financing and arms, as well as military advisers, for France's war against the Democratic Republic of Vietnam? The U.S. war in Vietnam is not so much a war without a definable beginning as a war defined by when one begins the story. And when one begins the story depends on what story one is telling. This is just as true for the narratives called history as for the narratives called fiction.

Curiously, fiction about the war helps define when and how it began. What many consider the classic novel about the American war in Vietnam—Graham Greene's *The Quiet American*—was begun in 1952 and published in 1955. Since it was based on actual events, the war must somehow have already begun. This, in fact, is a central theme of the novel.

Set during the period when French defeat was imminent, *The Quiet American* focuses on the American vanguard already positioning to replace them, embodied by Alden Pyle, a young, enthusiastic CIA officer committed to building a "Third Force," neither colonialist nor communist. Blinded to the social realities of Vietnam by his combination of all-American idealism and cold-war ideology, Pyle is gradually exposed as an archetypal representative of a nation capable of carrying out the most ruthless and bloody acts with the very best of intentions. As the British narrator says, "I never knew a man who had better motives for all the trouble he caused."

Pyle strikingly resembles Colonel Edward Lansdale, the man in charge of covert warfare and propaganda designed to establish and sustain a U.S. proxy regime in Saigon. In *The Ugly American*, the 1958 best-selling apologia for U.S. intervention in Vietnam written partly as a riposte to *The Quiet American*, William J. Lederer and Eugene Burdick present a far more favorable portrait of Lansdale in the character of all-American hero Colonel Edwin Hillandale. (Lansdale had already portrayed himself as a very similar heroic character in his top-secret reports, which came to light in 1971 with the publication of the *Pentagon Papers*.)

The Quiet American and *The Ugly American* drew battle lines for conflict over the war that would be contested far into the future. Yet both are in fundamental agreement that the archetypal American character is enthusiastic, idealistic, and, in key ways, innocent. If this can be taken as a before-Vietnam portrait of Americans, Robert Stone's 1974 *Dog Soldiers* offers an after-Vietnam picture as a terrifying contrast. Stone's novel consciously evokes *The Quiet American* in its unrelenting display of postwar America as a cesspool of disillusion, cynicism, greed, lust, and violence, in which the main characters destroy themselves and each other, replaying the war as a battle to possess a packet of pure heroin from Vietnam. According to the nightmarish tableaux of *Dog Solders*, the war did not so much change the nature of America as reveal it to itself. The protagonist puts it this way in Vietnam, as he recruits a fellow ex-marine to smuggle the heroin to America: "You can't blame us too much. We didn't know who we were till we got here. We thought we were something else."

In the two decades between *The Quiet American* and *Dog Soldiers*, approximately two hundred American novels about the Vietnam War were published. Most were militaristic adventure stories, many aimed directly at the juvenile and teenage market. A typical feature of this fiction was an elite unit or individual on a daring mission. The Special Forces had a cult status within this genre; in the wake of Robin Moore's 1965 best-seller, *The Green Berets,* came numerous works such as *The Pride of the Green Berets* (1966), *The Glory of the Green Berets* (1967), *Special Forces Trooper* (1967), and even *Women of the Green Berets* (1967). POW rescue stories began appearing at least as early as 1966 in *The Last Bridge,* foreshadowing the astonishingly potent POW/MIA cultural movement of the 1980s and 1990s, manifest not only in the POW/MIA rescue movies but in dozens of mass-market novels, including the popular *MIA Hunter* series.

While the glories of combat were being advertised by these novels to a mass audience, the war was being deglamorized by other fiction — and by glimpses of the war's reality beginning to slip through the nightly TV coverage, especially during and after the Tet Offensive of 1968. Trying to communicate what they perceived as this war's peculiar futility, special grotesqueness, and distinctive absurdity, the early novelists ranged through every mode of fiction from the gritty realism of David Halberstam's *One Long Hot Day* (1967) to the surrealism of William Eastlake's *The Bamboo Bed* (1969). Some of their finest successes appear in the first group of short stories, "Inside the War."

INSIDE THE WAR

Five of the six stories in this grouping are by combat veterans, three of whom (McCusker, Rottmann, and O'Brien) were wounded in action; the other is by war correspondent Tom Mayer, who ranged widely with several kinds of combat units. The first five, published in the 1971–1973 period, were all written while U.S. troops were still fighting in Indochina. Each story attempts to communicate some of the special and essential features of the Vietnam War from inside.

With one exception, none of America's earlier major wars had forced its fighters into protracted and personal contact with a radically alien culture. In the American Revolution and the War of 1812, "we" were fighting against the very empire from which "we" had come. The Civil War was fought between Americans. In World War I, the opponents were all Europeans whose descendants were part of America. In World War II and the Korean War, contact with the non-European enemies was mainly in pitched battles. The one exception was the war against the Indians, which went on for centuries and offered so many similarities that GIs often referred to Vietnam as "Injun country." American soldiers entered the villages of Vietnam just as their forebears had entered the villages of the Indians, whether to torch them or to engage in what President Eisenhower called "Winning Hearts and Minds"—the true meaning of which, as soon recognized in GI jokes, lay in its acronym, WHAM.

These six stories all explore a question generated by the very nature of this war and central to it: Who is the enemy? On the simplest level that question was a matter of survival. American soldiers were officially told that they were going to South Vietnam to prevent a communist takeover by repelling an invasion from North Vietnam. But when they got there, they discovered that their main enemies were men, women, and children living in South Vietnam, with whom they were required to have close, often intimate, contact. As W. D. Ehrhart puts it in his poem "Guerrilla War," "It's practically impossible/to tell civilians/from the Vietcong," so "after a while,/you quit trying." Moreover, it was not the Vietnamese soldiers from the north who evidently were looked on as invaders but the American soldiers and their allies from South Korea, Thailand, and Australia.

Thus the question "Who is the enemy?" also led to deeper questions of identity. Who *are* these people willing to fight endlessly to the death against the mightiest military power ever to wage war? Who *is* the alien or Other?

Larry Rottmann's "Thi Bong Dzu" and David Huddle's "The Interrogation of the Prisoner Bung by Mister Hawkins and Sergeant Tree" try to answer these questions by making an extraordinary imaginative displacement—becoming the enemy, the alien, the Other. Michael McCusker's "The Old Man" and Tim O'Brien's "The Man I Killed" turn the questions back onto those who, like the authors, discover the essential nature of the war through their involvement in the killing of these people about whom they knew so little. In Tom Mayer's aptly titled "Kafka for President," the narrator, a news photographer, becomes aware of his own alienation from all the participants, realizing that for him the Other includes not just the enemy and the "friendly" Vietnamese but also the American soldiers; he sees the central figure in the story as "a giant Negro" resembling "a black god," whose intense personal involvement in the action ends up as alienating as the narrator's disengagement. This view is almost the opposite of that of George Davis, who, like his protagonist Ben, was an African-American flight officer educated at an Ivy League college; Ben gradually perceives what he has in common with the Vietnamese fighting against white domination and begins to sense that the Other may be embodied by his fellow officers.

MICHAEL PAUL McCUSKER

Michael McCusker received two Purple Hearts while serving as a sergeant and combat correspondent in the U.S. First Marine Division in Vietnam from 1966 to 1967. Later he was an organizer of the Vietnam Veterans Against the War. Since 1980 he has been the editor and publisher of the North Coast Times Eagle *in Astoria, Oregon, where he still writes incisive commentaries on the war.*

"The Old Man," which McCusker wrote in Vietnam, compresses into two paragraphs some of the most crucial and revealing aspects of the U.S. military presence in the Vietnamese countryside. Fat Jack embodies one common response of American soldiers to the Vietnamese villagers; the narrator—another member of his unit, and just as thoroughly American—expresses an opposing vision. Fat Jack's actions suggest why an alien army could never win the "hearts and minds" of the people, while the narrator's recognition of the old man's humanity discloses the source of much of the literature by Vietnam veterans included in this volume.

The Old Man

He was just an old man. Bent and scabby-legged, sores all over his dark calloused feet; three long chin whiskers curling from his ancient crumbling jaw like nonsensical banners. He was waving one. A flag. Yellow with three red stripes. He was standing beside his hut. Kids were running everywhere yelling at the marines walking through the village. A tiny village alongside a river. Chickens, ugly pigs, scrawny old women with black teeth and frightened smiles because they thought the Americans might kill their men or burn down their homes.

So everybody pretended to be friendly and the old man hid his Viet Cong flag and brought out the Saigon absurdity, waving and smiling to beat hell. But Fat Jack saw him and Fat Jack had never shot down anybody in cold blood. Jack had this thing. He wanted to kill somebody. And there was that ridiculous old man. Who would miss him? Just an old man; he couldn't work in the fields anymore. Just another hungry stomach for a family loaded down with kids. So Jack walked up to him and the old man started bobbing his head up and down faster and smiling wider, but it didn't matter. Jack had the rifle in his face and the trigger pulled before the old man's body knew it was dead. He didn't fall. He just stood there without much of a face. A squashed, dripping berry. The back of his head looked like a busted balloon. Then he fell, old knees buckling on withered legs. His ass hit first, then the rest of him, sitting hunched over for a second, then collapsing on his side. "I don't feel nothin'," Jack shouted. The guys just smiled. The kids stopped running, quiet. The old women scooted back into their huts. A low wailing began to throb through the village, but Jack was walking away, shaking his head, telling his friends he just didn't feel nothin'. The old man, he had a lot of blood for such a small, skinny, used-up old man, he was left to lay there. Nobody touched him, not the kids, not the women, just the flies, coming from all over, from the village, the fields.

(1973)

LARRY ROTTMANN

Larry Rottmann, born in 1942, served in the U.S. Army, 1965–1968, including a year as infantryman in Vietnam, 1967–1968. As he tells in his poem "For Cissy Shellabarger, R.N., Wherever You Are" (page 306), he was so badly wounded during the 1968 Tet Offensive that he was triaged as too unlikely to survive to receive medical attention.

Rottmann is a key figure, both as a writer and as an editor, in the development of the literature by Vietnam War veterans. In 1972 he coedited, with Jan Barry and Basil T. Paquet, the first anthology of veterans' poetry, Winning Hearts and Minds: War Poems by Vietnam Veterans, *which has turned out to be the cradle of an important new literary creature, as discussed in the poetry section of this book. The following year he coedited, with Wayne Karlin and Basil T. Paquet,* Free Fire Zone: Short Stories by Vietnam Veterans, *an equally groundbreaking anthology. His poetry has been widely printed, and he has also published a novel,* American Eagle: The Story of a Navajo Vietnam Veteran *(1977), and* A History of the 25th Infantry Division in Vietnam *(1967).*

Rottmann's most recent book, Voices from the Vietnam Trail *(1993), is a unique volume of poetry, stunningly illustrated with photographs, that merges his own experience as a soldier in the war and as a frequent postwar visitor to Vietnam with stories told to him by hundreds of Vietnamese about their wartime and postwar experience. In still another act of artistic transmutation, Rottmann has turned* Voices from the Ho Chi Minh Trail *into a profoundly moving multimedia show that has toured widely. He currently teaches English at Southwest Missouri State University in Springfield.*

"Thi Bong Dzu," like a number of other selections in this volume, is a startling imaginative projection by an American combat veteran of the Vietnam War as seen from the view of the "enemy."

Thi Bong Dzu

It was the day before his birthday, and Thi Bong Dzu was a little bit excited. However, he knew it was important that he keep such feelings to himself, for if he failed to control his emotions, he could compromise the entire unit's mission that night.

Dzu rose early, for he had a lot of other work to do before the pre-arranged meeting time. Since the death of his father nearly six months before, Dzu had been the man-of-the-house to his mother, three younger sisters, and grandmother. As he crossed the packed earth of the yard on his way to the well, he could see faint luminescent trails of parachute flares low in the northeast sky. And a moment later, from somewhere in the south near Saigon, came the groundshuddering rumble of a B-52 bomb raid.

Drawing a full bucket, and holding his breath, Dzu doused himself with the cool water. He soaped his lean body vigorously, rinsed off with a couple more buckets, and shaking dry, trotted back to the hut shivering a little in the chill morning air.

He dressed quickly, pulling on a pair of faded trousers, a much-mended shirt, and his sandals, which he'd made himself from some rope and an old jeep tire. Moving quietly, so as not to wake his family, Dzu started a small fire in the cooking pit just outside the door. Into a battered tin pot he placed a few handfuls of rice, a few tiny dried minnows, and a bit of salt. He placed the pot on the low fire, and stirred it slowly until little bubbles started to appear. Dumping a small amount into a chipped bowl, he began eating it, pinching the rice between his thumb and forefinger.

As he ate, he watched the huge, blood-red ball of sun rise slowly. The air remained cool, and a thick mist hovered low over the flooded paddies surrounding the house. The sky was clear though, and Dzu knew that within the hour it would be steaming hot. Worse yet, the sky would probably still be clear that night. He frowned slightly at this prospect, for it would make their operation all the more difficult.

Swallowing the last few bites of breakfast, Dzu gently began to wake his family (all except grandmother, who'd been known to bite anyone who interrupted her sleep). As his mother and sisters began to move about, he took the rice sickle from the tool shelf, and squatting on the stoop, began to sharpen its well-worn cutting edge with a small sandstone. Back and forth, back and forth he moved the stone along the gentle curve of the blade, recalling how he had always been fascinated by the way his father had done it. Back and forth, back and forth, Dzu felt himself slipping into an almost hypnotic rhythm. Suddenly he was snapped from his near trance by a loud squawk from grandmother, who'd been playfully awakened by Dzu's sisters. Testing the sickle's edge, he was surprised to see a fine red line appear on his thumb where he'd drawn it across the steel. Satisfied, he replaced the sharpening stone and made ready to leave for the fields.

His mother had put some of the cooked rice in a small bucket, along with a piece of bread, for lunch. As Dzu took it from her, she noticed the blood on his thumb, and made him sit down while she washed out the cut and tied a too-large bandage around it. Dzu realized that she was making a lot of fuss over nothing, but he knew she was trying to let him know how much she loved him. Because he was now the head of the family, it wouldn't do for her to kiss him or fawn over him, so she expressed her concern in subtle, less obvious ways, like all this bother over a small cut.

But it was getting late, and already Dzu could see the other men of the hamlet heading for the fields. During rice harvest, no time could be wasted, and he was anxious to get started, especially since he'd have to stop a little early that day in order to get ready for the mission. He kissed each of his sisters, made a face at grandmother who was still grouching around, and took off down the path.

Dzu felt good, and for the second time allowed himself to think about his upcoming birthday. He knew that no matter how early he arose the next day, his mother would already be up, fixing a special breakfast. Even though they didn't have much, she would always manage to come up with a small bit of eel, some extra spices, or even fresh melons on birthdays. The girls would have some small, but hand-made and priceless, gift—like the red scarf from his last birthday that he wore on patrols. And even grandmother, despite her pretended gruffness, would have something for him too. But Dzu cared less for the presents than the special feeling of closeness that came on birthdays. Their home always seemed to have extra warmth and happiness then.

Dzu's thoughts were suddenly jarred by the roar of tanks. The path to the paddies paralleled Route 13, and a long U.S. convoy was approaching. Dzu paused as the vehicles rumbled by, and remembered the first armored task force that had passed his village, and how, as a small boy, he had stood clutching his father, frozen by fear at the sight of the seemingly endless parade of huge war machines. He recalled how the calloused hands of his father had trembled with fright, and yet how his jaw had clinched in anger and hatred. And he would never forget the words his usually quiet father had spat out at the disappearing Americans: "Bastards! Murderers! Animals!"

At that time, Dzu didn't know what it was that had caused his father to react so vehemently to the hairy strangers, but now he knew. As he watched the column roll by, and carefully counted the number of tanks, APC's, and supply trucks, he remembered the first air strike on his hamlet. The black, screaming planes had suddenly knifed through an overcast sky one afternoon, and for almost an hour had raked Ben

Cat with rockets, cannon fire, bombs, and napalm. In the attack, Dzu lost his older brother, his grandfather, two cousins, and a half-dozen playmates. The village's market place, temple, school—as well as over half its homes—were destroyed. Almost half the villagers were killed or wounded, and many still carried the scars caused by the sticking fire. That night most of the hamlet's able-bodied men joined the 271st Viet Cong Regiment. Dzu's father was among the volunteers, and he participated in many operations against the enemy. He was a brave fighter, and at the time of his death during the attack of an artillery fire support base, was still recovering from a wound suffered in an earlier action.

When his father was killed, Dzu took his place not only as head of the household, but also as a scout for the 271st recon platoon. In less than six months he had participated in nineteen separate engagements, had been decorated for bravery twice, and had risen from private to corporal. The platoon had lost nearly a third of its original men during that period, but had also recorded several surprising victories, each time against overwhelming odds and firepower. Dzu was the only man in the unit who hadn't been wounded, and had come to be regarded by them as something of a good luck charm. "Keep bullet holes out of Thi's shirt and we'll all be safe" was a frequently heard remark within the platoon.

Dzu's pulse was pounding as the end of the column approached. He thought of the night's mission and a bitter smile formed on his lips. As the last tank, laden with GI's, passed, Dzu raised his hand in a mock salute. One of the soldiers on the vehicle shouted "Hey, gook, you want smoke-smoke?" and laughing, threw a pack of C-Ration cigarettes at him. Grabbing them out of the air, Dzu stripped off the cellophane, removed the cigarettes, and turned the pack inside out. Taking a pencil stub from his pocket, he scribbled down the unit designations and makeup of the convoy. He folded the small paper, tucked it away, and puffing on one of the stale Camels, strode off down the path, his lunch pot and sickle flapping against his thin legs.

Arriving at the fields a few minutes later, Dzu stripped down to his shorts and went right to work. Again and again the sickle flashed in its smooth arc, severing the heavily laden stalks of rice from their submerged roots. With each easy swing, another sheave would slide neatly into Dzu's crooked left arm. When the shock felt exactly the right size and weight, he tied it about the middle with a piece of twine and laid it on the dike, away from the water. He worked tirelessly, his spare frame bent almost double and his legs immersed in water to mid-calf. He loved the squishy feel of the mud around his toes, and the rough tickle of the stubby, already cut-off rice shoots.

Dzu worked without a break until a little past mid-day. When he finally paused, he looked at the pile of shocks and realized he had already finished the day's quota. Taking his lunch, he walked to the bank of the nearby Hoc Mon River and sat down to eat. On the opposite bank, a young man about his age was fishing with a long, limber bamboo pole. It looked like the fish were biting well, but they were apparently too quick for the fisherman. Each time the float bobbed, he'd jerk the pole, but all he ever came up with was an empty hook which he'd rebait and throw back in. "Xin loi," laughed Dzu, "Too bad." For a moment he felt sorry for himself, wishing that he too could try his luck at catching the elusive cam roa. Perhaps on his birthday . . . ? But that thought lasted only a moment. Dzu remembered his responsibility to his family and to the liberation, and chided himself for such selfish reverie.

He finished his bread and rice and stretched out under a low pineapple scrub for a two-hour nap, just as he had done every day of his life. He knew the strength of the afternoon sun, and wondered to himself why only monkeys and U.S. soldiers dared defy it. He noted many similarities between the two, and was in the process of enumerating them when he fell asleep.

Dzu woke with a start to find his uncle standing over him, pointing a stick at his head and shouting, "Bang, bang, you're dead, you dirty Vee Cee!" "Don't make bad jokes, Uncle," Dzu replied as he jumped to his feet. Angry because he had allowed himself to be sneaked up on, Dzu grabbed the stick "gun," threw it into the stream, and without a backward glance, ran over to the road where his uncle's ox-cart was sitting and led the big water buffalo off toward the paddy.

When Dzu arrived at his pile of shocks, he immediately began tossing them one by one into the cart. By the time uncle had walked over from the river, they were all loaded but one. Dzu paused for a long moment, scanning the horizon and listening intently for the "whack-whack" of patrolling helicopters. Taking the remaining shock, he walked out to the middle of the paddy. He felt around a moment with his feet, then with a swift motion snatched an oblong object wrapped in plastic from beneath the water and concealed it within the rice bundle. Dzu placed this shock deep in the middle of the loaded cart, slipped into his shirt, and calling to uncle, "Make sure you deliver that load on time," he headed down the path for home.

As he made his way back to the village, Dzu noted that it was beginning to cloud up a little to the east. "A good sign," he thought to himself, and quickened his pace. His sisters saw him coming from a long way off, and ran to meet him. He was pleased, for he loved them dearly, but he also knew that part of their jubilance was due to their sharing of his birthday "secret." He embraced them all as they descended upon him in a maelstrom of laughter, and with one girl holding each hand and one riding piggy-back, he trotted the last hundred meters or so to the house. Shouting and giggling, they burst into the yard, almost tumbling over grandmother. "Not a very grownup way for the head of the house to behave," she groused, but she knew of Dzu's mission that night, and so she said no more.

A few minutes later mother returned from the market place where she'd been shopping for a breakfast treat. Out of sight of the girls, she handed Dzu a tai tom. He opened the hollow pineapple, removed the two dozen .45 caliber shells that had been hidden inside, and with an oily rag, carefully cleaned each one. Moving the sleeping platform to one side, he uncovered the entrance to a small tunnel. Wrapping the bullets in the rag, he put them in the families' tiny bomb shelter, then replaced the bed and went outside for supper.

Everyone else was in a gay mood during the meal, but Dzu couldn't keep his mind on the swirling conversation. He kept running over the plans for the night and casting anxious glances at the clearing sky. As they finished their supper, uncle arrived with the load of rice. Dzu removed his special bundle and took it inside while the rest of the family helped unload the cart. He again moved the bed and dropped into the tunnel beneath it. By the light of a small candle he unwrapped his package. With the skill that comes only from long practice, he broke the submachinegun down into its various parts and cleaned and recleaned each one. When he was satisfied that the weapon was spotless, he lightly oiled each piece, then quickly reassembled it. He also loaded his two magazines with the recently acquired cartridges.

Emerging from the tunnel, he could see that it was nearly dark outside, and time for him to leave. Dzu put on his black cotton shirt and pants, and a pair of black rubber-soled shoes. He tied the red scarf around his neck and fastened two hand grenades to his belt. He locked one loaded magazine into the gun and stuck the other in his waistband for easy access. Choosing a moment when the girls were busy at play, he slipped outside, and after pausing only long enough to make sure mother had replaced the bed, Dzu disappeared into the darkness.

Alert and careful, Dzu padded silently along the path toward the rendezvous point. The sky was again overcast, and a thick fog was forming along the ground. Dzu's spirits rose, and he anticipated another successful operation. He felt sure he would be home in plenty of time to get some sleep before his birthday breakfast. Dzu started thinking about grumpy grandmother and didn't see the first soldier's slight movement. He was imagining the antics of his sisters and didn't hear the faint click of the safety on the second GI's rifle. He was seeing the shy smile of his proud mother and didn't feel the tug of the flare trip-wire until too late.

Dzu stood paralyzed by the sudden explosive blaze of light, and in the instant before his body was riddled by the bullets of two machine guns and a dozen M-16's; in that half-moment before thousands of razor-sharp fragments from Claymores and grenades tore at his flesh, Dzu realized that he wasn't ever going to have another birthday. He realized that he was never going to be twelve.

(1973)

DAVID HUDDLE

Born in Virginia in 1942, David Huddle served in the U.S. Army from 1964 to 1967, as a paratrooper and with a tour as sergeant in the Twenty-fifth Military Intelligence Detachment in Vietnam, 1966–1967, where he was awarded a Bronze Star. His numerous books include four collections of short stories—A Dream with No Stump Roots in It *(1975),* Only the Little Bone *(1986),* The High Spirits *(1988), and* Intimates *(1993)—and three volumes of poetry*—Paper Boy *(1979),* Stopping by Home *(1988), and* The Nature of Yearning *(1992). He currently teaches literature and creative writing at the University of Vermont and the Bread Loaf School of English.*

Reprinted frequently, "The Interrogation of the Prisoner Bung by Mister Hawkins and Sergeant Tree" has withstood a test of time. For today's readers, the story not only presents insights into the war but also reveals something of the cultural state of America at the end of 1970, when it hit the newsstands in the January 1971 issue of Esquire.

The Interrogation of the Prisoner Bung by Mister Hawkins and Sergeant Tree

The land in these provinces to the south of the capital city is so flat it would be possible to ride a bicycle from one end of this district to the other and to pedal only occasionally. The narrow highway passes over kilometers and kilometers of rice fields, laid out square and separated by slender green lines of grassy paddy-dikes and by irrigation ditches filled with bad water. The villages are far apart and small. Around them are clustered the little pockets of huts, the hamlets where the rice farmers live. The village that serves as the capital of this district is just large enough to have a proper marketplace. Close to the police compound, a detachment of Americans has set up its tents. These are lumps of new green canvas, and they sit on a concrete, French-built tennis court, long abandoned, not far from a large lily pond where women come in the morning to wash clothes and where policemen of the compound and their children come to swim and bathe in the late afternoon.

The door of a room to the rear of the District Police Headquarters is cracked for light and air. Outside noises—chickens quarreling, children playing, the mellow grunting of the pigs owned by the police chief—these reach the ears of the three men inside the quiet room. The room is not a cell; it is more like a small bedroom.

The American is nervous and fully awake, but he forces himself to yawn and sips at his coffee. In front of him are his papers, the report forms, yellow notepaper, two pencils and a ball-point pen. Across the table from the American is Sergeant Tree, a young man who was noticed by the government of his country and taken from his studies to be sent to interpreter's school. Sergeant Tree has a pleasant and healthy face. He is accustomed to smiling, especially in the presence of Americans, who are, it happens, quite fond of him. Sergeant Tree knows that he has an admirable position working with Mister Hawkins; several of his unlucky classmates from interpreter's school serve nearer the shooting.

The prisoner, Bung, squats in the far corner of the room, his back at the intersection of the cool concrete walls. Bung is a large man for an Asian, but he is squatted down close to the floor. He was given a cigarette by the American when he was first brought into the room, but has finished smoking and holds the white filter inside his fist. Bung is not tied, nor restrained, but he squats perfectly still, his bare feet laid out flat and large on the floor. His hair, cut by his wife, is cropped short and uneven; his skin is dark, leathery, and there is a bruise below one of his shoulder blades. He looks only at the floor, and he wonders what he will do with the tip of the cigarette when the interrogation begins. He suspects that he ought to eat it now so that it will not be discovered later.

From the large barracks room on the other side of the building comes laughter and loud talking, the policemen changing shifts. Sergeant Tree smiles at these sounds. Some of the younger policemen are his friends. Hawkins, the American, does not seem to have heard. He is trying to think about sex, and he cannot concentrate.

"Ask the prisoner what his name is."

"What is your name?"

The prisoner reports that his name is Bung. The language startles Hawkins. He does not understand this language, except the first ten numbers of counting, and the words for yes and no. With Sergeant Tree helping him with the spelling, Hawkins enters the name into the proper blank.

"Ask the prisoner where he lives."

"Where do you live?"

The prisoner wails a string of language. He begins to weep as he speaks, and he goes on like this, swelling up the small room with the sound of his voice until he sees a warning twitch of the interpreter's hand. He stops immediately, as though corked. One of the police chief's pigs is snuffing over the ground just outside the door, rooting for scraps of food.

"What did he say?"

"He says that he is classed as a poor farmer, that he lives in the hamlet near where the soldiers found him, and that he has not seen his wife and his children for four days now and they do not know where he is.

"He says that he is not one of the enemy, although he has seen the enemy many times this year in his hamlet and in the village near his hamlet. He says that he was forced to give rice to the enemy on two different occasions, once at night, and another time during the day, and that he gave rice to the enemy only because they would have shot him if he had not.

"He says that he does not know the names of any of these men. He says that one of the men asked him to join them and to go with them, but that he told this man that he could not join them and go with them because he was poor and because his wife and his children would not be able to live without him to work for them to feed them. He says that the enemy men laughed at him when he said this but that they did not make him go with them when they left his house.

"He says that two days after the night the enemy came and took rice from him, the soldiers came to him in the field where he was working and made him walk with them for many kilometers, and made him climb into the back of a large truck, and put a cloth over his eyes, so that he did not see where the truck carried him and did not know where he was until he was put with some other people in a pen. He says that one of the soldiers hit him in the back with a weapon, because he was afraid at first to climb into the truck.

"He says that he does not have any money, but that he has ten kilos of rice hidden beneath the floor of the kitchen of his house. He says that he would make us the gift of this rice if we would let him go back to his wife and his children."

When he has finished his translation of the prisoner's speech, Sergeant Tree smiles at Mister Hawkins. Hawkins feels that he ought to write something down. He moves the pencil to a corner of the paper and writes down his service number, his Social Security number, the telephone number of his girl friend in Silver Spring, Maryland, and the amount of money he has saved in his allotment account.

"Ask the prisoner in what year he was born."

Hawkins has decided to end the interrogation of this prisoner as quickly as he can. If there is enough time left, he will find an excuse for Sergeant Tree and himself to drive the jeep into the village.

"In what year were you born?"

The prisoner tells the year of his birth.

"Ask the prisoner in what place he was born."

"In what place were you born?"

The prisoner tells the place of his birth.

"Ask the prisoner the name of his wife."

"What is the name of your wife?"

Bung gives the name of his wife.

"Ask the prisoner the names of his parents."

Bung tells the names.

"Ask the prisoner the names of his children."

The American takes down these things on the form, painstakingly, with help in the spelling from the interpreter, who has become bored with this. Hawkins fills all the blank spaces on the front of the form. Later, he will add his summary of the interrogation in the space provided on the back.

"Ask the prisoner the name of his hamlet chief."

"What is the name of your hamlet chief?"

The prisoner tells this name, and Hawkins takes it down on the notepaper. Hawkins has been trained to ask these questions. If a prisoner gives one incorrect name, then all names given may be incorrect, all information secured unreliable.

Bung tells the name of his village chief, and the American takes it down. Hawkins tears off this sheet of notepaper and gives it to Sergeant Tree. He asks the interpreter to take this paper to the police chief to check if these are the correct names. Sergeant Tree does not like to deal with the police chief because the police chief treats him as if he were a farmer. But he leaves the room in the manner of someone engaged in important business. Bung continues to stare at the floor, afraid the American will kill him now that they are in this room together, alone.

Hawkins is again trying to think about sex. Again, he is finding it difficult to concentrate. He cannot choose between thinking about sex with his girl friend Suzanne or with a plump girl who works in a souvenir shop in the village. The soft grunting of the pig outside catches his ear, and he finds that he is thinking of having sex with the pig. He takes another sheet of notepaper and begins calculating the number of days he has left to remain in Asia. The number turns out to be one hundred and thirty-three. This distresses him because the last time he calculated the number it was one hundred and thirty-five. He decides to think about food. He thinks of an omelet. He would like to have an omelet. His eyelids begin to close as he considers all the things that he likes to eat: an omelet, chocolate pie, macaroni, cookies, cheeseburgers, black-cherry Jell-O. He has a sudden vivid image of Suzanne's stomach, the path of downy hair to her navel. He stretches the muscles in his legs, and settles into concentration.

The clamor of chickens distracts him. Sergeant Tree has caused this noise by throwing a rock on his way back. The police chief refused to speak with him and required him to conduct his business with the secretary, whereas this secretary gloated over the indignity to Sergeant Tree, made many unnecessary delays and complications before letting the interpreter have a copy of the list of hamlet chiefs and village chiefs in the district.

Sergeant Tree enters the room, goes directly to the prisoner, with the toe of his boot kicks the prisoner on the shinbone. The boot hitting bone makes a wooden sound. Hawkins jerks up in his chair, but before he quite understands the situation, Sergeant Tree has shut the door to the small room and has kicked the prisoner's other shinbone. Bung responds with a grunt and holds his shins with his hands, drawing himself tighter into the corner.

"Wait!" The American stands up to restrain Sergeant Tree, but this is not necessary. Sergeant Tree has passed by the prisoner now and has gone to stand at his own side of the table. From underneath his uniform shirt he takes a rubber club, which he has borrowed from one of his policeman friends. He slaps the club on the table.

"He lies!" Sergeant Tree says this with as much evil as he can force into his voice.

"Hold on now. Let's check this out." Hawkins' sense of justice has been touched. He regards the prisoner as a clumsy, hulking sort, obviously not bright, but clearly honest.

"The police chief says that he lies!" Sergeant Tree announces. He shows Hawkins the paper listing the names of the hamlet chiefs and the village chiefs. With the door shut, the light in the small room is very dim, and it is difficult to locate the names on the list. Hawkins is disturbed by the darkness, is uncomfortable being so intimately together with two men. The breath of the interpreter has something sweetish to it. It occurs to Hawkins that now, since the prisoner has lied to them, there will probably not be enough time after the interrogation to take the jeep and drive into the village. This vexes him. He decides there must be something unhealthy in the diet of these people, something that causes this sweet-smelling breath.

Hawkins finds it almost impossible to read the columns of handwriting. He is confused. Sergeant Tree must show him the places on the list where the names of the prisoner's hamlet chief and village chief are written. They agree that the prisoner has given them incorrect names, though Hawkins is not certain of it. He wishes these things were less complicated, and he dreads what he knows must follow. He thinks regretfully of what could have happened if the prisoner had given the correct names: the interrogation would have ended quickly, the prisoner released; he and Sergeant Tree could have driven into the village in the jeep, wearing their sunglasses, with the cool wind whipping past them, dust billowing around the jeep, shoeshine boys shrieking, the girl in the souvenir shop going with him into the back room for a time.

Sergeant Tree goes to the prisoner, kneels on the floor beside him, and takes Bung's face between his hands. Tenderly, he draws the prisoner's head close to his own, and asks, almost absentmindedly, "Are you one of the enemy?"

"No."

All this strikes Hawkins as vaguely comic, someone saying, "I love you," in a high-school play.

Sergeant Tree spits in the face of the prisoner and then jams the prisoner's head back against the wall. Sergeant Tree stands up quickly, jerks the police club from the table, and starts beating the prisoner with random blows. Bung stays squatted down and covers his head with both arms. He makes a shrill noise.

Hawkins has seen this before in other interrogations. He listens closely, trying to hear everything: little shrieks coming from Sergeant Tree's throat, the chunking sound the rubber club makes. The American recognizes a kind of rightness in this, like the final slapping together of the bellies of a man and a woman.

Sergeant Tree stops. He stands, legs apart, facing the prisoner, his back to Hawkins. Bung keeps his squatting position, his arms crossed over his head.

The door scratches and opens just wide enough to let in a policeman friend of Sergeant Tree's, a skinny, rotten-toothed man, and a small boy. Hawkins has seen this boy and the policeman before. The two of them smile at the American and at Sergeant Tree, whom they admire for his education and for having achieved such an excellent position. Hawkins starts to send them back out, but decides to let them stay. He does not like to be discourteous to Asians.

Sergeant Tree acknowledges the presence of his friend and the boy. He sets the club on the table and removes his uniform shirt and the white T-shirt beneath it. His chest is powerful, but hairless. He catches Bung by the ears and jerks upward until the prisoner stands. Sergeant Tree is much shorter than the prisoner, and this he finds an advantage.

Hawkins notices that the muscles in Sergeant Tree's buttocks are clenched tight, and he admires this, finds it attractive. He has in his mind Suzanne. They are sitting in the back seat of the Oldsmobile. She has removed her stockings and garter belt, and now she slides the panties down from her hips, down her legs, off one foot, keeping them dangling on one ankle, ready to be pulled up quickly in case someone comes to the car and catches them. Hawkins has perfect concentration. He sees her panties glow.

Sergeant Tree tears away the prisoner's shirt, first from one side of his chest and then the other. Bung's mouth sags open now, as though he were about to drool.

The boy clutches at the sleeve of the policeman to whisper in his ear. The policeman giggles. They hush when the American glances at them. Hawkins is furious because they have distracted him. He decides that there is no privacy to be had in the entire country.

"Sergeant Tree, send these people out of here, please."

Sergeant Tree gives no sign that he has heard what Hawkins has said. He is poising himself to begin. Letting out a heaving grunt, Sergeant Tree chops with the police club, catching the prisoner directly in the center of the forehead. A flame begins in Bung's brain; he is conscious of a fire, blazing, blinding him. He feels the club touch him twice more, once at his ribs and once at his forearm.

"Are you the enemy?" Sergeant Tree screams.

The policeman and the boy squat beside each other near the door. They whisper to each other as they watch Sergeant Tree settle into the steady, methodical beating. Occasionally he pauses to ask the question again, but he gets no answer.

From a certain height, Hawkins can see that what is happening is profoundly sensible. He sees how deeply he loves these men in this room and how he respects them for the things they are doing. The knowledge rises in him, pushes to reveal itself. He stands up from his chair, virtually at attention.

A loud, hard smack swings the door wide open, and the room is filled with light. The Police Chief stands in the doorway, dressed in a crisp, white shirt, his rimless glasses sparkling. He is a fat man in the way that a good merchant might be fat—solid, confident, commanding. He stands with his hands on his hips, an authority in all matters. The policeman and the boy nod respectfully. The Police Chief walks to the table and picks up the list of hamlet chiefs and village chiefs. He examines this, and then he takes from his shirt pocket another paper, which is also a list of hamlet chiefs and village chiefs. He carries both lists to Sergeant Tree, who is kneeling in front of the prisoner. He shows Sergeant Tree the mistake he has made in getting a list that is out of date. He places the new list in Sergeant Tree's free hand, and then he takes the rubber club from Sergeant Tree's other hand and slaps it down across the top of Sergeant Tree's head. The Police Chief leaves the room, passing before the American, the policeman, the boy, not speaking or looking other than to the direction of the door.

It is late afternoon and the rain has come. Hawkins stands inside his tent, looking through the open flap. He likes to look out across the old tennis court at the big lily pond. He has been fond of water since he learned to water-ski. If the rain stops before dark, he will go out to join the policemen and the children who swim and bathe in the lily pond.

Walking out on the highway, with one kilometer still to go before he comes to the village, is Sergeant Tree. He is alone, the highway behind him and in front of him as far as he can see and nothing else around him but rain and the fields of wet, green rice. His head hurts and his arms are weary from the load of rice he carries. When he returned the prisoner to his hamlet, the man's wife made such a fuss Sergeant Tree had to shout at her to make her shut up, and then, while he was inside the prisoner's hut conducting the final arrangements for the prisoner's release, the rain came, and his policeman friends in the jeep left him to manage alone.

The ten kilos of rice he carries are heavy for him, and he would put this load down and leave it, except that he plans to sell the rice and add the money to what he has been saving to buy a .45 caliber pistol like the one Mister Hawkins carries at his hip. Sergeant Tree tries to think about how well-received he will be in California because he speaks the

American language so well, and how it is likely that he will marry a rich American girl with very large breasts.

The prisoner Bung is delighted by the rain. It brought his children inside the hut, and the sounds of their fighting with each other make him happy. His wife came to him and touched him. The rice is cooking, and in a half hour his cousin will come, bringing with him the leader and two other members of Bung's squad. They will not be happy that half of their rice was taken by the interpreter to pay the American, but it will not be a disaster for them. The squad leader will be proud of Bung for gathering the information that he has—for he has memorized the guard routines at the police headquarters and at the old French area where the Americans are staying. He has watched all the comings and goings at these places, and he has marked out in his mind the best avenues of approach, the best escape routes, and the best places to set up ambush. Also, he has discovered a way that they can lie in wait and kill the Police Chief. It will occur at the place where the Police Chief goes to urinate every morning at a certain time. Bung has much information inside his head, and he believes he will be praised by the members of his squad. It is even possible that he will receive a commendation from someone very high.

His wife brings the rifle that was hidden, and Bung sets to cleaning it, savoring the smell of the rice his wife places before him and of the American oil he uses on the weapon. He particularly enjoys taking the weapon apart and putting it together again. He is very fast at this.

(1971)

GEORGE DAVIS

George Davis was born in West Virginia in 1939. He spent seven years (1961–1968) in the U.S. Air Force, rising to the rank of captain at the age of twenty-seven. In 1967 and 1968 he was based in Thailand as a navigator on KC-135s that midair refueled fighter-bombers and B-52s attacking Vietnam; he also flew forty-seven reconnaissance missions over Vietnam. From 1968 to 1970, he was a reporter and editor for the Washington Post *and the* New York Times.

"Ben" consists of two extracts from his 1972 novel Coming Home, *based on his wartime experience in Thailand, as they appeared in* Free Fire Zone *in 1973. Central to the novel is the profound alienation of the African-American protagonist — even though he is a Harvard-educated flying officer—and his growing sense that he may be fighting on the wrong side.*

Davis's subsequent publications include the novel Love, Black Love *(1978) and* Black Life in Corporate America *(1982; coauthored with Glegg Watson). He is currently director of journalism at the Newark campus of Rutgers University.*

Ben

The Blue Sky is almost empty. I walk to the rear and ask Papa-San to fix some fried rice for me. Then I walk over and sit on the concrete floor near the well. The other G.I.'s have gone to the bungalows to sleep with their girls, or back to the air base. I don't want to sleep with anyone. My head hurts from too much scotch.

Papa-san watches me while he cooks, but I don't want to pretend that I am cheerful in order to prevent him from feeling sad that I am alone.

He cooks over a small blazing fire in a pan which he never sets down unless to add more ingredients. The food sizzles, and he lets the smoke come up into his face as the small flames lick up from a bed of rocks and touch the bottom of the pan. He serves the fried rice in a wooden bowl. I pay him a quarter. There are large reddish shrimp in the mixture but I don't feel like eating.

"Lieutenant?" he says, "Lieutenant?"

I smile.

He goes back to the fire, whispers something in the ear of his youngest son and sends the boy off on an errand. I hear the boy running barefoot on the stones outside the rear compound fence. The old man is plump. The faces of his family are lit by the light from the flames. They sit without eating, without talking; they are simply there.

The son returns with a thin, youngish girl. Her clothing is wet in spots, which makes it apparent that she's been working in a bathhouse. Papa-san pushes her toward me, saying, "You sleep with her tonight, Lieutenant."

She takes the last few steps toward me as if she has not lost the momentum from his push. She is a dainty, eighty- or ninety-pound girl with shoulder-length hair and a small mannish shirt covering her pointed teen-age breasts. She tucks her head and blushes. Her shorts are white like the shirt and she has a Scottish-plaid belt holding them up. She would look tinier yet if she didn't have high-heel shoes on over her white bobbysocks. She is amusingly beautiful. Papa-san and his family are happy that I have someone for the night.

"No, Papa-san," I say.

"She no have VD," he says. His voice quickens and rises to assure me. He shows me her card which has a blue circle on it to show that she has passed her last VD inspection. He takes my hand and places it to my ear. I know I am supposed to take wax out of my ear and rub it in her pussy to see if it burns her, but I do not. "I don't want to pom-pom," I say.

The family laughs at the way I say pom-pom. The youngest son urges me by slapping his hands together to make the sound that two bodies make slapping together.

The entire family has turned to look at me—four children, a wife and a mother. I hear a transistor radio playing from one of the bungalows.

The girl is embarrassed. "We walk," I say.

"Chi," she says, and the old toothless woman sitting on the other side of the flames shakes her head Yes.

"Beautiful, poo ying," I say.

We leave along the back path in front of the dark wooden bungalows where several GI's are sitting out with their girls.

The bungalows are in a row like a series of outhouses in back of an old Southern church. A wooden platform runs along in front of them and a naked shiny-skinned GI runs down the platform to where the vat of water is. He squats and washes his privates, then tiptoes back past us into his bungalow.

For a while the narrow path leads into the jungle before it turns toward the main road. The girl and I hold hands as we walk along the ditch that carries waste from the tapioca mill down to the ocean. The girl laughs and holds her nose at the wet-dog odor of the ditch. I laugh.

For a moment I wonder what would happen if I disappeared forever into the human and bamboo jungles of Asia.

We reach the road and walk along the stony shoulder. She takes off her highheels and walks in her socks for a while, then she takes them off, too. In some places the air is chilly, and in others we walk through warm air. Walking through ghosts, we used to call it down South, before Harvard, before everything became literal and scientific, and then became more unreal than it ever was before, leading straight to Vietnam. Before a million explanations came down between me and what I want to feel, and then all the explanations proved to be lies.

As I walk I feel strangely free, and I dread the thought of going back to America. I don't know how I can ever feel right about America again, after what they got weak-assed me to do over here.

I want to go to graduate school, but I know I'll never sit in a class and learn from a white man. And who will I work for, and where will I go.

The road turns out of the trees and runs along the beach. The gulf is empty and the black morning is peppered with stars. The air on the beach is cool. I feel the presence of billions of people around me whose lives are menaced in the same way that mine is. Like the millions of Chinese who were slaves in their own country for centuries.

We walk down toward the water's edge. There is nothing man-made in sight except for a puny wooden dock where the trucks come down to pick up the ammunition and jet fuel from the ships anchored in deep water.

"Pom-pom?" the girl says in a weak voice and sits down and begins to undo her shorts.

"No," I say, and take out my wallet and give her five dollars anyway. Tomorrow I want to bring Damg on this same walk. We could sit on the edge of this continent which has been kept under the foot of white men until finally China had to get an H-bomb and say, "No more." And the people I am fighting, me, in Vietnam had to say, "You can kill me but you can't enslave me any more."

I look out across the water. Bangkok, Rangoon, Kuala Lumpur, Djakarta, Calcutta—dark music—and then across the Indian Ocean to Africa.

The street is silent. I feel almost as if I'm floating through the night air with stoppers in my ears. Everything seems far away. I don't want to think about tomorrow.

The African Star sits on the main street, but farther down, in a quieter section behind a small garden. It is owned by three black ex-GI's who got out of the Army and stayed in Bangkok.

The place looks good, better than I thought it would. I go inside. Warm. A lot of laughter comes from upstairs and I can hear a live jazz band playing. I can tell by the sound that they're black. The downstairs room is about half-full. I find a table, sit down, and order a drink. More music and laughter comes from upstairs whenever the door at the top of the stairs is opened. People come in and go straight upstairs. I wish that I was in the mood for a good party. The noise reminds me of the Hollywood Club in Washington, but the downstairs room of the Hollywood is long, while this room is square and darker.

I remember how the guy at the top of the stairs at the Hollywood would take your dollar and stamp your hand so you wouldn't have to pay again no matter how many times you ran in and out. And we used to do a lot of running between there and Chez Maurice next door, and the Bohemian Caverns around the corner on U Street, Ninth and U Street, or Eleventh and U. Damn, I can't remember, and we used to do it almost every Saturday night when I was stationed at Andrews.

A tall bright-skinned black man comes in the African Star with three Thai girls following him. The bartender knows him. They joke. The bartender is a slender Thai man. The three girls perch on three barstools while the two men talk across the bar.

The bartender digs behind the counter and brings up three packs of black market cigarettes. He gives them to the girls and they slip them into their handbags. The girls sit on the stools and talk among themselves while the two men continue talking. Red slacks, blue slacks, mini-skirt with nice little legs spinning and wiggling.

The bar is made of blue mirrors, and there is a long blue mirror along the wall in back of the row of liquor bottles. A blue ball made of octagonal mirrors spins above the bartender's head.

Several GI's sit with their girls eating soul food in the dim room. The door at the top of the stairs opens. Laughter comes down followed by a round, laughing black GI with a cigar in his mouth. "Hey, Nick, my man," he says as his head emerges out of the stairwell.

"Hey, my man," the tall guy says.

"What's happening?" The black man is wearing a silk suit.

"Nothing."

"Nothing? Man, I thought your name was synonymous with what's happening." He slaps the tall guy on the shoulder.

"Shit, not me."

"Three foxes." He looks at the three girls.

"Friends and cousins of friends," the tall guy says.

"Yeah, how about that."

I listen rather mindlessly to their conversation, happy to be hearing familiar tones and familiar rhythms. A young-looking black man sits at the far end of the bar, drinking by himself. He has long well-shaped sideburns. The waitress brings my scotch and water. I give her a dollar, and she gives me change in baht. I watch her small hands counting out the baht on the tabletop.

"Have you heard the band at the Lido?" the tall guy asks. I begin to drink slowly.

"Where're you from, my man?" a voice very close to my ear says.

I look up and see it is the young guy from the far end of the bar. "Washington, D.C." I make a sign for him to sit down.

"Greensboro."

"Close."

"Neighbors. What's happening?"

"Nothing."

"Yeah, I know this shit's a bitch. Army?"

"No, Air Force."

"I'm Army, infantry, Vietnam. What're you, in CD?"

"No, I'm a pilot."

He leans back and takes another look. "Oh, shit, a glory boy. Officer."

I laugh.

"Wilton Smith."

"Ben Williams."

"Yeah, so you an officer?"

"I guess."

We sit and talk for a while. The waitress brings two more drinks. "What do you fly?" he asks after a while, as if he has not let the thought out of his mind.

"F-105's."

"That's nice. Super Thuds," he smiles. He drums his fingers on the table for a moment. "I was going to be an officer, but I had to drop out of college—A & T."

"It's not that much difference."

He laughs. "No, man, there's a world of difference. It's a whole different war down in the mud."

"I'm quitting flying anyway," I say to put myself back on equal footing with him.

"Yeah." He drinks slowly. Then he leans back and drums the table. "I haven't been in combat in twenty-one days," he says, as if to put himself ahead of me again. "I been AWOL twenty-one days. I'm not going back. They don't even know where to find me, and if they wait a few more days, I'll be in Sweden somewhere," he whispers as if he trusts me but does not trust the people who might overhear us. "If you a cop, then you a cop, but I ain't going back. Not alive, I ain't."

"I'm not a cop."

"Well, an officer might be the same thing."

"Shit, man, why would I turn you in?" I say to turn away some of the growing hostility in his manner.

"I don't see why you would go back. They gon' put your ass in jail. The minute you tell them you ain't gon' kill no more of these people they gon' put you in jail."

"I don't feel like running away."

"I want to live, man," there is rage in his voice now. "I want to live. Shit."

"We been running away long enough," I say angrily.

"*You* been running. I ain't been running nowhere. I was born in the shit and I want a chance to live. That's all. I shot a kid, man. I shot a little Vietnamese kid right in the back, man. The night before I left the 'Nam. I was on patrol in a village near Thuc Yen and this little kid came up to me in an alley and asked me did I want a shoeshine. And sometimes they have bombs in those little boxes. So I told him to set his box down and back off, and he turned and ran, and I shot him in the back." His voice cracks and he is silent for a moment. "Then I went up and looked in his little box and do you know what I found?"

"I don't know."

"Shoe polish, man. Not a goddam thing but shoe polish. I went back to base and packed my shit and left. I ain't ever gon' kill no more innocent people, man. And I ain't going to no jail either. I'm still young."

"Okay."

"Not that I'm coming down on you. I thought about the shit too, but if you go to jail, you just as well be dead. Just as well call yourself a dead martyr, and we got enough of them. Don't go to no jail on a bull-shit tip, man. I been in jail. You die in jail. There are some Buddhists on Rama One Road near Wat Suthat who can help you get to Japan, and up through Russia to Sweden." He stands up. "I'm going to go back to my hotel," he says. "I didn't mean to come down on you so hard." He laughs. "Ain't your fault that you an officer."

"Good luck," I say as he goes out. I sit down and think about all the black men who have been hitting the road, catching trains. Then I think about all the black men in prisons or on Southern prison farms. I try and weigh one group against another as I pay my check and go out the door.

I go back through the late night streets of Bangkok. I stop at a small all-night coffee shop in the Loom Hotel. I sip the coffee slowly, and think. Then I catch a cab back to our hotel. Damg is asleep when I get there. I turn on the small lamp on the dresser. She is small and beautiful in the dim light. I go into the bathroom and write a note by the small night light above the mirror. Then I pack my things, leave the note and a hundred dollars on the dresser, go out into the hallway and pull the door closed behind me.

(1973)

TOM MAYER

Born in Chicago in 1943, Tom Mayer published his first book of short stories,
Bubble Gum and Kipling, *in 1964. He went to Vietnam as a freelance
magazine correspondent and came back with the material for* The Weary
Falcon, *his 1971 volume of five searing and penetrating short stories, including "Kafka for President." Mayer now describes himself as "a writer who lives
in New Mexico."*

*When Mayer actually saw "Kafka for President" lettered on the helmet
of an American infantryman, he found the appropriate title for this story.*

Kafka for President

In Danang I talked with Captain Hendricks, the head Marine Public Information Officer, about various Combined Action Companies.
These were squad size Marine units posted in hamlets and villages with
comparable size Popular Force units, the idea being that American ag-
gressiveness and know-how would rub off on the Vietnamese, who
would then be able to provide security for their own homes. As everyone was always saying, pacification, the uprooting of the Viet Cong infrastructure, was impossible without security.

Hendricks said a good CAC, one that hadn't received much publicity, was CAC 8, just off the road to Hoi An. The PIO, an ex-halfback
from Ann Arbor and a recruiting poster Marine, heavy shouldered,
lean, blond hair cropped so close the scalp gleamed, was delighted I
was going to shoot the piece, and enthusiastically explained the operation. Without actually lying about anything he tried to leave me with
the impression that the program was achieving phenomenal success,
was the answer to pacification. I did not blame him. In fact, I had expected it.

From his point of view it was a perfect story, one that couldn't be
told often enough. Instead of zippo-ing villages Marines were protecting them, instead of killing civilians or creating refugees they were
helping, providing security from the marauding Cong, medicines, no
squatting prisoners, no crying mothers, only Christian brotherhood
and American social work. A story to which not even the most militant
Vietnik could take objection.

Hendricks sent me down to the 1/27 command post the next
morning, with a lance corporal as a bodyguard and chauffeur. We went

out by the short cut across the airfield, past the revetments for the delta-wing F-102 Interceptors, and a C-54 with the tail assembly removed, onto Highway One. It was pocked with holes, some from mines, but most from use. We passed a Marine company on a road sweep, two long files of men, spaced out and walking with weapons at the ready, the machine-gunners wearing belts of shining ammunition, pop art necklaces, around their necks. Through towns with the familiar sloppy half-uniformed PFs lounging at the roadsides. I saw one tossing a white phosphorous grenade in the air and catching it as casually as if it were a rubber ball or an Indian club. ARVNs guarded every bridge. They lived with their women in dank straw-floored bunkers beside the road. Five or six kilometers from Hoi An we turned off.

We drove into the 1/27 CP, a sandbagged and barbwire fortress on top of a sand dune, and I checked in with the battalion executive officer, who turned me over to an ancient goliath of a gunnery sergeant named Ingersoll. One of his ears was shot away, the other so cauliflowered even his own mother could never have recognized it.

I threw my stuff in the back of the gunny's mule. We went through a hamlet and out onto a country lane lined with coconut palms. The day was clear and cool from the recent monsoons. The palms ended and paddies stretched away to the treelines. A little boy was riding a water buffalo, whacking its neck and flanks with a stick. We passed a Buddhist graveyard, lumpy grass-covered mounds, a few headstones, one with ornate carving on it, and an old French blockhouse, a hexagonal bullet-pocked concrete bunker with beveled firing slits.

"How much farther?" I asked.

"Across the river," he said, and pointed ahead to a treeline.

I didn't see any river.

"Is this road secure?"

"Supposed to be," he said. "Ain't nobody been shot on it yet."

I laughed politely.

"Who you work for?" he asked.

"Free lance. I'm doing this job for the *New York Times*."

The gunny gargled and spat. I gathered he didn't approve of the *Times*.

"Sometimes I work for UPI," I offered.

"We don't get many reporters here."

I could see now that in front of the treeline was a river, spanned by a girdered bridge. On the near side was a sandbagged position. We clattered across. The Marine compound was a miniature of the CP, a

living tent with sandbags halfway up the sides, a small stone house
sprouting radio antennae, three sandbagged bunkers, one covering the
bridge, the others the approaches from the hamlet beyond, a two-seat
crapper that at first I mistook for a position, a shower made from a
fifty-five-gallon drum perched on a stilt platform, the inevitable layers
of concertina. A small basketball court had been scraped out behind the
living tent and six Marines, one a giant Negro built along the lines of
Jimmy Brown, were playing.

The hamlet beyond the wire was of the one-street variety.
Thatched roof huts, dirt paths worn dusty smooth by bare feet, chickens, dogs, pigs, old women in black pajamas and conical hats, the usual.
At the far end of the street sand dunes began, and on top of the first
one was another French blockhouse.

"This-here's it," gunny said.

The basketball game broke up and the Marines, shirtless and
sweating, crowded around the mule.

"Hey, gunny man," the big Negro said. "You bring the fuckin'
beer?"

Gunny didn't answer, got out of the mule, and I followed him into
the stone house, which contained several radios and a field phone, a
desk, a couple of cots with air mattresses. A skinny, shirtless Negro,
much lighter than the giant, was sitting by the radio reading a comic
book, and a sergeant was writing at the desk.

"Sergeant Bernays," the gunny said.

"What do you know, gunny? You got beer?"

"This here is Mr. Bender from the *New York Times.*"

Bernays stood up and we shook hands.

"Mr. Bender wants to look around a little. The major says you
should extend him every courtesy."

"Glad to meet you," Bernays said.

I explained that I wanted to spend a day or two, shoot a few pictures. Bernays said that would be fine, they'd fix me a cot in here. He
sent the light Negro, his name was Wright, to get my stuff.

Gunny left and Bernays introduced me to the Marines—there
were seventeen of them, including one corpsman, a heavy squad—and
we had lunch, C-rations heated on primitive stoves and washed down
with Cokes and Dr. Peppers. The soft drinks were supplied by three
Vietnamese houseboys, called Bugs Bunny and Fucky and Stinky, who
brought them from a store in the hamlet for 15 piastres.

The Marines, except for Bernays, a veteran of the retreat from the

Yalu in Korea, seemed very young and not particularly on the ball, high school dropout types. Hendricks had told me proudly that they were all proven veterans—CAC was not a place for malingerers, no one was considered for a CAC assignment until he had done six months in a line company. "These boys," he had concluded, "have all been in some good firefights." But they seemed very naive, innocent, if you could apply the terms to someone who had spent six months in a Marine line company.

The living conditions, compared even to a Special Forces A-camp, were Stone Age. No refrigerator, no electricity, cots instead of bunks, X-rations instead of canned and frozen foods, beer came irregularly and in limited amounts, no hard liquor. And the defensive system seemed to me fairly flimsy. There was no artillery, not even any mortars or a machine gun, only two full automatic M-14s, which were notoriously hard to hold down. I asked Bernays about it, and he said, "Battalion says a detached squad don't rate no automatic weapons." The chief recreations were basketball, and, when it was warm, floating around under the bridge on air mattresses.

John Northup, a private from Chicago who had been drafted after two years of college because of low grades, and the corpsman, a boy named Lowenstein with a fierce Cossack mustache, offered to show me around the hamlet. They were evidently the unit intellectuals, and were eager to get to know the visiting reporter. I asked Northup if there were other draftees in the unit and he said no. I asked him if he'd been surprised when they'd sent him to the Marines.

"Shit yes," he said. "I didn't even know the Corps took draftees."

"Are you glad now?"

"Are you kidding?" he said. "Christ, in the Army I'd have a soft job, be a fucking clerk or something. In the Corps everybody's a rifleman. Who wants to be a rifleman?"

We walked down the hut-lined street, past a well constructed stone house with a concertina roll for a front fence, a PF with a carbine standing guard. Lowenstein said it was the PF barracks. We stopped in front of a seamstress shop. There were two treadle sewing machines, one operated by an old woman and the other by a pretty girl wearing fresh light blue pajamas.

"That's Betty Lou," Lowenstein said, pointing to the pretty girl, who smiled at us coyly. "Prime slope cunt."

"Greer's giving it to her," Northup said.

"Which one's Greer?" I didn't know which names went with which faces yet.

"The big coon," Lowenstein said.

At the end of the street was a schoolhouse with a bare metal flag-pole in the yard. Lowenstein said he held Medcap, or first aid sessions, here three times a week, and asked if I wanted to come. I said sure. We had a Coke at the store on the way back.

At 1700 Bernays sent out a patrol, six Vietnamese and six Marines, and I went along. The Marines wore flak jackets with no shirts under them and steel pots. Greer, a corporal, was the patrol leader. He showed me where we were going, tracing a route along the seashore—I had not realized we were so close to the ocean—and through some woods and a hamlet, which he said was deserted, and back to camp along the riverbank. His finger was the thickness of a rifle barrel, only blacker.

He put a Vietnamese on point, then an American, and so on. "If we don't alternate," he said, "the slopes bunches up on you. You gotta watch the little mothers all the time." I was in the middle with Lowenstein.

We moved out down the street, past the seamstresses' establishment—Greer grinned at Betty Lou and she giggled and Lowenstein said, "Look at the ass man"—and the store, through barbwire at the edge of town, by two positions which I assumed the Vietnamese manned at night, and along the dunes under the French fort. A dungpit smell emanated from the fort and Lowenstein said, "That's the town shitter up there."

We hiked on, sinking into the fine deep sand, but it was pleasantly cool. A breeze blew over the dunes, smelling of sea salt and carrying the sound of waves. Greer motioned a redhead named Monday out onto the left flank. Monday had a bad sunburn and his bare arms protruding out of the flak jacket looked like half-cooked sausages.

I shot a good deal of film, trying always to include both Viets and Americans. The PFs in their motley uniforms—one was barefoot and two wore white tennis shoes and another faded jeans—and carrying carbines, looked like children out with Christmas present cap guns alongside the Marines.

After a half-hour's march we approached the woods, and people began to scan the treeline, train weapons on every modulation in the dunes. Suddenly Greer motioned us down. Lowenstein ducked behind a bush, drew his .45, cocked it. I got behind a low hummock of sand and knelt, shooting quickly. We waited a few seconds, crouched, poised, ready to fire and cringe and burrow into the sand, staring at the treeline, trying to detect some giveaway movement, some unnatural feature, but all I saw were bushes and palms swaying in the breeze.

Greer got us up, passed word back he'd seen something. I followed along after Lowenstein, my torso bent forward as far as it would go without my falling on my face. I tried to take bent-kneed steps, to make myself as small a target as possible, and picked likely cover to dive behind.

Then we were at the trees and nothing had happened. A bird squawked raucously and Lowenstein spun, his .45 held in front of him. The Vietnamese behind me laughed and Lowenstein said, "Shut up, you fuckheaded slope."

We came into a clearing with the remains of a few houses and huts, the hamlet shown on the map. The huts had been burned down and all that was left were piles of ashes and a few charred poles. The houses were roofless and the walls were pocked and had holes in them such as a round from a recoilless rifle might make. A stench hung over the place, so cloying it was almost visible, and I looked around for a body and saw a dead dog. Insects had eaten out its eyes but its stomach had not burst yet, was grotesquely distended.

We went on through a hedge and by another burned-down shack into a new clearing. At the far end was a half-destroyed house. A very old Vietnamese couple stood with their backs to one of the shattered walls, their hands clasped in front of them, while Greer and a PF covered them. The other Marines and PFs set up a perimeter on the edges of the clearing.

Lowenstein and I went to the house and I began taking pictures.

"Not these two again," Lowenstein said.

"Yeah man," Greer said. "They the same ones."

"They won't leave," Lowenstein explained. "All the people from here are supposed to be in the village, but these two stay here. We find them every time we patrol down here."

"Tell 'em," Greer said to the PF. "Why ain't they in the village where they belongs?"

The PF translated and the old woman began to cry, tears navigating down the creases at her eye corners and in her cheeks, and the old man shook his head and talked, slowly, and with dignity, addressing himself to Greer, his beard jerking as he spoke. He ended with a short bow. All through it his eyes had been expressionless, not calculating or begging or questioning or afraid, just flat.

"Say not have place go," the PF said. "Here home."

"Shit man," Greer said. "Don't give me that shit. Tell him again. Tell him if he stay here we gonna zap him sure. Tell him I seen him back there and I almost zap him this time."

"And tell that old lady to shut the fuck up," the corpsman said. The woman had not stopped crying.

"Can't we take them in with us?" I asked.

"We done that twice," Greer said.

When the PF had finished translating the old man went through his routine again. The woman kept wailing.

"He say not like village," the PF said. "Here home."

Greer drew his bayonet and held it to the old man's throat. The blade was black, but the cutting edges gleamed, were honed to a fineness worthy of a Gillette ad. Greer's biceps, black as anthracite and knotted, were thicker than the old man's neck. Greer put the tip of the bayonet under the old man's chin, forced his head up and back against the wall. The woman was on her knees, moaning and wailing. I was taking pictures.

"Tell him," Greer said. "The nex' time I zap him. Tell him I think they was VC here and I think the motherfuckers split while he talkin' and his old lady cryin'."

Greer drew the bayonet tip across the underside of the chin, behind the old man's beard, then wiped the blade on his pants and sheathed it. A few drops of bright blood dripped down the sparse hair of the beard. Without waiting for the PF to translate Greer said, "Aw right. Move out."

We formed up, followed a path out of the clearing. I glanced back just before plunging through the bamboo curtain. The woman was on her feet, dabbing at the man's chin with a rag of some sort, but she was still crying. Her man had not moved, was leaning against the wall, his head back and his hands folded in front of him.

We went up a small hill, the trail sandy, jungle undergrowth on all sides. The track veered every few yards and I closed up on Lowenstein, wanted him in sight in case we came to a fork. We reached the river, turned up it toward base. The water was still, layered with scum, perhaps a hundred yards across. The path now was packed, easy walking.

We passed more shot-up houses, several deserted rice paddies. In front of a temple Greer called a halt. We found places beside the trail behind fallen logs and sat down with our backs against them.

Lowenstein said that just beyond here they'd gotten into a firefight about a week before, killed two Cong and gotten some papers that indicated the Cong were planning to hit the hamlet. One paper was a diagram of positions and another was a list of all the Marine and PF weapons. Greer, who was sitting with us, said, "Some of them mothers in that vil is Congs."

Monday, the sausage-armed redhead, had missed a VC at about twenty meters, shot an entire clip at him on full auto.

"Shit man," Greer said, laughing. "The Corps spends thousands of dollars teachin' the mother to shoot and he see a Cong and forget to aim."

Monday, several logs up the trail, heard and said, "Fuck you, Greer."

One of the Vietnamese brought us three green coconuts.

"He wants your bayonet," the doc said.

Greer hacked holes in the nuts and we drank the sweet cool milk.

Greer got us up, said to recon by fire. Instantly Monday cut loose a clip into the temple, sending up sprays of plaster and stone and tile. Lowenstein drew his .45 and assumed the classic pose of a pistol marksman, right arm extended but not rigid, feet apart and braced, left hand on hip, and began to shoot very deliberately at a coconut tree a few yards away. The PFs were clattering away with their carbines, but all were careful not to shoot at the temple. The one who had done the interpreting was trying to shoot down a cluster of coconuts, but hit several instead and the thin white fluid came down in streams. Greer walked up behind him and kicked him in the tail and shouted over the din, "This ain't no fuckin' nut hunt."

It was 1800 and getting dark quickly when we got back to base. A pair of PFs with a BAR and carbine were in one of the holes outside the wire. I was glad to see the BAR, hoped the PFs knew how to use it. Another PF pulled a roll of concertina across the trail behind us.

After dinner I talked with Bernays in the communications hut. The PF commander, a little sergeant named Hoa, was there, sitting on a blanket on the floor cleaning his carbine. Bernays talked to me about what he was trying to do in the village—put another room on the schoolhouse, get in some cheap cloth for the seamstresses, maybe get a battery-powered sewing machine, if there was such a thing, find some lumber for carpenters to make trunks with. He said all the Marines wanted trunks to send home souvenirs in. I got out my brandy flask, gave a shot to Bernays and one to Hoa, but he did not like it.

Later I walked with Bernays through the hamlet to check the sentries. They were in place, but the PFs outside the wire were smoking. We could see the coals from fifty yards, which meant so could a Cong crawling around out on the dunes.

"They ought to cup them," I said. "You can't see a cigarette if you cup it."

"I know," Bernays said. "I told them, but they didn't pay no attention and I ain't gonna tell them again. It's their fucking asses."

In the huts kerosene lamps burned softly. Bernays stopped in front of the seamstresses' hut, and said, "You in there, Greer?"

"Yeah man."

"The ambush goes out at 2300."

"I know, man."

"You getting any?"

Greer laughed.

We walked on and Bernays explained that every night he put out four-man Marine ambushes, listening posts really. He varied the times and places.

In the morning I went with Lowenstein to the schoolhouse for Medcap. He brought several bottles of antibiotic and vitamin pills and a huge bottle of antibiotic ointment, his instruments, and a cardboard box full of half-bars of soap. I asked him why he gave out the soap in pieces instead of whole, and he said, "I tried giving it to the fuck faces whole, but then they sell it. I want them to use it."

People swarmed into the school yard after us. Lowenstein set up his material on the steps.

"Watch how the little shits try to steal stuff," he said.

He got the people into line, children first. Some had nothing wrong, only wanted the big purple vitamins, but most had festering sores on the legs and ankles, or colds. Lowenstein explained that their blood did not coagulate well, that most were anemic, thanks to their poor diet, and any cut or insect bite was likely to infect. He yanked the scabs off with forceps, swabbed the wounds out with dabs of cotton dipped in the vaseline-like ointment, gave the patient a vitamin pill and an antibiotic pill, and watched while he took them. Several times he grabbed children by the necks and pried their mouths open and fished the pills out unswallowed. When that happened he dropped the pills on the ground and stamped on them.

"They take them home to their parents," he said. "I don't give a shit about their parents. If their parents got something wrong, they can come themselves."

Several children tried to sneak back in line, but Lowenstein picked them out, spanked them, threw dirt clods at them until they ran out of the yard. All the children laughed and giggled, except when having their scabs yanked off.

Next came the mothers with babies. Lowenstein gave both parent and child vitamins, and the mother a half bar of soap. Most of the babies had hideous rashes and scabs. Three had ringworm. Lowenstein cleaned them and shouted at each mother, "Wash the little shit. Use the fucking soap. He wouldn't have this rash if you washed him, you filthy pig."

The mothers nodded dumbly and smiled and tucked the soap inside their blouses.

"Half these kids oughta be in the hospital," the doc said.

Last were a few men, all war cripples or very old, and a dozen cackling old women. The men were very grave, smiled stiffly while their scabs were being yanked and bowed polite thank yous for their pills. The harridans squawked when Lowenstein hurt them. He could find nothing wrong with several and swatted them hard on the back and shoved them toward the gate, where they turned and spat betel juice at us and bawled what I was sure were the foulest of Vietnamese obscenities.

"They want pills," Lowenstein said. "And it gives them the ass if I don't give them any. They're too fucking old to waste pills on."

We collected the medicines and went back and I washed very carefully, scrubbed at my hands and forearms and face with a rough-grained medical soap, before lunch.

The afternoon patrol was to go in the opposite direction from yesterday's, through an inhabited but unsecured hamlet to a swift boat base. Swift boats were patrol vessels that the Navy used to try to intercept smugglers. Bernays said it was always a good patrol, because the Navy had a generator and a refrigerator and plenty of beer.

Northup was on this patrol and I noticed written across his helmet was *Kafka for President*. Almost all Marines and soldiers wrote things on their helmets, but usually they were predictably obscene or the names of their girl friends.

"That's quite a slogan you have," I said.

"Shit," he said. "It's a fucking Kafkaesque war, isn't it?"

I said I guessed it was.

Again a Vietnamese was on point, an American second, etc. Bernays was patrol leader and Greer, unhappy at missing the beer, stayed home. Bernays carried a carbine he'd taken from a dead VC instead of an M-14. I asked him if he always put a Vietnamese on point.

"Fucking A," he said. "It's their country. The least they can do is run point."

Hoa went along too, and Monday told me, "That shit-face don't hardly ever stir out of the vil unless he thinks he'll get some beer."

We went behind the dunes in the other direction, the sea on our left flank this time, and into the inhabited hamlet. Bernays explained to me that within the month the Marines were going to depopulate the area, move the people either into his village or refugee camps. The place was filled with VC or VC sympathizers, which amounted to the same thing, and Battalion couldn't spare the men to start another CAC unit. The Marines had gotten intelligence about a VC meeting one night about a month before and had tried to ambush it. They'd been moving into the hamlet—he pointed to a burned down hut and scarred palm—when an old woman had set off the alarm, had seen or sensed them and started wailing.

"Just like that old bitch yesterday," Lowenstein said.

A machine gun had opened up, enfiladed the trail, killed one Marine and wounded another.

"Good kids," Bernays said. "I wanted to burn this place down the next day."

The people acted friendly enough, smiled at us, and the children ran beside the column and shouted and the dogs sniffed, but I noticed Bernays' carbine's safety was off. Hoa knew everybody, smiled and waved and stopped to chat.

At the swift-boat base we had a couple of cans of icy beer, more out of a sense of duty than any burning thirst, because it wasn't very hot. We took a different route home, worked along the shore of the stagnant lagoon. Bernays said we were looking for a VC .50 cal. machine gun which had been shooting at planes, and of course you never went back the same way you came out if you could help it. It was very hard going, vines and roots and walls of bamboo and stickers and wide ditches, mud-slimy trails and narrow dike tops. Insects dropped inside my shirt and limbs whipped across my face. My camera straps snagged every other step. The Marines were all tense, walked carefully with weapons held ready, but the Vietnamese appeared unconcerned.

They barged through the brush and talked noisily to each other and Hoa played a transistor radio. Nasal Vietnamese music preceded us at about a billion decibels. Bernays told him to shut it off. He pretended not to understand, but finally turned it down. I was hot and itchy and scared. The water, where we could see it through the curtains of vines, was filmed with a heavy scum of sick green. Reeds thrust up in little islands. Hoa turned his radio back up again, or anyway to my straining ears it sounded as if he did, and I said, "Why don't you take it away from him?"

"He'll bitch to his officers," Bernays said. "And then they bitch to Battalion and Battalion shits on me."

"I just hope there aren't any Cong in here," I said. "If there are, nobody's going to have a chance to bitch to anybody."

"At least they know where we are," Bernays said, grinning weakly. "They can keep away if they want to."

The radio played all the way back to the base but nothing happened.

That night Greer and Bernays planned an operation. There was an inhabited village on the river almost to the spot where it ran into the sea, well below the hamlet in which we'd found the old couple. They planned to move out in two columns at 0400 the next morning. One column would march down the beach, then sweep inland across paddies into the village, while the other would sneak down the riverbank and act as a blocking force. The two Marines decided they'd go with the beach column and let Hoa command the river group. I decided to go with the river group, because it had much less walking to do. I asked Bernays if he was going to brief Hoa tonight.

"Shit no," Bernays said.

"Why not?" I asked.

"Half his people will DD off to Hoi An," Bernays said. "They always bug off if they know about an operation. I'll wake him at 0300."

Bernays called Battalion, cleared the operation with them, gave them map coordinates. Then we walked over to the tent and he told the Marines. They bitched a little, but began cleaning weapons and laying out gear.

We went back to the house and I got Bernays talking about Hoa. He said he wasn't bad as PFs went. Anyway he trusted him. It was just that he hadn't had much training and most of his people had none at all. Hoa was very good at intelligence, at interrogating prisoners and assessing information. It was Hoa who had found out about the meeting in the village and he had killed one of the three Cong in the firefight. We had some brandy and turned in.

Bernays shook me awake at 0330. It was cold and completely dark. I got into my clothes and pulled on my boots, shivering. The Marines were forming up, joking and grumbling and cursing, but the PFs were quiet. Bernays made sure everyone was with the correct group, walked up and down the two columns shining a flashlight in each man's face, while we smoked last cigarettes.

Just outside the village we split up. Bernays' group plunged up the dune, by the French fort and over to the beach, while we worked toward the river. I was with Doc Lowenstein again. Hoa was ahead of him, then Northup. No one talked, but it seemed to me we were making enough noise to wake the dead, crashing through brush and tripping over roots. The PFs tinkled as they walked, grenades and clips ticking against each other and the eyelets in the webbing, sling swivels tapping stocks. The Marines had covered their swivels with green tape and made sure that grenades were secure, hung where they would not make noise, the handles held down by tape or rubber bands.

We found the river trail and stopped making so much noise. I could discern the outlines of the temple's winged roof as we passed it, but mostly I walked with my eyes down, picking my way, glancing up to make sure Lowenstein was close ahead. I developed the old familiar craving for tobacco, remembered on a night patrol in the rain once when I had put an unlit cigarette between my lips and sucked on it until it had gotten soggy and disintegrated.

We stopped for a minute, and two or three men ahead a match flared and steadied and I could see Hoa lighting a cigar. He waved the flame out as casually as if we had been on a Sunday morning stroll. We started again and I saw the glowing tip bobbing. I was furious. I wanted to run past Lowenstein and snatch the cigar away and stamp it out. I did not think he was even making an effort to cup the thing.

We cut in from the river, climbed several dunes, legs driving in the slipping sand, and scrambled back down to the water's edge, and ahead always was the bright glow. We stopped again and another PF, farther ahead, lit a cigarette with a match flare I was sure you could see in Hanoi. Lowenstein moved up to Hoa and told him to throw the cigar away. His voice was tight with rage. We started again, still the bobbing glow. I wanted to beat the man, tackle him and sit on him and choke him and stuff the cigar down his throat. We crossed several clearings and I imagined a VC machine-gunner thumbing the safety off and aiming just below the glow and squeezing a burst and then raking down the column and I wondered if I would be quick enough to get down and scanned the dark trailsides for a place to dive.

But again, as with the transistor radio, nothing happened.

Dawn came and in the first half light we were still moving along the river. The pace quickened and we came to a hut with a kerosene lamp lit inside. Hoa sent two PFs in, and they hauled out an old man and two women, one with a baby, the other pregnant, and three small children. We herded them ahead of us. One of the children started to cry and Hoa slapped him. Another hut, a barking dog sent whimpering by a blow from Hoa's rifle butt. The PFs went in and collected an old woman, who came out rubbing her eyes, then went back for her conical hat.

By 0630 we had rounded up all the people who lived along the riverbank and herded them into a clearing in front of a schoolhouse. Two PFs guarded them. The other PFs and Marines were strung out on the riverbank behind logs and trees. I sat with Lowenstein on the schoolhouse steps and watched the prisoners. They squatted in the dirt, chatted. Occasionally one of the younger women would move away, turn her back and drop her trousers. The crones and children relieved themselves where they were. Several mothers breastfed their babies, and Lowenstein said, "Did you ever see such ugly tits?"

We heated C-ration ham and eggs and washed it down with coconut milk. Then I walked down the trail to where Northup had positioned himself behind a fallen tree. He had the radio, said Bernays hadn't had any contact yet, but had collected twenty-three women and children. I took a picture of a PF BAR man eating a bowl of rice, went back to the schoolhouse and stretched out on the top step, using my camera bag as a pillow.

I had just gotten comfortable when firing broke out. There were two bursts, and the BAR down the bank started. Several rounds whined overhead and smacked through the palm leaves. I rolled off the steps, crouched against the side of the schoolhouse, where Lowenstein joined me. Another burst, followed by the concussive whump of hand grenades.

The Vietnamese civilians were in panic. The PF guards had disappeared. The old women jabbered and the children were crying. A woman scurried off up the trail and Lowenstein yelled at her to come back but she was out of sight around a bend. A young one, carrying her baby, broke, and Lowenstein drew his pistol and shot at her. The ejected round tinked against one of my cameras. Lowenstein shot again and missed and she was gone too, but he turned the pistol on the others. They stopped talking, none moved, even the smallest children, and watched him.

"Now stay where you fucking are," he said. "Or somebody's going to get hurt."

I got some good shots of him and the people. Several old women were squatting in piles of offal, had stained their pants. There was no more firing, and I ducked and dodged down the trail to Northup. He was lying behind his log, the muzzle of his M-14 poking around one end. I dropped beside him and asked what had happened. He didn't know. We waited perhaps five minutes—it seemed like a year—until Bernays called. Wright, the other Negro, had been wounded. One PF was dead. Two Cong killed, they were bringing in a female suspect. I went up the trail, told Doc to get ready.

A stream of civilians, exactly like the ones Lowenstein was guarding, ambled up the trail driven by PFs. The new group mingled with the old, squatted down, spat betel. Two PFs came up the trail carrying a body wrapped in a poncho. The hood was not snapped and blood dripped out of it. Then came Greer, carrying Wright in his arms as if he were a child. He also carried both rifles. Wright's flak vest, and Wright's webbing hung around his neck. Monday and Bernays prodded a young woman ahead of them, and each had an extra weapon, a carbine for Monday and an old bolt-action rifle for Bernays. The girl was rather pretty, neatly dressed in a fresh white shirt and black pajama trousers that weren't as baggy as most.

Greer laid Wright on the top step. He was pale, as if bleach had been poured over his smoke-colored skin, and his eyes were shut. His teeth were clenched and you could hear each breath distinctly. A hastily applied field dressing covered his right elbow and a tourniquet was tied around the biceps above. He groaned as Greer set him down. Doc had his bag open and went to work, took the dressing off and checked the tourniquet, straightened the arm and strapped it to Wright's side.

"You give him morphine?" he asked Greer.

"Yeah man."

"How many Syrettes?"

"One."

"How's it feel, Danny?"

"Shitty," Wright said.

"We'll have you out of here in a little."

Doc ripped Wright's trousers and jabbed a Syrette in his thigh. "Don't sweat it."

"I ain't."

Bernays said he thought the Medevac could set down in the school yard and told Monday to move the civilians. Hoa and the interpreter were checking their IDs. Northup came up, said he had the Medevac. I could hear a chopper, a giant flapping in the distance.

It grew louder and an H-34 flew over and then a whining flapping and a Huey gunship, mounting four machine guns and fourteen rockets, came over so low the fronds trembled and a rotten coconut fell. Bernays threw out a smoke grenade which burst green, and the H-34 pilot's voice came over the radio saying he could make it and the ship lowered in. Greer picked Wright up and loaded him on and ducked away, and Wright gave us a thumbs up with his good hand as the chopper lifted, turned toward us, dipped its nose, and rushed at us across the yard like an airborne bull with whirling horns. It raised a wall of dust and knocked my hat off with the blast and barely cleared the school, then turned back across the river, straining for altitude.

I found my hat and dusted off my cameras. The Vietnamese were dust covered and clearly frightened. Hoa began checking their cards again. One out of every eight or ten did not have a card or had one that was out of date or possibly forged. These people were grouped to one side, and the others were released.

I sat on the steps with Doc and Greer and Bernays, who was gouging open a coconut, and asked what had happened. Bernays said they had been sweeping across a paddy, almost to the hamlet, and had come to a hut. Wright and the PF had gone in and brought out the girl in the neat blouse, who had tried to stall them. She had known a little English and did not have a card, went through a long story about how she had lost it. Greer and Bernays had listened to her, and the PF and Wright had gone around behind the hut and surprised two armed Cong trying to climb into a well. The Cong had killed the PF and wounded Wright, although Wright had wounded one of them. They tried to run away, the unhurt man helping his friend, and Greer had come around the hut and cut them both down. Then he had grenaded the well. They'd left the bodies there.

Doc said Wright's elbow had probably been shattered, he would lose most of the use of it, if they didn't have to amputate. Greer was eating from a tin of steak and potatoes, and did not say anything, did not appear to be listening to us, just moved the plastic spoon back and forth between can and mouth.

When Hoa had finished with the civilians, he commandeered six sampans with boat women, and we loaded ourselves and the dead PF and the suspects, eight of them including the girl, and began to pole up the river toward base. I asked Bernays if it wasn't dangerous going up the river like this, and he said no, we'd swept one side, and Company had positions all along the other.

The sun was out but not too hot and I rested in the bottom of the sampan and let myself relax with the thrusting and gliding of the poling and felt the sun on my face. I started to doze again and then jerked awake at the sound of two explosions. I couldn't place what they were, and sat up, almost tipping the sampan over, in time to hear a third, and see a great fountain of scummy brown water lift up in front of a sampan filled with PFs. The water settled lazily. Bernays was laughing at me.

"They're fishing," he said.

A PF in another sampan stood up, his legs braced, the narrow craft tipping, the boat woman balancing with her pole, and pulled the pin from a grenade and threw it out ahead. Another explosive lifting of dirty water. Ahead of the first sampan the water was dotted with silver spots, fish that had risen to the surface, killed by the concussion. One fish swam crazily along the top of the water, its head out like a girl who doesn't want to get her hair wet, and a PF dove in after it.

It was almost 1300 when we got to base. The boat women drove the bows of the sampans into the shore mud and we unloaded. The PFs herded the suspects into a one-room hut with no windows. All of the prisoners were women, but the girl Greer and Bernays had picked up stood out. She was younger, better dressed, much cleaner, and did not talk and cackle with the others, but walked by herself, her arms tied behind her, head up. The last sampan to be unloaded carried the dead PF and many dead fish. The hood of the poncho was crusted with blood, but had stopped dripping, and smelled of fish.

Lowenstein and Northup and I opened some cans and sent Bugs Bunny for Cokes.

"What happens now?" I asked.

"We'll torture them, probably," Northup said.

"That's one thing Hoa is good for," Doc said. "He can make the little fuckers talk."

"And after that?"

Northup shrugged.

Bernays came over and Doc asked, "When do we start?"

"Start what," Bernays laughed.

"You know fucking well."

"Hoa wants to let them stew awhile."

After lunch we shot baskets until the torturing began, at about 1500, in a small dark hut. I tried to bring my cameras, but Bernays shook his head. The hut was too dark to have gotten anything anyway.

Hoa and the PF translator were the only Viets there, but most of the Americans crowded into the room. The only furniture was a straight-backed chair, occupied by Hoa, and a low wooden bench. Greer brought the girl in, her hands still tied behind her. She looked at us, her glance seeming to stop for a moment on each face, but did not appear frightened. Hoa spoke to her in Vietnamese and she sat down on the bench. He questioned her for a half hour, making notes in a little spiral pad.

"What's she saying," Bernays asked.

"Nothing," the interpreter said. "Say not live here. Visit friend. Lie."

Hoa kept repeating the same questions and the girl shook her head, answered briefly or not at all, looked down. Hoa's voice became angry, she shook her head again. Hoa nodded to Greer. He untied her hands and forced her to lie down on the bench on her back. Then he tied her hands and feet together under the bench.

Hoa spoke to her again, his voice level and smooth. She shook her head. Her eyes were shut. Hoa nodded to the translator, who went outside and dragged in a five-gallon water tin. Hoa pulled a washcloth-size rag out of his pocket and a bar of soap, and placed the rag over the girl's face. He lit a cigarette and tipped back his chair.

"She's scared pissless now," Monday said.

"You'd better believe it," Doc said.

"I don't know," Northup said. "You can't tell. She may have been expecting this."

"I don't give a shit if she was expecting it or not," Monday said. "She's gotta be scared. She knows Hoa ain't fucking around."

The girl turned her head and the cloth fell off. Hoa leaned forward and his arm whiplashed out and his open palm popped into her cheek. Tears gathered in her eyes. Hoa put the cloth back and began to question her. She shook her head, the cloth fell, he slapped her again. She shouted something at him and he laughed, replaced the cloth, nodded to the interpreter.

Greer held the girl's head in his massive hands and the interpreter poured some water onto the cloth. The girl gasped. Hoa leaned forward, rubbed soap into the wet cloth until it lathered, then nodded to the interpreter again. He poured water, and the girl began to struggle, to heave and twist her head against Greer's vise grip. Her hips twisted as if she were doing a belly dance, and Monday said, "Look at that. She looks like she's humping."

Hoa took the cloth away and the girl jerked her head from side to side, spluttering and sucking air, and threw up. Soap bubbles were mixed with her vomit, and some of it went down her neck and onto her blouse. She kept gasping and vomiting for some time more or less simultaneously. Then Hoa questioned her and again she shook her head. He put the cloth back and rubbed in more soap and nodded to the interpreter.

It went on like that for an hour and a half before she broke. All the Marines but Greer and Bernays had left, though from time to time they dropped in to find out how things were going. Finally, after the interpreter had emptied two tins of water and Hoa's soap was worn to a sliver, the girl began to babble and cry. I thought her nerves had snapped, that she was out of her head, but Hoa smiled at Bernays. He asked more questions, which she now answered volubly, and wrote furiously in his notebook.

The interpreter translated in snatches. She was a VC schoolteacher. She had been trained in North Vietnam. She was new in this area. She had relatives here. She was born in Quang Ngai. Hoa wanted to know how many local VC there were, what units, and did not like her answer, put the cloth back. She gave the names and numbers of some local force units and Bernays and Hoa seemed pleased. Then Hoa asked who were VC sympathizers and agents in town. She hesitated and he dangled the cloth. She started to talk. Hoa looked sharply at Greer, then at Bernays.

"Betty Lou, she say," the interpreter said.

Greer didn't say anything, but put one of his huge hands on her throat and began to squeeze. Her breath came hoarsely as he bore down on her windpipe. Hoa motioned him away, but he did not release her, just lessened the pressure slightly. She spoke quickly.

"Betty Lou fucky VC," the interpreter said.

Greer was looking down at her and I shall never forget his expression. There was something of the hurt animal in it, a look such as you sometimes see on the faces of the mortally wounded just after they have been hit, a sudden and complete comprehension of the worst, but also the loss of bearing and perspective, the enveloping numbness, that comes with severe shock.

"Knock it off, Greer," Bernays said. "Take a break."

Greer stood up and went outside.

Hoa kept questioning. Betty Lou was the one who had furnished the diagram of the positions and the list of weapons. Two other women had relatives in the local VC. Hoa wanted to know if there were any plans to attack. She said no, one of the VC the Marines had killed had been the local CO, and anyway the VC knew the Marines had found the diagram. Hoa put the cloth back over her, but she repeated the story exactly.

It was past 1800 when they finished. Bernays said to come get some food, they'd work on Betty Lou after dinner. One of the PFs had been sent to arrest her and the other two women when the girl had talked.

I was not hungry, and walked out onto the bridge and watched the water and the sunset. Two Marines were manning the position at the far end. I could hear the murmur of their voices but not what they said. A 106mm recoilless rifle fired somewhere across the river, made a long whining whooshing and detonated in the distance.

I went into the tent. Lowenstein and Monday and Northup and a lance corporal named Mitchell were playing hearts. Greer was lying on a cot in shorts. I stopped and started to say something, but his eyes were closed. Northup motioned me away with a wave of his hand and shook his head.

After Bernays and Hoa had eaten they started on Betty Lou. They took her into the interrogation hut and lit a lamp. Hoa did not go through the polite preliminaries, just had the interpreter tie her down. She was very frightened. Her legs and arms trembled. Without Greer there to hold her head, Hoa had to get out of his chair and help with the work. After one long douse she was crying hysterically, and Hoa began to question her. Yes, she had made the diagram. Yes, she did have a VC boyfriend. She named other VC sympathizers.

Hoa was writing again. The lamplight flickered across his face. I looked to the door and Greer stood there. He was in the shadows and I could not make out his expression. I watched him for some time, but he did not move.

Hoa asked the girl where she met her boyfriend. No answer. He slapped her. No answer. He put the cloth on, soaped it, poured water. She gasped, vomited. In a rice paddy on the other side of the river. When? How did they arrange the meetings? She was sobbing and he poured more water and she retched. The boyfriend was a farmer. He had papers. When did they meet? He slapped her very hard. Every other Thursday when she went to Hoi An to buy cloth. She had to walk to Route One, where she caught a Lambretta bus. He met her in the afternoons on the way back.

"Maybe can kill," Hoa said.

Bernays nodded.

Hoa continued questioning her, going over the same ground again and again, trying to catch her in a lie, or get her to expand the information she had already given. I was very tired, had a headache, and did not want to hear any more. Greer was in the doorway as I left, and I said good night, but he did not answer.

During the night it rained.

The next morning was fresh and bright. The sun was out and the air was cool and very clear. I ate with Bernays, asked him what would happen to the prisoners. He said they would be turned over to Battalion, a jeep was coming for them in an hour or so. I said I was about ready to shove off myself, I had plenty of material, and he said he'd call Battalion and ask for transportation. He didn't think there would be room for me in the first jeep. I asked if they were going to send all the prisoners, and he said no, just the girl, who was really hard core, and Betty Lou. The others would go to a refugee camp, but there was no hurry about it.

I played basketball with Monday and Northup, then shaved and packed my rucksack. I was just finishing when the jeep came for Betty Lou and the girl. It carried two Marines. The driver held a shotgun and the guard an M-14.

A PF brought out the prisoners. Both were red-eyed from the soap but otherwise looked all right. The girl had managed to clean most of the vomit off her shirt, and had recovered her resolve. In fact, they both looked resigned, but sullen and determined and not scared. I thought the girl must have given Betty Lou a talking. Their hands were tied.

They got in the back seat and the Marines tied their bonds to the seats. Most of the CAC Marines were gathered around, including Greer, who stood on Betty Lou's side, trying to catch her eye. Both of the girls stared straight ahead. The driver started the motor. Bernays was on his side, his hand on the windshield post.

"Tell gunny to bring out the beer," he said.

"Gunny ain't supposed to come out here today," the driver said.

"Yes he is," Bernays said. "He's coming to pick up this reporter." He nodded at me. "Remind him we ain't had no beer in two weeks."

Greer stepped up to the side of the jeep and put his hand on Betty Lou's shoulder. She turned and spat full in his face.

"All right," the driver said. "I'll tell him."

Greer stepped back and wiped his arm across his face. The guard twisted around in his seat, put the muzzle of his rifle under Betty Lou's chin, said, "Cut that shit out, you hear?"

The driver put the jeep in gear and pulled away. Greer went into the tent.

"Fucking slope cunt," Lowenstein said.

The group broke up, some going to the basketball court and others into the tent or to the village. Doc started off for Medcap and asked if I wanted to come. I did not.

Gunny Ingersoll drove up promptly at 1100.

"You bring beer?" Bernays asked him.

"What beer?" Gunny said. "There ain't a can of beer in the whole fucking Battalion."

I shook hands with all the Marines who were nearby, and thanked Bernays. He said to come back any time. I threw my gear in the back of the mule and got in. Gunny turned around and we started out onto the bridge. Greer was standing on the edge in the middle, wearing only shorts. He looked like a sculptor's model for a black god. Gunny slowed as we went past and I said, "So long, Greer. Take it easy."

"Yeah man," he said.

We reached the other side and I turned for a last look at the place. Greer sprang away from the bridge and flung out his arms and arched his back, hung suspended, then nosed over and arrowed for the water and hit and a plume of spray geysered up behind his heels. He stayed down until I was holding my own breath and the bank threatened to interfere with my line of sight. I stood up in the bouncing mule, gripping the windshield and the seat back, and he came up, snorted, and swam toward the bank.

(1971)

TIM O'BRIEN

Tim O'Brien is one of the most influential and highly regarded writers of Vietnam War fiction. Born in Minnesota in 1946, he was drafted shortly after he graduated from college in 1968 and served two years in the U.S. Army. During his year as an infantryman in Vietnam he became a sergeant and received a Purple Heart.

Each of the six books O'Brien has published so far flows from the Vietnam War. If I Die in a Combat Zone, Box Me Up and Ship Me Home (1973) is an anecdotal and somewhat fictionalized account of his wartime experience. Northern Lights (1975) centers on the relationship between a Vietnam veteran and his brother. Going After Cacciato (1978), winner of the National Book Award for 1979, is a narrative tour de force that constructs layer upon layer of fictive reality from the imaginings of a GI in Vietnam. The protagonist of The Nuclear Age (1981, 1985), which is set in the near future, is a former anti–Vietnam War radical. The central theme of In the Lake of the Woods (1994) is denial of the Vietnam War and its devastating consequences, dramatized in the nightmarish fate of a man who futilely attempted to erase all memory and records of his participation in the My Lai massacre.

"The Man I Killed" is one of the interlinked stories in The Things They Carried (1990), a work that shows just how spectacularly O'Brien's art has advanced from his first book. Although conspicuously subtitled A Work of Fiction, The Things They Carried is narrated by a central character named Tim O'Brien, who surely is employing this "fiction" to explore the most painful revelations about the author's own experience. Tim O'Brien the narrator introduces "On the Rainy River," an early section of the book, as "one story I've never told before" because of its unbearable "shame." It is his confession that he allowed himself to be drafted, rather than fleeing to Canada, "because I was embarrassed not to": "I was a coward. I went to the war." Writing and publishing "The Man I Killed," however, is an act of courage and bravery, evidently offered in part as an atonement for such personal — and national — cowardice.

The Man I Killed

His jaw was in his throat, his upper lip and teeth were gone, his one eye was shut, his other eye was a star-shaped hole, his eyebrows were thin and arched like a woman's, his nose was undamaged, there was a slight tear at the lobe of one ear, his clean black hair was swept upward into a cowlick at the rear of the skull, his forehead was lightly freckled, his fingernails were clean, the skin at his left cheek was peeled back in three ragged strips, his right cheek was smooth and hairless, there was a butterfly on his chin, his neck was open to the spinal cord and the blood there was thick and shiny and it was this wound that had killed him. He lay face-up in the center of the trail, a slim, dead, almost dainty young man. He had bony legs, a narrow waist, long shapely fingers. His chest was sunken and poorly muscled—a scholar, maybe. His wrists were the wrists of a child. He wore a black shirt, black pajama pants, a gray ammunition belt, a gold ring on the third finger of his right hand. His rubber sandals had been blown off. One lay beside him, the other a few meters up the trail. He had been born, maybe, in 1946 in the village of My Khe near the central coastline of Quang Ngai Province, where his parents farmed, and where his family had lived for several centuries, and where, during the time of the French, his father and two uncles and many neighbors had joined in the struggle for independence. He was not a Communist. He was a citizen and a soldier. In the village of My Khe, as in all of Quang Ngai, patriotic resistance had the force of tradition, which was partly the force of legend, and from his earliest boyhood the man I killed would have listened to stories about the heroic Trung sisters and Tran Hung Dao's famous rout of the Mongols and Le Loi's final victory against the Chinese at Tot Dong.[1] He would have been taught that to defend the land was a man's highest duty and highest privilege. He had accepted this. It was never open to question. Secretly, though, it also frightened him. He was not a fighter. His health was poor, his body small and frail. He liked books. He wanted someday to be a teacher of mathematics. At night, lying on his mat, he could not picture himself doing the brave things his father had done, or his uncles, or the heroes of the stories. He hoped in his heart that he would never be tested. He hoped the Americans would go away. Soon, he hoped. He kept hoping and hoping, always, even when he was asleep.

---

[1] In A.D. 40, the Trung sisters led an insurrection against Chinese occupation that freed Vietnam for three years. In 1285 and 1287, General Tran Hung Dao led the Vietnamese in defeating two massive invasions by the Mongol armies of Kublai Khan that had already conquered China and much of Europe. Between 1418 and 1427, the Vietnamese under Le Loi drove out the Chinese occupiers, leading to the establishment of an independent Vietnam. [Ed.]

"Oh, man, you fuckin' trashed the fucker," Azar said. "You scrambled his sorry self, look at that, you *did*, you laid him out like Shredded fuckin' Wheat."

"Go away," Kiowa said.

"I'm just saying the truth. Like oatmeal."

"Go," Kiowa said.

"Okay, then, I take it back," Azar said. He started to move away, then stopped and said, "Rice Krispies, you know? On the dead test, this particular individual gets A-plus."

Smiling at this, he shrugged and walked up the trail toward the village behind the trees.

Kiowa kneeled down.

"Just forget that crud," he said. He opened up his canteen and held it out for a while and then sighed and pulled it away. "No sweat, man. What else could you do?"

Later, Kiowa said, "I'm serious. Nothing *anybody* could do. Come on, stop staring."

The trail junction was shaded by a row of trees and tall brush. The slim young man lay with his legs in the shade. His jaw was in his throat. His one eye was shut and the other was a star-shaped hole.

Kiowa glanced at the body.

"All right, let me ask a question," he said. "You want to trade places with him? Turn it all upside down—you *want* that? I mean, be honest."

The star-shaped hole was red and yellow. The yellow part seemed to be getting wider, spreading out at the center of the star. The upper lip and gum and teeth were gone. The man's head was cocked at a wrong angle, as if loose at the neck, and the neck was wet with blood.

"Think it over," Kiowa said.

Then later he said, "Tim, it's a *war*. The guy wasn't Heidi—he had a weapon, right? It's a tough thing, for sure, but you got to cut out that staring."

Then he said, "Maybe you better lie down a minute."

Then after a long empty time he said, "Take it slow. Just go wherever the spirit takes you."

The butterfly was making its way along the young man's forehead, which was spotted with small dark freckles. The nose was undamaged. The skin on the right cheek was smooth and fine-grained and hairless. Frail-looking, delicately boned, the young man would not have wanted to be a soldier and in his heart would have feared performing badly in battle. Even as a boy growing up in the village of My Khe, he had often worried about this. He imagined covering his head and lying in a deep hole and closing his eyes and not moving until the war was over. He had no stomach for violence. He loved mathematics. His eyebrows were thin and arched like a woman's, and at school the boys sometimes teased him about how pretty he was, the arched eyebrows and long shapely fingers, and on the playground they mimicked a woman's walk and made fun of his smooth skin and his love for mathematics. The young man could not make himself fight them. He often wanted to, but he was afraid, and this increased his shame. If he could not fight little boys, he thought, how could he ever become a soldier and fight the Americans with their airplanes and helicopters and bombs? It did not seem possible. In the presence of his father and uncles, he pretended to look forward to doing his patriotic duty, which was also a privilege, but at night he prayed with his mother that the war might end soon. Beyond anything else, he was afraid of disgracing himself, and therefore his family and village. But all he could do, he thought, was wait and pray and try not to grow up too fast.

"Listen to me," Kiowa said. "You feel terrible, I know that."

Then he said, "Okay, maybe I *don't* know."

Along the trail there were small blue flowers shaped like bells. The young man's head was wrenched sideways, not quite facing the flowers, and even in the shade a single blade of sunlight sparkled against the buckle of his ammunition belt. The left cheek was peeled back in three ragged strips. The wounds at his neck had not yet clotted, which made him seem animate even in death, the blood still spreading out across his shirt.

Kiowa shook his head.

There was some silence before he said, "Stop *staring.*"

The young man's fingernails were clean. There was a slight tear at the lobe of one ear, a sprinkling of blood on the forearm. He wore a gold ring on the third finger of his right hand. His chest was sunken and poorly muscled—a scholar, maybe. His life was now a constellation of possibilities. So, yes, maybe a scholar. And for years, despite his family's poverty, the man I killed would have been determined to continue his education in mathematics. The means for this were arranged, perhaps, through the village liberation cadres, and in 1964 the young man began attending classes at the university in Saigon, where he avoided politics and paid attention to the problems of calculus. He devoted himself to his studies. He spent his nights alone, wrote romantic poems in his journal, took pleasure in the grace and beauty of differential equations. The war, he knew, would finally take him, but for the time being he would not let himself think about it. He had stopped praying; instead, now, he waited. And as he waited, in his final year at the university, he fell in love with a classmate, a girl of seventeen, who one day told him that his wrists were like the wrists of a child, so small and delicate, and who admired his narrow waist and the cowlick that rose up like a bird's tail at the back of his head. She liked his quiet manner; she laughed at his freckles and bony legs. One evening, perhaps, they exchanged gold rings.

Now one eye was a star.

"You okay?" Kiowa said.

The body lay almost entirely in shade. There were gnats at the mouth, little flecks of pollen drifting above the nose. The butterfly was gone. The bleeding had stopped except for the neck wounds.

Kiowa picked up the rubber sandals, clapping off the dirt, then bent down to search the body. He found a pouch of rice, a comb, a fingernail clipper, a few soiled piasters, a snapshot of a young woman standing in front of a parked motorcycle. Kiowa placed these items in his rucksack along with the gray ammunition belt and rubber sandals.

Then he squatted down.

"I'll tell you the straight truth," he said. "The guy was dead the second he stepped on the trail. Understand me? We all had him zeroed. A good kill—weapon, ammunition, everything." Tiny beads of sweat glistened at Kiowa's forehead. His eyes moved from the sky to the dead man's body to the knuckles of his own hands. "So listen, you best pull your shit together. Can't just sit here all day."

Later he said, "Understand?"

Then he said, "Five minutes, Tim. Five more minutes and we're moving out."

The one eye did a funny twinkling trick, red to yellow. His head was wrenched sideways, as if loose at the neck, and the dead young man seemed to be staring at some distant object beyond the bell-shaped flowers along the trail. The blood at the neck had gone to a deep purplish black. Clean fingernails, clean hair—he had been a soldier for only a single day. After his years at the university, the man I killed returned with his new wife to the village of My Khe, where he enlisted as a common rifleman with the 48th Vietcong Battalion. He knew he would die quickly. He knew he would see a flash of light. He knew he would fall dead and wake up in the stories of his village and people.

Kiowa covered the body with a poncho.

"Hey, you're looking better," he said. "No doubt about it. All you needed was time—some mental R&R."

Then he said, "Man, I'm sorry."

Then later he said, "Why not talk about it?"

Then he said, "Come on, man, talk."

He was a slim, dead, almost dainty young man of about twenty. He lay with one leg bent beneath him, his jaw in his throat, his face neither expressive nor inexpressive. One eye was shut. The other was a star-shaped hole.

"Talk," Kiowa said.

(1990)

AGAINST THE WAR

When did Americans begin to oppose the Vietnam War? A few spoke out even while the Eisenhower administration was maneuvering to shift from financing the French war to supplanting the French. For example, on May 15, 1954, just a week after the fall of Dien Bien Phu and the opening of the Geneva peace conference, Paul Sweezy and Leo Huberman argued in "What Every American Should Know about Indo-China":

> The American people, by and large, are against colonialism and aggression, and believe in the right of every country to manage its own affairs free from outside interference.
>
> Rarely have these simple principles been so clearly and grossly violated as in present United States policy towards Indo-China. . . . [If] we send American forces into Indo-China, as Dulles and other high government spokesmen have repeatedly threatened to do in the last two months, we shall be guilty of aggression. . . .
>
> Are we going to take the position that anti-Communism justifies anything, including colonialism, interference in the affairs of other countries, and aggression? That way, let us be perfectly clear about it, lies war and more war leading ultimately to full-scale national disaster.

This early protest concluded with a prophetic call for action:

> There never has been and never will be a clearer test case than Indo-China. The time for decision is now. Let everyone who cares about the future of our country stand up and speak out today. Tomorrow may be too late.[1]

These were the feelings of ever-growing numbers of Americans in the next two decades. And for most of this period, the main form of antiwar action was to "speak out"—in the form of letters to editors, appeals to Congress, articles and books, petitions and advertisements, sermons and teach-ins, banners and picket signs, leaflets and graffiti, resolutions and demands, referenda and slogans. Although there was some organized opposition to the war in the late 1950s and early 1960s, the first nationwide action against U.S. participation in Vietnam combat was campaigning in 1964 for the presidential candidate who was pledging never to send American troops to Vietnam—Lyndon Johnson.

When the bombing of North Vietnam began in February 1965, less than three weeks after President Johnson's inauguration, and when the first acknowledged American combat troops went ashore in March, the antiwar movement appeared for the first time as a national phenomenon distinct from electoral politics. The first teach-ins began in late March. Back in December 1964 an obscure little organization called Students for a Democratic Society (SDS) had issued a call for people to go to Washington on April 17, 1965, to march against the war. Only a few thousand were expected. But when the march took place, it turned out to be the largest antiwar demonstration in Washington's history—25,000 people, most neatly dressed in jackets and ties or skirts and dresses.

What seemed at the time very large demonstrations continued throughout 1965, with 15,000 marching in Berkeley on October 15; 20,000 marching in Manhattan the same day; and 25,000 marching again in Washington on November 27. These early demonstrations would have been imperceptible in such later giant protests as the April 1967 New York demonstration of 300,000 to 500,000 people or among the half million or more who converged on Washington in November 1969 and again in the spring of 1971. In the nationwide antiwar Moratorium of October 15, 1969, millions of Americans—at least ten times the half million then stationed in Indochina—demonstrated against the war.

Demonstrations were one form of the attempt to go beyond mere words. Other forms appeared as early as 1965. Many of the activists were veterans of the civil rights movement, who now began to apply its use of civil disobedience and moral witness. That summer, the Vietnam Day Committee in northern California attempted to block munitions trains by lying on the tracks, hundreds of people were arrested for civil disobedience in Washington, and public burnings of draft cards began. Moral witness was taken to its ultimate by Norman Morrison, a thirty-two-year-old Quaker who drenched himself with gasoline and set himself on fire outside the Pentagon; pacifist Roger La Porte, who immolated himself at the United Nations; and eighty-two-year-old Alice Herz, who burned herself to death in Detroit to protest against the Vietnam War. By 1971 civil disobedience was so widespread that the number *arrested* in that spring demonstration in Washington— 14,000—would have been considered a good-size march in 1965.

Whether the majority of Americans at any point supported the government's policies in Vietnam (or even knew what they were) is a matter of debate. Certainly most Americans never supported the war strongly enough to agree to pay for it with new taxes, or even to demonstrate for it in significant numbers, much less to go willingly to fight in it. Nor were they ever willing to vote for any national candidate who pledged to fight until "victory." In fact, from 1964 through the end of the war, every nominee for president of both major parties, except for Barry Goldwater in 1964, ran as some kind of self-professed peace candidate.

Who opposed the war? Contrary to the impression prevailing today, opposition to the war was not concentrated among affluent college students. In fact, opposition to the war was *inversely* proportional to both wealth and education. Blue-collar workers generally considered themselves "doves" and tended to favor withdrawal from Vietnam, whereas those who considered themselves "hawks" and supported participation in the war were concentrated among college-educated, high-income strata.[2]

Opposition was especially intense among nonwhite people, although they tended not to participate heavily in the demonstrations called by student and pacifist organizations. One reason for their caution was that nonwhites often had to pay a heavy price for protesting the war. For speaking out in 1966 against drafting black men to fight in Vietnam, Julian Bond was denied his seat in the Georgia legislature. World heavyweight boxing champion Muhammad Ali was stripped of his boxing title and criminally prosecuted for draft resistance. When 25,000 Mexican Americans staged the Chicano Moratorium, the largest antiwar demonstration held in Los Angeles, the police attacked not just with clubs but with guns, killing three, including the popular television news director and *Los Angeles Times* reporter Ruben Salazar.

Certainly the campus antiwar movement was spectacular. The teach-ins of the spring of 1965 swept hundreds of campuses and involved probably hundreds of thousands of students. By the late 1960s, millions of students were intermittently involved in antiwar activities ranging from petitions and candlelight marches to burning down ROTC buildings and going to prison for draft resistance. In May 1970 the invasion of Cambodia was met by the largest student protest movement in American history, a strike that led to the shutdown of hundreds of campuses, as well as the killing of students by national guardsmen at Kent State and by police at Jackson State.

There are three important misconceptions about the college movement. First, it was not motivated by students' selfish desires to avoid the draft, which was relatively easy for them. In fact, by physically disrupting campus draft-deferment tests, student demonstrators protested *against* their own exemptions as privileges unfair to young men unable to attend college. Second, most college students were not affluent, and some of the largest and most militant demonstrations were at public universities that could hardly be labeled sanctuaries of the rich, such as Michigan, Maryland, Wisconsin, San Francisco State, and Kent State. Third, although college antiwar activism did hamper those in Washington trying to conduct the war without hindrance, the most decisive opposition to the war came ultimately not from the campuses but from within the cities and the army itself.

To understand the antiwar movement, one must perceive its relations with the other powerful mass movement hamstringing the Pentagon—the upsurge among African Americans. The civil rights movement of the late 1950s and early 1960s had not achieved economic progress for the majority of black people, whose conditions were made even worse as the war brought conscription and inflation to the inner cities. In the summer of 1964, rebellions broke out in several urban ghettos. Rioting spread in the summer of 1965, and by 1966 the pattern of "long, hot summers" seemed to be intensifying each year. In April 1967, Martin Luther King linked the ghetto violence directly to the war in Vietnam, declaring "I could never again raise my voice against the violence of the oppressed in the ghettos without having first spoken clearly to the greatest purveyor of violence in the world today —my own government." That summer the uprisings reached new heights, especially in blue-collar cities such as Newark and Detroit. Then, in April 1968, during the week following the assassination of Dr. King, rebellions broke out simultaneously in 125 U.S. cities.

The black movement had been helping to energize the antiwar movement at least since 1965, when a number of leading civil rights activists and organizations had condemned the war as an assault on another people of color. Stokely Carmichael in 1966 was the main speaker at the first rally against napalm. In 1968, dozens of black soldiers, many of them Vietnam veterans, were arrested and courtmartialed for refusing mobilization against antiwar demonstrators outside the Democratic convention. It was the situation inside the armed forces that made the convergence of the black and antiwar movements especially dangerous.

Especially after the 1968 Tet Offensive, antiwar sentiment spread widely among the combat troops in Vietnam, where peace symbols and antiwar salutes became commonplace. Some units even organized their own antiwar demonstrations to link up with the movement at home. For example, to join the November 1969 antiwar Mobilization, a unit stationed at Pleiku fasted against the war and boycotted the Thanksgiving Day dinner; of the 141 soldiers classified below the rank of Spec 5, only 8 showed up for the traditional meal.[3] When Bob Hope introduced General Creighton Abrams, commander of all U.S. forces in Vietnam, to the 30,000 troops assembled for a Christmas show at the sprawling Long Binh base, the entire throng leaped to their feet and held their hands high in the salute of the peace movement.[4] Individual acts of rebellion, ranging from desertion to "fragging" officers who ordered hazardous search-and-destroy missions, merged into sporadic mutinies and large-scale resistance. In January 1970 *The Naval War College Review* published "Constraints of the Negro Civil Rights Movement on American Military Effectiveness," an alarming article that pointed out the explosive combination of the black movement and antiwar movement within the military. By June 1971 the *Armed Forces Journal* was running an article accurately titled "The Collapse of the Armed Forces," arguing that the situation verged on revolution.

Like many of the authors whose works are collected in this book, thousands of those who fought in Vietnam moved to the forefront of the antiwar movement after they returned to the United States. For example, the vanguard of that Washington demonstration by half a million people in the spring of 1971 was a contingent of a thousand Vietnam veterans, many in wheelchairs and on crutches, who conducted an operation they called Dewey Canyon III. About eight hundred marched up to a barricade hastily erected to stop them and hurled their Purple Hearts, Bronze Stars, Silver Stars, and campaign ribbons at the Capitol.

Many of the poems in the final section of this volume flow directly out of the history just summarized. Parts of that history are brought to life in the three stories grouped together here, which portray some of the very different kinds of activities and arenas of the antiwar movement. Each tale also reveals the intensity of the war's contradictions in the lives of individuals. Ward Just's "The Congressman Who Loved Flaubert," drawing on the author's deep experience in both Vietnam and Washington, dramatizes the kind of struggle waged in the halls of Congress. When the protagonist of Mary Hazzard's *Idle and Disorderly*

Persons finds herself, much to her own surprise, engaging in an act of civil disobedience, she exposes and transfigures her identity as a faculty wife. In Wayne Karlin's "Moratorium," with its multilevel title, the experience of one antiwar Vietnam veteran compresses the agonies, discoveries, and transformation of an epoch.

Notes

1. Paul M. Sweezy and Leo Huberman, "What Every American Should Know about Indo-China," *Monthly Review*, 6 (June 1954), 1–23.

2. Harlan Hahn, "Dove Sentiments Among Blue-Collar Workers," *Dissent*, 17 (May–June 1970), 202–205; Richard F. Hamilton, "A Research Note on the Mass Support for "'Tough' Military Initiatives," *American Sociological Review*, 33 (June 1968), 439–445; William L. Lunch and Peter W. Sperlich, "American Public Opinion and the War in Vietnam," *Western Political Quarterly*, 32 (March 1979), 21–44.

3. *New York Times*, November 28, 1969. In *Home Before Morning: The True Story of an Army Nurse in Vietnam* (New York: Warner Books, 1984), Lynda Van Devanter describes her participation in the Pleiku protest and notes that the antiwar fast "spread to units all over Vietnam" (p. 184).

4. *San Francisco Chronicle*, December 23, 1968.

WARD JUST

Ward Just was born in 1935, the son and grandson of Illinois newspaper publishers. From 1957 to 1965 he worked as a journalist, including several years as a Newsweek *reporter in Chicago, London, and Washington, where he covered the political scene. In 1965 he became a foreign correspondent for the* Washington Post, *which sent him to Vietnam, where he spent two years covering the war. He still carries grenade fragments from wounds he received in a 1966 battle in the central highlands. He returned to the United States in 1967 and wrote his first book, the nonfictional* To What End: Report from Vietnam *(1968). He left journalism in 1969 and, since that time, has published ten novels and three collections of short stories.*

Most of Just's early fiction was about the Vietnam War, and almost all of his works draw on his rich knowledge of Washington politics. As he told an interviewer, "The milieu I knew as a reporter is the milieu I write about—the world of journalists, politicians, diplomats, and soldiers." Julian Moynahan has written this about his fiction: "Mr. Just bids to be considered the political novelist of his generation. He may even be considered for a rarer title, that of national novelist."

"The Congressman Who Loved Flaubert," which appeared first in the Atlantic Monthly *in October 1972, offers invaluable insights into the dialectic between the antiwar movement and the Washington political scene during the war. But perhaps what is most striking (and disheartening) about the story is its timeliness decades later. We discover that the Washington that Ward Just so brilliantly dramatized decades ago has not, alas, changed very much.*

The Congressman Who Loved Flaubert

The deputation was there: twelve men in his outer office and he would have to see them. His own fault, if "fault" was the word. They'd called every day for a week, trying to arrange an appointment. Finally his assistant, Annette, put it to him: Please see them. Do it for me. Wein is an old friend, she'd said. It meant a lot to Wein to get his group before a congressman whose name was known, whose words had weight. LaRuth stood and stretched; his long arms reached for the ceiling. He was his statuesque best that day: dark suit, dark tie, white shirt, black beard neatly trimmed. No jewelry of any kind. He rang his secretary and told her to show them in, to give them thirty minutes, and then ring again; the committee meeting was at eleven.

"What do they look like?"

"Scientists," she said. "They look just as you'd expect scientists to look. They're all thin. And none of them are smoking." LaRuth laughed. "They're pretty intense, Lou."

"Well, let's get on with it."

He met them at the door as they shyly filed in. Wein and his committee were scientists against imperialism. They were physicists, biologists, linguists, and philosophers. They introduced themselves, and LaRuth wondered again what it was that a philosopher did in these times. It had to be a grim year for philosophy. The introductions done, LaRuth leaned back, a long leg hooked over the arm of his chair, and told them to go ahead.

They had prepared a congressional resolution, a sense-of-the-Congress resolution, which they wanted LaRuth to introduce. It was a message denouncing imperialism, and as LaRuth read it he was impressed by its eloquence. They had assembled hard facts: so many tons of bombs dropped in Indochina, so many "facilities" built in Africa, so many American soldiers based in Europe, so many billions in corporate investment in Latin America. It was an excellent statement, not windy as so many of them are. He finished reading it and turned to Wein.

"Congressman, we believe this is a matter of simple morality. Decency, if you will. There are parallels elsewhere, the most compelling being the extermination of American Indians. Try not to look on the war and the bombing from the perspective of a Westerner looking east but of an Easterner facing west." LaRuth nodded. He recognized that it was the war that truly interested them. "The only place the analogy breaks down is that the Communists in Asia appear to be a good deal more resourceful and resilient than the Indians in America. Perhaps that is because there are so many more of them." Wein paused to smile. "But it is genocide either way. It is a stain on the American Congress not to raise a specific voice of protest, not only in Asia but in the other places where American policy is doing violence . . ."

LaRuth wondered if they knew the mechanics of moving a congressional resolution. They probably did; there was no need for a civics lecture. Wein was looking at him, waiting for a response. An intervention. "It's a very fine statement," LaRuth said.

"Everybody says that. And then they tell us to get the signatures and come back. We think this ought to be undertaken from the inside.

In that way, when and if the resolution is passed, it will have more force. We think that a member of Congress should get out front on it."

An admirable toughness there, LaRuth thought. If he were Wein, that would be just about the way he'd put it.

"We've all the people you'd expect us to have." Very rapidly, Wein ticked off two dozen names, the regular antiwar contingent on the Democratic left. "What we need to move with this is not the traditional dove but a more moderate man. A moderate man with a conscience." Wein smiled.

"Yes," LaRuth said.

"Someone like you."

LaRuth was silent a moment, then spoke rapidly. "My position is this. I'm not a member of the Foreign Affairs Committee or the Appropriations Committee or Armed Services or any of the others where . . . war legislation or defense matters are considered. I'm not involved in foreign relations, I'm in education. It's the Education and Labor Committee. No particular reason why those two subjects should be linked, but they are." LaRuth smiled. "That's Congress for you."

"It seems to us, Congressman, that the war—the leading edge of imperialism and violence—is tied to everything. Education is a mess because of the war. So is labor. And so forth. It's all part of the war. Avoid the war and you avoid all the other problems. The damn thing is like the Spanish Inquisition, if you lived in Torquemada's time, fifteenth-century Spain. If you did try to avoid it you were either a coward or a fool. That is meant respectfully."

"Well, it is nicely put. Respectfully."

"But you won't do it."

LaRuth shook his head. "You get more names, and I'll think about cosponsoring. But I won't front for it. I'm trying to pass an education bill right now. I can't get out front on the war, too. Important as it is. Eloquent as you are. There are other men in this House who can do the job better than I can."

"We're disappointed," Wein said.

"I could make you a long, impressive speech." His eyes took in the others, sitting in chilly silence. "I could list all the reasons. But you know what they are, and it wouldn't do either of us any good. I wish you success."

"Spare us any more successes," Wein said. "Everyone wishes us success, but no one helps. We're like the troops in the trenches. The administration tells them to go out and win the war. You five hundred thousand American boys, you teach the dirty Commies a lesson. Storm the hill, the administration says. But the administration is far away from the shooting. We're right behind you, they say. Safe in Washington."

"I don't deny it," LaRuth said mildly.

"I think there are special places in hell reserved for those who see the truth but will not act." LaRuth stiffened but stayed silent. "These people are worse than the ones who love the war. You are more dangerous than the generals in the Pentagon, who at least are doing what they believe in. It is because of people like you that we are where we are."

Never justify, never explain, LaRuth thought; it was pointless anyway. They were pleased to think of him as a war criminal. A picture of a lurching tumbrel in Pennsylvania Avenue flashed through his mind and was gone, an oddly comical image. LaRuth touched his beard and sat upright. "I'm sorry you feel that way. It isn't true, you know." One more number like that one, he thought suddenly, and he'd throw the lot of them out of his office.

But Wein would not let go. "We're beyond subtle distinctions, Mr. LaRuth. That is one of the delightful perceptions that the war has brought us. We can mumble all day. You can tell me about your responsibilities and your effectiveness, and how you don't want to damage it. You can talk politics and I can talk morals. But I took moral philosophy in college. An interesting academic exercise." LaRuth nodded; Wein was no fool. "Is it true you wrote your Ph.D. thesis on Flaubert?"

"I wrote it at the Sorbonne," LaRuth replied. "But that was almost twenty years ago. Before politics." LaRuth wanted to give them something to hang on to. They would appreciate the irony, and then they could see him as a fallen angel, a victim of the process; it was more interesting than seeing him as a war criminal.

"Well, it figures."

LaRuth was surprised. He turned to Wein. "How does it figure?"

"Flaubert was just as pessimistic and cynical as you are."

LaRuth had thirty minutes to review his presentation to the committee. This was the most important vote in his twelve years in Congress, a measure which, if they could steer it through the House, would release a billion dollars over three years' time to elementary schools throughout the country. The measure was based on a hellishly complicated formula which several legal experts regarded as unconstitutional; but one expert is always opposed by another when a billion dollars is involved. LaRuth had to nurse along the chairman, a volatile personality, a natural skeptic. Today he had to put his presentation in exquisite balance, giving here, taking there, assuring the committee that the Constitution would be observed, and that all regions would share equally.

It was not something that could be understood in a university, but LaRuth's twelve years in the House of Representatives would be justified if he could pass this bill. Twelve years, through three Presidents. He'd avoided philosophy and concentrated on detail, his own time in a third-rate grade school in a Southern mill town never far from his mind: that was the reference point. Not often that a man was privileged to witness the methodical destruction of children before the age of thirteen, before they had encountered genuinely soulless and terrible events: the war, for one. His bill would begin the process of revivifying education. It was one billion dollars' worth of life, and he'd see to it that some of the money leaked down to his own school. LaRuth was lucky, an escapee on scholarships, first to Tulane and then to Paris, his world widened beyond measure; Flaubert gave him a taste for politics. *Madame Bovary* and *A Sentimental Education* were political novels, or so he'd argued at the Sorbonne; politics was nothing more or less than an understanding of ambition, and the moral and social conditions that produced it in its various forms. The House of Representatives: *un stade des arrivistes.*[1] And now the press talked him up as a Southern liberal, and the Northern Democrats came to him for help. Sometimes he gave it, sometimes he didn't. They could not understand the refusals— Lou, you won with sixty-five percent of the vote the last time out. What do you want, a coronation? They were critical that he would not get out front on the war and would not vote against bills vital to Southern interests. (Whatever they were, now that the entire region was dominated by industrial combines whose headquarters were in New York or Chicago—and how's that for imperialism, Herr Wein?) They didn't, or couldn't, grasp the paper-thin depth of his support. The Birchers and the segs were everywhere, and each time he voted with the liberals in the House he'd hear from a few of them. *You are being watched.* He preferred a low silhouette. All those big liberals didn't understand that a man with enough money could still buy an election in

---

[1] *un stade des arrivistes:* a stage for opportunists. [Ed.]

his district; he told them that LaRuth compromised was better than no LaRuth at all. That line had worked well the first four or five years he'd been in Washington; it worked no longer. In these times, caution and realism were the refuge of a scoundrel.

The war, so remote in its details, poisoned everything. He read about it every day, and through a friend on the Foreign Affairs Committee saw some classified material. But he could not truly engage himself in it, because he hadn't seen it firsthand. He did not know it intimately. It was clear enough that it was a bad war, everyone knew that; but knowing it and feeling it were two different things. The year before, he'd worked to promote a junket, a special subcommittee to investigate foreign aid expenditures for education. There was plenty of scandalous rumor to justify the investigation. He tried to promote it in order to get a look at the place firsthand, on the ground. He wanted to look at the faces and the villages, to see the countryside that had been destroyed by the war, to observe the actual manner in which the war was being fought. But the chairman refused, he wanted no part of it; scandal or no scandal, it was not part of the committee's business. So the trip never happened. What the congressman knew about the war he read in newspapers and magazines and saw on television. But that did not help. LaRuth had done time as an infantryman in Korea and knew what killing was about; the box did not make it as horrible as it was. The box romanticized it, cleansed it of pain; one more false detail. Even the blood deceived, coming up pink and pretty on the television set. One night he spent half of Cronkite fiddling with the color knob to get a perfect red, to insist the blood look like *blood.*

More. Early in his congressional career, LaRuth took pains to explain his positions. He wanted his constituents to know what he was doing and why, and two newsletters went out before the leader of his state's delegation took him aside one day in the hall. Huge arms around his shoulders, a whispered conference. Christ, you are going to get killed, the man said. *Don't do that.* Don't get yourself down on paper on every raggedy-ass bill that comes before Congress. It makes you a few friends, who don't remember, and a lot of enemies, who do. Particularly in your district: you are way ahead of those people in a lot of areas, but don't advertise it. You've a fine future here; don't ruin it before you've begun. LaRuth thought the advice was captious and irresponsible, and disregarded it. And very nearly lost re-election, after some indiscretions to a newspaperman. *That* son of a bitch, who violated every rule of confidence held sacred in the House of Representatives.

His telephone rang. The secretary said it was Annette.

"How did it go?" Her voice was low, cautious.

"Like a dream," he said. "And thanks lots. I'm up there with the generals as a war criminal. They think I make lamp-shades in my spare time."

Coolly: "I take it you refused to help them."

"You take it right."

"They're very good people. Bill Wein is one of the most distinguished botanists in the country."

"Yes, he speaks very well. A sincere, intelligent, dedicated provocateur. Got off some very nice lines, at least one reference to Dante. A special place in hell is reserved for people like me, who are worse than army generals."

"Well, that's one point of view."

"You know, I'm tired of arguing about the war. If Wein is so goddamned concerned about the war and the corruption of the American system, then why doesn't he give up the fat government contracts at that think tank he works for—"

"That's unfair, Lou!"

"Why do they think that anyone who deals in the real world is an automatic sellout? Creep. A resolution like that one, *even if passed*, would have no effect. Zero effect. It would not be binding, the thing's too vague. They'd sit up there and everyone would have a good gooey warm feeling, *and nothing would happen.* It's meaningless, except of course for the virtue. Virtue everywhere. Virtue triumphant. So I am supposed to put my neck on the line for something that's meaningless —" LaRuth realized he was near shouting, so he lowered his voice. "Meaningless," he said.

"You're so hostile," she said angrily. "Filled with hate. Contempt. Why do you hate everybody? You should've done what Wein wanted you to do."

He counted to five and was calm now, reasonable. His congressional baritone: "It's always helpful to have your political advice, Annette. Very helpful. I value it. Too bad you're not a politician yourself." She said nothing, he could hear her breathing. "I'll see you later," he said, and hung up.

LaRuth left his office, bound for the committee room. He'd gone off the handle and was not sorry. But sometimes he indulged in just a bit too much introspection and self-justification, endemic diseases in politicians. There were certain basic facts: his constituency supported the war, at the same time permitting him to oppose it so long as he did it quietly and in such a way that "the boys" were supported. Oppose the war, support the troops. A high-wire act—very Flaubertian, that situation; it put him in the absurd position of voting for military appropriations and speaking out against the war. Sorry, Annette; that's the way we think on Capitol Hill. It's a question of what you *vote* for. Forget the fancy words and phrases, it's a question of votes. Up, down, or "present." Vote against the appropriations, and sly opponents at home would accuse him of "tying the hands" of American troops and thereby comforting the enemy. Blood on his fingers.

LaRuth was forty; he had been in the House since the age of twenty-eight. Some of his colleagues had been there before he was born, moving now around the halls and the committee rooms as if they were extensions of antebellum county courthouses. They smelled of tobacco and whiskey and old wool, their faces dry as parchment. LaRuth was amused to watch them on the floor; they behaved as they would at a board meeting of a family business, attentive if they felt like it, disruptive if their mood was playful. They were forgiven; it was a question of age. The House was filled with old men, and its atmosphere was one of very great age. Deference was a way of life. LaRuth recalled a friend who aspired to a position of leadership. They put him through his paces, and for some reason he did not measure up; the friend was told he'd have to wait, it was not yet time. He'd been there eighteen years and was only fifty-two. Fifty-two! Jack Kennedy was President at forty-three, and Thomas Jefferson had written the preamble when under thirty-five. But then, as one of the senior men put it, this particular fifty-two-year-old man had none of the durable qualities of Kennedy or Jefferson. That is, he did not have Kennedy's money or Jefferson's brains. Not that money counted for very much in the House of Representatives; plutocrats belonged in the other body.

It was not a place for lost causes. There were too many conflicting interests, too much confusion, too many turns to the labyrinth. Too many *people:* four hundred and thirty-five representatives and about a quarter of them quite bright. Quite bright enough and knowledgeable enough to strangle embarrassing proposals and take revenge as well. Everyone was threatened if the eccentrics got out of hand. The political coloration of the eccentric didn't matter. This was one reason why it was so difficult to build an ideological record in the House. A man with ideology was wise to leave it before reaching a position of influence, because by then he'd mastered the art of compromise, which had nothing to do with dogma or public acts of conscience. It had to do with simple effectiveness, the tact and strength with which a man dealt with legislation, inside committees, behind closed doors. That was where the work got done, and the credit passed around.

LaRuth, at forty, was on a knife's edge. Another two years and he'd be a man of influence, and therefore ineligible for any politics outside the House—or not ineligible, but shopworn, no longer new, no longer fresh. He would be ill-suited, and there were other practical considerations as well, because who wanted to be a servant for twelve or fourteen years and then surrender an opportunity to be master? Not LaRuth. So the time for temporizing was nearly past. If he was going to forsake the House and reach for the Senate (a glamorous possibility), he had to do it soon.

LaRuth's closest friend in Congress was a man about his own age from a neighboring state. They'd come to the Hill in the same year, and for a time enjoyed publicity in the national press, where they could least afford it. *Two Young Liberals from the South*, that sort of thing. Winston was then a bachelor, too, and for the first few years they shared a house in Cleveland Park. But it was awkward, there were too many women in and out of the place, and one groggy morning Winston had come upon LaRuth and a friend taking a shower together and that had torn it. They flipped for the house and LaRuth won, and Winston moved to grander quarters in Georgetown. They saw each other frequently and laughed together about the curiosities of the American political system; Winston, a gentleman farmer from the plantation South, was a ranking member of the House Foreign Affairs Committee. The friendship was complicated because they were occasional rivals: Who would represent the New South? They took to kidding each other's press notices: LaRuth was the "attractive liberal," Winston the "wealthy liberal." Thus, LaRuth became Liberal Lou and Winston was Wealthy Warren. To the extent that either of them had a national reputation, they were in the same category: they voted their consciences, but were not incautious.

It was natural for Wein and his committee of scientists to go directly to Winston after leaving LaRuth. The inevitable telephone call came the next day, Winston inviting LaRuth by for a drink around six;

"small problem to discuss." Since leaving Cleveland Park, Warren Winston's life had become plump and graceful. Politically secure now, he had sold his big house back home and bought a small jewel of a place on Dumbarton Avenue, three bedrooms and a patio in back, a mirrored bar, and a sauna in the basement. Winston was drinking a gin and tonic by the pool when LaRuth walked in. The place was more elegant than he'd remembered; the patio was now decorated with tiny boxbushes, and a magnolia tree was in full cry.

They joked a bit, laughing over the new Southern manifesto floating around the floor of the House. They were trying to find a way to spike it without seeming to spike it. Winston mentioned the "small problem" after about thirty minutes of small talk.

"Lou, do you know a guy named Wein?"

"He's a friend of Annette's."

"He was in to see you, then."

"Yeah."

"And?"

"We didn't see eye to eye."

"You're being tight-lipped, Liberal Lou."

"I told him to piss off," LaRuth said. "He called me a war criminal, and then he called me a cynic. A pessimist, a cynic, and a war criminal. All this for some cream-puff resolution that will keep them damp in Cambridge and won't change a goddamned thing."

"You think it's *that* bad."

"Worse, maybe."

"I'm not sure. Not sure at all."

"Warren, *Christ.*"

"Look, doesn't it make any sense at all to get the position of the House on the record? That can't fail to have some effect downtown, and it can't fail to have an effect in the country. It probably doesn't stand a chance of being passed, but the effort will cause some commotion. The coon'll be treed. Some attention paid. It's a good thing to get on the record, and I can see some points being made."

"What points? Where?"

"The newspapers, the box. Other places. It'd show that at least some of us are not content with things as they are. That we want to change . . ."

LaRuth listened carefully. It was obvious to him that Winston was trying out a speech, like a new suit of clothes; he took it out and tried it on, asking his friend about the color, the fit, the cut of it.

". . . the idea that change can come from within the system . . ."

"Aaaaaoh," LaRuth groaned.

"No?" Innocently.

"How about, *and so, my fellow Americans, ask not what you can do for Wein, but what Wein can do for you.* That thing is loose as a hound dog's tongue. Now tell me the true gen."

"Bettger's retiring."

"You don't say." LaRuth was surprised. Bettger was the senior senator from Winston's state, a living Southern legend.

"Cancer. No one knows about it. He'll announce retirement at the end of the month. It's my only chance for the next four years, maybe *ever*. There'll be half a dozen guys in the primary, but my chances are good. If I'm going to go for the Senate, it's got to be now. This thing of Wein's is a possible vehicle. I say possible. One way in. People want a national politician as a senator. It's not enough to've been a good congressman, or even a good governor. You need something more: when people see your face on the box they want to think *senatorial*, somehow. You don't agree?"

LaRuth was careful now. Winston was saying many of the things he himself had said. Of course he was right: a senator needed a national gloss. The old bulls didn't need it, but they were operating from a different tradition, pushing different buttons. But if you were a young man running statewide for the first time, you needed a different base. Out there in television land were all those followers without leaders. People were pulled by different strings now. The point was to identify which strings pulled strongest.

"I think Wein's crowd is a mistake. That resolution is a mistake. They'll kill you at home if you put your name to that thing."

"No, Lou. You do it a different way. With a little rewording, that resolution becomes a whole lot less scary; it becomes something straight out of Robert A. Taft. You e-*liminate* the fancy words and phrases. You steer *clear* of words like 'corrupt' and 'genocide' and 'violence.' You and I, Lou, we know: our people *like* violence, it's part of our way of life. So you don't talk about violence, you talk about American traditions, like 'the American tradition of independence and individuality. Noninterference!' Now you are saying a couple of *other* things when you're saying that, Lou. You dig? That's the way you get at imperialism. You don't call it imperialism, because that word's got a bad sound. A foreign sound."

LaRuth laughed. Winston had it figured out. He had to get Wein to agree to the changes, but that should present no problem. Wealthy Warren was a persuasive man.

"Point is, I've got to look to people down there like I can make a difference . . ."

"I think you've just said the magic words."

"Like it?"

"I think so. Yeah, I think I do."

"*To make the difference. Winston for Senator.* A double line on the billboards, like this." Winston described two lines with his finger and mulled the slogan again. "*To make the difference. Winston for Senator.* See, it doesn't matter what kind of difference. All people know is that they're fed up to the teeth. *Fed up and mad at the way things are.* And they've got to believe that if they vote for you, in some unspecified way things will get better. Now I think the line about interference can do double duty. People are tired of being hassled, in all ways. Indochina, down home." Winston was a gifted mimic, and now he adopted a toothless expression and hooked his thumbs into imaginary galluses. "Ah think Ah'll vote for that-there Winston. Prob'ly won't do any harm. Mot do some good. Mot mek a diff'rence."

"Shit, Warren."

"You give me a little help?"

"Sure."

"Sign the Wein thing?"

LaRuth thought a moment. "No," he said.

"What the hell, Lou? Why not? If it's rearranged the way I said. Look, Wein will be out of it. It'll be strictly a congressional thing."

"It doesn't mean anything."

"Means a whole lot to me."

"Well, that's different. That's political."

"If you went in too, it'd look a safer bet."

"All there'd be out of that is more Gold Dust Twins copy. You don't want that."

"No, it'd be made clear that I'm managing it. I'm out front. I make all the statements, you're back in the woodwork. Far from harm's way, Lou." Winston took his glass and refilled it with gin and tonic. He carefully cut a lime and squeezed it into the glass. Winston looked the part, no doubt about that. Athlete's build, big, with sandy hair beginning to thin; he could pass for an astronaut.

"You've got to find some new names for the statement."

"Right on, brother. Too many Jews, too many foreigners. Why are there no scientists named Robert E. Lee or Thomas Jefferson? Talmadge, Bilbo." Winston sighed and answered his own question. "The decline of the WASP. Look, Lou. The statement will be forgotten in six weeks, and that's fine with me. I just need it for a little national coverage at the beginning. Hell, it's not decisive. But it could make a difference."

"You're going to *open* the campaign with the statement?"

"You bet. Considerably revised. It'd be a help, Lou, if you'd go along. It would give them a chance to crank out some updated New South pieces. The networks would be giving that a run just as I announce for the Senate and my campaign begins. See, it's a natural. Bettger is Old South, I'm New. But we're friends and neighbors, and that's a fact. It gives them a dozen pegs to hang it on, and those bastards love *you*, with the black suits and the beard and that cracker accent. It's a natural, and it would mean a hell of a lot, a couple of minutes on national right at the beginning. I wouldn't forget it. I'd owe you a favor."

LaRuth was always startled by Winston's extensive knowledge of the press. He spoke of "pieces" and "pegs," A.M. and P.M. cycles, facts "cranked out" or "folded in," who was up and who was down at CBS, who was analyzing Congress for the editorial board of the *Washington Post*. Warren Winston was always accessible, good for a quote, day or night; and he was visible in Georgetown.

"Can you think about it by the end of the week?"

"Sure," LaRuth said.

He returned to the Hill, knowing that he thought better in his office. When there was any serious thinking to be done, he did it there, and often stayed late, after midnight. He'd mix a drink at the small bar in his office and work. Sometimes Annette stayed with him, sometimes not. When LaRuth walked into his office she was still there, catching up, she said; but she knew he'd been with Winston.

"He's going to run for the Senate," LaRuth said.

"Warren?"

"That's what he says. He's going to front for Wein as well. That statement of Wein's—Warren's going to sign it. Wants me to sign it, too."

"Why you?"

"United front. It would help him out. No doubt about that. But it's a bad statement. Something tells me not to do it."

"Are you as mad as you look?"

He glanced at her and laughed. "Does it show?"

"To me it shows."

It was true; there was no way to avoid competition in politics. Politics was a matter of measurements, luck, and ambition, and he and Warren had run as an entry for so long that it disconcerted him to think of Senator Winston; Winston up one rung on the ladder. He was irritated that Winston had made the first move and made it effortlessly. It had nothing to do with his own career, but suddenly he felt a shadow on the future. Winston had seized the day all right, and the fact of it depressed him. His friend was clever and self-assured in his movements; he took risks; he relished the public part of politics. Winston was expert at delivering memorable speeches on the floor of the House; they were evidence of passion. For Winston, there was no confusion between the private and the public; it was all one. LaRuth thought that he had broadened and deepened in twelve years in the House, a man of realism, but not really a part of the apparatus. Now Winston had stolen the march, he was a decisive step ahead.

LaRuth may have made a mistake. He liked and understood the legislative process, transactions that were only briefly political. That is, they were not public. If a man kept himself straight at home, he could do what he liked in the House. So LaRuth had become a fixture in his district, announcing election plans every two years from the front porch of his family's small farmhouse, where he was born, where his mother lived still. The house was filled with political memorabilia; the parlor walls resembled huge bulletin boards, with framed photographs, testimonials, parchments, diplomas. His mother was so proud. His life seemed to vindicate her own, his successes hers; she'd told him so. His position in the U.S. Congress was precious, and not lightly discarded. The cold age of the place had given him a distrust of anything spectacular or . . . capricious. The House: no place for lost causes.

Annette was looking at him, hands on hips, smiling sardonically. He'd taken off his coat and was now in shirt sleeves. She told him lightly that he shouldn't feel bad, that if *he* ran for the Senate he'd have to shave off his beard. Buy new clothes. Become prolix, and professionally optimistic. But, as a purchase on the future, his signature . . .

"Might. Might not," he said.

"Why not?"

"I've never done that here."

"Are you refusing to sign because you don't want to, or because you're piqued at Warren? I mean, Senator Winston."

He looked at her. "A little of both."

"Well, that's foolish. You ought to sort out your motives."

"That can come later. That's my business."

"No. Warren's going to want to know why you're not down the line with him. You're pretty good friends. He's going to want to know *why*."

"It's taken me twelve years to build what credit I've got in this place. I'm trusted. The Speaker trusts me. The chairman trusts me."

"Little children see you on the street. Gloryosky! There goes trustworthy Lou LaRuth—"

"Attractive, liberal," he said, laughing. "Well, it's true. This resolution, if it ever gets that far, is a ball buster. It could distract the House for a month and revive the whole issue. Because it's been quiet we've been able to get on with our work, I mean the serious business. Not to get pompous about it."

"War's pretty important," she said.

"Well, is it now? You tell me how important it is." He put his drink on the desk blotter and loomed over her. "Better yet, you tell me how this resolution will solve the problem. God forbid there should be any solutions, though. Moral commitments. Statements. Resolutions. They're the great things, aren't they? Fuck solutions." Thoroughly angry now, he turned away and filled the glasses. He put some ice and whiskey in hers and a premixed martini in his own.

"What harm would it do?"

"Divert a lot of energy. Big play to the galleries for a week or two. Until everyone got tired. The statement itself? No harm at all. Good statement, well done. No harm, unless you consider perpetuating an illusion some kind of harm."

"A lot of people live by illusions, *and what's wrong with getting this House on record?*"

"But it won't be gotten on record. That's the point. The thing will be killed. It'll just make everybody nervous and divide the place more than it's divided already."

"I'd think about it," she said.

"Yeah, I will. I'll tell you something. I'll probably end up signing the goddamned thing. It'll do Warren some good. Then I'll do what I can to see that it's buried, although God knows we won't lack for gravediggers. And then go back to my own work on the school bill."

"I think that's better." She smiled. "One call, by the way. The chairman. He wants you to call first thing in the morning."

"What did he say it's about?"
"The school bill, dear."
Oh shit, LaRuth thought.
"There's a snag," she said.
"Did he say what it was?"
"I don't think he wants to vote for it anymore."

Winston was after him, trying to force a commitment, but LaRuth was preoccupied with the school bill, which was becoming unstuck. It was one of the unpredictable things that happen; there was no explanation for it. But the atmosphere had subtly changed, and support was evaporating. The members wavered, the chairman was suddenly morose and uncertain; he thought it might be better to delay. LaRuth convinced him that was an unwise course and set about repairing damage. This was plumbing, pure and simple: talking with members, speaking to their fears. LaRuth called it negative advocacy, but it often worked. Between conferences a few days later, LaRuth found time to see a high school history class, students from his alma mater. They were touring Washington and wanted to talk to him about Congress. The teacher, sloe-eyed, stringy-haired, twenty-five, wanted to talk about the war; the students were indifferent. They crowded into his outer office, thirty of them; the secretaries stood aside, amused, as the teacher opened the conversation with a long preface on the role of the House, most of it inaccurate. Then she asked LaRuth about the war. What was the congressional role in the war?

"Not enough," LaRuth replied, and went on in some detail addressing the students.

"Why not a congressional resolution demanding an end to this terrible, immoral war?" the teacher demanded. "Congressman, why can't the House of Representatives take matters into its own hands?"

"Because"—LaRuth was icy, at once angry, tired, and bored—"because a majority of the members of this House do not want to lose Asia to the Communists. Irrelevant, perhaps. You may think it is a bad argument. I think it is a bad argument. But it is the way the members feel."

"But why can't that be *tested?* In votes."

The students came reluctantly awake and were listening with little flickers of interest. The teacher was obviously a favorite, their mod pedagogue. LaRuth was watching a girl in the back of the room. She resembled the girls he'd known at home, short-haired, light summer dress, full-bodied; it was a body that would soon go heavy. He abruptly steered the conversation to his school bill, winding into it, giving them a stump speech, some flavor of home. He felt the students with him for a minute or two, then they drifted away. In five minutes they were somewhere else altogether. He said good-bye to them then and shook their hands on the way out. The short-haired girl lingered a minute; she was the last one to go.

"It would be good if you could do something about the war," she said.

"Well, I've explained."

"My brother was killed there."

LaRuth closed his eyes for a second and stood without speaking.

"Any gesture at all," she said.

"Gestures." He shook his head sadly. "They never do any good."

"Well," she said. "Thank you for your time." LaRuth thought her very grown-up, a well-spoken girl. She stood in the doorway, very pretty. The others had moved off down the hall; he could hear the teacher's high whine.

"How old was he?"

"Nineteen," she said. "Would've been twenty next birthday."

"Where?"

"They said it was an airplane."

"I'm so sorry."

"You wrote us a letter, don't you remember?"

"I don't know your name," LaRuth said gently.

"Ecker," she said. "My brother's name was Howard."

"I remember," he said. "It was . . . some time ago."

"Late last year," she said, looking at him.

"Yes, that would be just about it. I'm very sorry."

"So am I," she said, smiling brightly. Then she walked off to join the rest of her class. LaRuth stood in the doorway a moment, feeling the eyes of his secretary on his back. It had happened before; the South seemed to bear the brunt of the war. He'd written more than two hundred letters, to the families of poor boys, black and white. The deaths were disproportionate, poor to rich, black to white, South to North. Oh well, he thought. Oh hell. He walked back into his office and called Winston and told him he'd go along. In a limited way. For a limited period.

Later in the day, Winston dropped by. He wanted LaRuth to be completely informed and up to date.

"It's rolling," Winston said.

"Have you talked to Wein?"

"I've talked to Wein."

"And what did Wein say?"

"Wein agrees to the revisions."

"Complaining?"

"The contrary. Wein sees himself as the spearhead of a great national movement. He sees scientists moving into political positions, cockpits of influence. His conscience is as clear as rainwater. He is very damp."

LaRuth laughed; it was a private joke.

"Wein is damp in Cambridge, then."

"I think that is a fair statement, Uncle Lou."

"How wonderful for him."

"He was pleased that you are with us. He said he misjudged you. He offers apologies. He fears he was a speck . . . harsh."

"Bully for Wein."

"I told everyone that you would be on board. I knew that when the chips were down you would not fail. I knew that you would examine your conscience and your heart and determine where the truth lay. I knew you would not be cynical or pessimistic. I know you want to see your old friend in the Senate."

They were laughing together. Winston was in one of his dry, mordant moods. He was very salty. He rattled off a dozen names and cited the sources of each member's conscience: money and influence. "But to be fair—always be fair, Liberal Lou—there are a dozen more who are doing it because they want to do it. They think it's *right*."

"*Faute de mieux.*"

"I am not schooled in the French language, Louis. You are always flinging French at me."

"It means 'in the absence of anything better.'"

Winston grinned, then shrugged. LaRuth was depressed, the shadow lengthened, became darker.

"I've set up a press conference, a half-dozen of us. All moderate men. Men of science, men of government. I'll be out front, doing all the talking. OK?"

"Sure." LaRuth was thinking about his school bill.

"It's going to be jim-dandy."

"Swell. But I want to see the statement beforehand, music man."

Winston smiled broadly and spread his hands wide. Your friendly neighborhood legislator, concealing nothing; merely your average, open, honest fellow trying to do the right thing, trying to do his level best. "But of course," Winston said.

Some politicians have it; most don't. Winston has it, a fabulous sense of timing. Everything in politics is timing. For a fortnight, the resolution dominates congressional reportage. "An idea whose time has come," coinciding with a coup in Latin America and a surge of fighting in Indochina. The leadership is agitated, but forced to adopt a conciliatory line; the doves are in war paint. Winston appears regularly on the television evening news. There are hearings before the Foreign Affairs Committee, and these produce pictures and newsprint. Winston, a sober legislator, intones *feet to the fire*. There are flattering articles in the news magazines, and editorial support from the major newspapers, including the most influential paper in Winston's state. He and LaRuth are to appear on the cover of *Life*, but the cover is scrapped at the last minute. Amazing to LaRuth, the mail from his district runs about even. An old woman, a woman his mother has known for years, writes to tell him that he should run for President. Incredible, really: the Junior Chamber of Commerce composes a certificate of appreciation, commending his enterprise and spirit, "an example of the indestructible moral fiber of America." When the networks and the newspapers cannot find Winston, they fasten on LaRuth. He becomes something of a celebrity, and wary as a man entering darkness from daylight. He tailors his remarks in such a way as to force questions about his school bill. He finds his words have effect, although this is measurable in no definite way. His older colleagues are amused; they needle him gently about his new blue shirts.

He projects well on television, his appearance is striking; his great height, the black suits, the beard. So low-voiced, modest, diffident; no hysteria or hyperbole. (An intuitive reporter would grasp that he has contempt for "the Winston Resolution," but intuition is in short supply.) When an interviewer mentions his reticent manner, LaRuth smiles and says that he is not modest or diffident, he is pessimistic. But his mother is ecstatic. His secretary looks on him with new respect. Annette thinks he is one in a million.

No harm done. The resolution is redrafted into harmless form and is permitted to languish. The language incomprehensible, at the end it becomes an umbrella under which anyone could huddle. Wein is disillusioned, the media look elsewhere for their news, and LaRuth returns to the House Education and Labor Committee. The work is backed up;

the school bill has lost its momentum. One month of work lost, and now LaRuth is forced to redouble his energies. He speaks often of challenge and commitment. At length the bill is cleared from committee and forwarded to the floor of the House, where it is passed; many members vote aye as a favor, either to LaRuth or to the chairman. The chairman is quite good about it, burying his reservations, grumbling a little, but going along. The bill has been, in the climactic phrase of the newspapers, watered down. The three years are now five. The billion is reduced to five hundred million. Amendments are written, and they are mostly restrictive. But the bill is better than nothing. The President signs it in formal ceremony, LaRuth at his elbow. The thing is now law.

The congressman, contemplating all of it, is both angry and sad. He has been a legislator too long to draw obvious morals, even if they were there to be drawn. He thinks that everything in his life is meant to end in irony and contradiction. LaRuth, at forty, has no secret answers. Nor any illusions. The House of Representatives is no simple place, neither innocent nor straightforward. Appearances there are like appearances elsewhere: deceptive. One is entitled to remain fastidious as to detail, realistic in approach.

Congratulations followed. In his hour of maximum triumph, the author of a law, LaRuth resolved to stay inside the belly of the whale, to become neither distracted nor moved. Of the world outside, he was weary and finally unconvinced. He knew who he was. He'd stick with what he had and take comfort from a favorite line, a passage toward the end of *Madame Bovary*. It was a description of a minor character, and the line had stuck with him, lodged in the back of his head. Seductive and attractive, in a pessimistic way. *He grew thin, his figure became taller, his face took on a saddened look that made it nearly interesting.*

(1972)

MARY HAZZARD

Born in upstate New York in 1928, Mary Hazzard is a dramatist and poet as well as a writer of fiction for adults and children. She has been writer-in-residence at the College of William and Mary and has received Yaddo and MacDowell fellowships, as well as a playwright grant from the National Endowment for the Arts. She now lives in Waban, Massachusetts.

Hazzard won a scroll from the Mystery Writers of America for her first novel, Close His Eyes *(published in 1961 under the pseudonym Olivia Dwight), a mystery exposing murderous ambition in a midwestern university. In both* Sheltered Lives *(set in 1969, completed in 1973, but not published until 1980) and* Idle and Disorderly Persons *(1981), Hazzard shows how the Vietnam War, the antiwar movement, and the closely associated emergence of feminist consciousness stripped away layers of illusion and self-deception from the lives of many ordinary middle-class women in the late 1960s and early 1970s. In each novel, the coming of the antiwar movement to a college campus forces a faculty wife to confront and transform her own buried identity.* Idle and Disorderly Persons, *from which the following excerpt comes, is one of the finest literary expressions of the impact of the war on people whose lives seemed most remote from it.*

From Idle and Disorderly Persons
Risk

The ridges of ice on the sidewalk in front of the draft board were hard as metal under the soles of Phoebe's boots, and her fingers, in spite of sheepskin gloves, felt solid with pain and permanently welded to the handle of the sign that said, to her discomfiture, "War is not healthy for children and other living things." She envied her pediatrician, tramping along in his Henry Higgins hat with his "End the Draft" sign. Perhaps he would be willing to trade. The sentiment she was carrying was particularly appropriate for him, and he might not be bothered by the wording. In fact, he surely wouldn't; Phoebe had never discovered anyone yet who shared her opinion of the artless tone of the slogan. "Healthy," she found herself muttering inside her head. "War *is* healthy. It has never been healthier."

At least fifty people were there, not bad for five-thirty in the morning, and most of them were adults. Phoebe was sorry to see a few high-school students in the group, with their antiestablishment costumes and dirty-word signs. It shouldn't be part of their lives to parade around like this or to feel an obligation to go to jail. Although she had deliberately not told Paul about the demonstration, he had heard about it at school and considered for a day and then told her that he wasn't coming. He had deep-set eyes like hers, which gave him the same serious expression and made it difficult to tell how much emotion might lie behind anything he said. "You go if you want, Mom. It's your right. I've decided I believe in working within the system." Phoebe hoped he didn't think she was disappointed in him, but she hadn't wanted him to see, either, how relieved she was.

More demonstrators were arriving, waving and making V signs at each other. There were over a hundred people by now. Phoebe recognized two teachers and a librarian. The thirty-seven people who had volunteered to be arrested stood near the curb, stamping their feet on the frozen sidewalk and trying to make friends with the police. "Pity about the riot helmets," someone whispered. "They must feel like fools." The policemen were lined up in the street next to the curb, feet apart, hands clasped behind their backs, staring glumly past the faces of the demonstrators through the plastic shields on their helmets.

The people on the edge of the crowd stopped talking and began to look down the street. The ones near the curb poised themselves for action, and the police shifted their feet. A bus was approaching—an ordinary green bus with cigarette ads on the sides. It pulled up to the curb and the door opened. Phoebe hadn't expected the bus to look so normal. She felt her eyes stinging.

When the draftees came out of the building behind her, she was surprised again. For some reason she had left them out of the mental picture she had formed in which the only participants were the demonstrators and the police. But of course the demonstration wasn't just symbolic. For any concrete effect it would have on these boys, it might as well be; they would eventually be taken away in the bus, no matter how many people sat down in front of it. But the boys themselves were real. They wore jeans and boots and school jackets like the boys who were picketing, and their faces as they came out of the doorway didn't show much besides an effort not to show anything. She felt like a source of embarrassment to them, as if she were a mother rushing to school at recess with forgotten mittens.

As the boys approached the bus, three of the protesters moved forward and sat down on the curb, blocking the entrance. Two more sat in the street in front of the bus. Phoebe clutched the handle of her sign and held it higher. A murmur went through the crowd as two of the police gingerly picked up a white-haired philosophy professor and carried him to a paddy wagon. Edith Levine was next, a motherly woman with a crown of auburn braids, beaming between peace-symbol earrings. "Where's the press, anyway?" Phoebe heard someone ask. "Channel 5 definitely said they'd be here." But there were plenty of photographers, whether from the newspapers or the FBI, and she could see at least one television camera.

The draftees stood awkwardly, as if they hadn't been told what to do.

Each demonstrator who was carried away was replaced by another, until only two people were sitting in the frozen street—one of the high-school boys and ferocious, heavy Gayle Pierce. Two of the police began to approach Gayle, bracing themselves with a show of resignation, and Phoebe was apprehensive, remembering Gayle's references to police as "pigs" during the planning session.

But Gayle was disposed of without extra excitement, and the pony-tailed boy was left sitting alone. The man in charge of the draftees motioned to them, and they started to walk toward the bus.

Phoebe couldn't bear the sight. If she was just going to stand there, she might as well be at home. She took a breath and leaned her sign against the brick wall of the building behind her. Then she walked quickly toward the bus and sat down on the cold cement. The boy who was sitting there looked up, as surprised as she was. She blinked as a flashbulb went off and thought, I've done it again; the album at home was full of pictures of her with her eyes closed.

She didn't have time to wonder what she thought she was doing, before she felt herself being picked up by the elbows. Phoebe had not had practice in going limp, and she was sure she was doing it wrong. She was glad when she was finally sitting in the wagon.

Gayle was hunched forward on the seat next to her, squinting at a number written on the inside of her wrist. Ordinarily Gayle wore contact lenses, but the demonstrators had been advised against them. "Can you see what that says?" she asked.

Phoebe read the number to her. "What is it for?"

"Legal assistance. Didn't you write it down?"

"I wasn't expecting to be arrested." Phoebe felt apologetic.

"I can call if somebody has to. You'll want to use your phone call to get hold of your husband." Gayle didn't approve of husbands, it was well known.

Daniel. Phoebe had mentioned the demonstration to him the night before, and she knew she had told him she was planning to picket, though she wasn't sure it had registered; he had been immersed in the *Trojan Women* translation that was his contribution to the anti-war effort.[1] Still, she certainly hadn't warned him that she might do something that would get her arrested. She had, in fact, given him all her customary arguments against doing anything of the sort. What she had said to Daniel last night had amounted to a promise. It fitted into the terms of the unspoken contract that Phoebe considered an essential part of marriage, an agreement that neither of them, except in extreme circumstances, would do anything that might cause unnecessary trouble or pain to the other. The present circumstances could be considered extreme, she supposed, and her reaction had been unpredictable, but she did not feel easy about Daniel.

Phoebe wondered whether her near-sightedness had made her especially daring. She had left her glasses at home, and she wasn't sure now that the precaution had been wise. She was able to see fairly well without them, but the lack of detail gave her a feeling of being removed from events around her—as if she herself had fuzzy edges.

Daniel would be teaching his Ideals of Greek Culture class right now. She imagined herself calling the Classics Department and trying to leave a message the secretary could transmit without decoding. It couldn't be done. But of course there was no need to call him. The phone call was a right, not a requirement. Phoebe might even be home before he was, and it would be easier to talk to him in person. "I don't believe I will," she said, and thought Gayle seemed respectful.

Phoebe was in the kitchen that afternoon when Daniel came in. She was wearing an embroidered apron and stirring a pot of chili with a wooden spoon and singing rounds with Louisa, who was making her

---

[1]*The Trojan Women* (415 B.C.), by the Greek dramatist Euripides, offers a scathing indictment of the atrocities perpetrated by the Greek victors on the women and children of the conquered city of Troy. [Ed.]

first batch of oatmeal bread. They were just finishing "Scotland's Burning" as Daniel came in, and Phoebe was envying Louisa's volume. She might speak up more often in meetings if she had a louder voice. "Daniel, could you come here for a minute?" She left Louisa kneading dough and walked into the living room.

Daniel followed reluctantly, and Phoebe was a little ashamed of having staged such a pretty domestic scene for him. As soon as he appeared in the doorway, she sat on the couch and told him about her morning. She and the other demonstrators had been charged with being idle and disorderly persons. The charge was a graver one than they had anticipated, but it meant that they were unlikely to be convicted. On the advice of their lawyer, they had pleaded innocent. "It's simpler than I thought," Phoebe said. "We go to court in about six weeks, and if we're found guilty, we pay a fine."

"Oh, God," Daniel said, and sat heavily beside her. He began to rub his temple with a circular motion, and Phoebe could see it turning pink.

"I'm at least as surprised as you are," she said. "But when I saw those boys walking toward the bus, I couldn't stand it. I'm sorry."

"Are you really?"

"No. I'm glad, actually. If I *hadn't* sat in front of the bus, I would be sorry." She stood up and ran her hands through her hair, making it stick out like the hair of an impulsive, irrational person if nothing worse. "I can pay the fine with my own money."

"Will you sit down, Phoebe?" She couldn't tell how he felt. "I don't mind what you did," he said. "There's no need to apologize."

"It's not you; it's me. It seemed unfair to do something like that without warning you. Besides," she said, "you did mind. You said, 'Oh, God.'"

"That was natural. I was surprised."

"So it's all right?"

"Of course. Will you let me pay the fine?"

"You could count it as my birthday present."

He put his arms around her. "Phoebe, I'm proud of you. Okay?"

Idle and Disorderly Persons

A layer of speckled sand on the sidewalks still showed the patterns made by melting snow, and the grass lay in colorless, flattened clumps scored with muddy plow tracks, but the air was soft, and water trickled into the drains. It was the wrong sort of day for a trial, Phoebe thought, and then wondered whether grim, cold weather would have made it any easier for her to go to the courthouse.

"Look how yellow the willow branches are already." She heard herself chattering like a dean's wife at a faculty party. Daniel, in the car beside her, didn't bother to answer, and she didn't blame him. The trouble was that nothing in her life so far had prepared her for the events of the last six weeks. She had even felt furtive about the things she had been doing to make sure the household would run smoothly in case she should have to serve a jail sentence. The lawyer had explained to Phoebe and the others that there was no danger of their being unable to go home right after the trial. They would almost certainly be found innocent. If by any chance they weren't, they could simply pay their fine and leave. Yet Phoebe had quietly stocked the freezer, made her children's spring dental appointments, returned all the library books, and paid the bills.

Daniel parked the car on a side street and waited while she searched through her bag for money for the meter. "This isn't the day to get a ticket," he said cheerfully. He really was being very forbearing.

As they approached the courthouse, Phoebe could see a crowd of people on the lawn of the church across the street. There was Jenny's face, round and peasantish above a heavy gray sweater. Annette was standing in profile, her poor back looking long and straight as a yardstick. Roslyn Rose slouched like a fashion model in her eye shadow and liner and mascara and base and blusher and frosted hair and her custom-tailored suede suit. The handles of signs had been stuck into the hedge: "End the Draft," "WFP Supports Resisters," "Stop Killing Our Sons." Phoebe held onto Daniel's arm, smiled toward a television camera, and went up the steps.

The judge, a known liberal, had a kind, clever face with wild eyebrows. The defendants, he said, were among the least idle and disorderly members of the community. They had broken the law only to protest a grave injustice. He wished he could have been with them himself. "Why wasn't he, then?" Phoebe heard Gayle mutter.

The judge seemed to be about to find them not guilty. Phoebe realized that she was disappointed. It might be only a question of terms, but surely they were guilty of something. If it was legal to sit in front of a bus, why had they done it?

But she was staring so hard at the judge that she had stopped listening. He was saying now, not that the defendants were innocent, but that they had obstructed a public roadway. The case would be continued, and after the summer all charges would be dropped.

She could feel the relief around her, as the other defendants broke into smiles. "Thank God," a man said to her. "Linda was afraid we wouldn't get to the Cape till August."

"What does 'continued' mean?" Everyone but Phoebe seemed to understand.

"Not a thing. Just that you won't have a record. They'll erase the whole business unless you rob a bank before the end of the summer. Terrific, nicht?"

"Why won't we have a record?" She looked around, hoping for an explanation.

"A trick. A conspiracy!" Phoebe wasn't the only one after all. Gayle's face blazed. "Are we going to let him get away with this?" She seized her attorney.

There were thirty-eight people in the room who had expected either to be found innocent or to be punished, and now most of them seemed pleased at what appeared to be a weakly reasoned compromise. Phoebe supposed it was nice of the judge, but how had be been able to find them guilty of something they hadn't been charged with?

"It's all right." Gayle turned from her lawyer, exultant. "We can demand to be sentenced right away. We can go to jail after all."

Twenty dollars or twenty days. Daniel reached for his wallet, but Phoebe put her hand on his. "You're not serious," he said, staring at her.

"Yes. We can't pay it. It wouldn't be right."

She was holding her head so high and her mouth so firm that Daniel was dismayed. "God bless Captain Vere,"[2] he said, but couldn't tell whether Phoebe heard. "Oh, come on," he said in desperation. "You can't go to jail. You wouldn't be able to stand it." The wrong thing to say, he knew, as he saw her clench her teeth. "All right," he said, "I wouldn't be able to."

"I'm sorry," Phoebe said, looking quite ruthless. "You'll just have to be brave."

---

[2]In Herman Melville's novella *Billy Budd, Sailor*, these are the final words of Billy Budd before he is hanged, as ordered by Captain Vere. [Ed.]

In the end, three of the women and five of the men chose jail. "Cowards," cried Gayle to the others. "If you're not part of the solution, you're part of the problem!"

The third prisoner was Leslie, a tall young woman that Phoebe almost didn't recognize because she had never seen her before without two children in a stroller and another in a pack on her back. "Thank God for people like you," Gayle said, looking from Leslie to Phoebe. "I'll never trust any of them again." She jerked her chin back over her shoulder.

"I'm not sure how long I can stay," Leslie said. She looked worried, and her nose was pink.

"It isn't fair to blame them," Phoebe said. "We can't know their reasons."

"They made a commitment." Gayle stamped along.

Leslie said, "I think I'm coming down with a cold."

The physical exam was what Phoebe was most apprehensive about. She had heard that the matrons might try to humiliate her, and as far as she was concerned, they wouldn't even have to try; the prospect of even the most ordinary check-up with her own doctor was enough to ruin a day. But the exam turned out to be mainly a series of questions. If there was anything wrong with her, they didn't want to find it. Most of the questions were the usual ones, but there were others.

"What drugs do you take, dear?"

She didn't suppose they meant aspirin. "None." But the matron kept her pencil poised. "Nothing at all," Phoebe said.

The matron wrote something, probably a question mark, and went on. "Diseases?" The pencil was ready to check them off.

"Just the usual ones."

"Measles? Mumps? Syphilis? Gonorrhea?"

"Yes. Yes. No, of course not." She supposed they had their reasons.

"Did you go to high school, dear?"

"Yes."

The matron looked at her consideringly. "College?"

"Yes." It seemed to Phoebe like an admission.

"Good for you, dear. Any graduate work by any chance?"

"I have an M.A. in biology." Then what are you doing here? she expected to be asked.

But the matron beamed. "Good for you!"

Leslie was sniffing as she came out of the examining room. "They took away my antihistamine pills. And my Bible."

"Subversive literature." Gayle was delighted. "What did you want with a Bible, anyhow?"

"I thought I might find some quotations."

"Look what they let me keep!" Gayle waved a small red book. *Thoughts of Chairman Mao.*

The prison was old, with real stone walls like a prison in a book. It could have held the Count of Monte Cristo or Hester Prynne.[3] Phoebe was surprised to find that she had a cell of her own, with her own wash basin and toilet. There was a bed too, not a bunk like the ones in jail cartoons. It was on casters which made it possible for her to move it so that the head was against the bars on the front of the cell. By draping a blanket over the end, she was able to create at least the idea of privacy. The mattress was impossible, but that wasn't surprising. Because of Gayle's inquiries among friends who had spent time in jail, Phoebe knew enough to ask for a toothbrush, soap, sheet, and blanket. One thing she hadn't been prepared for was the amount of noise. All the time, day and night, there was competing music from different people's radios.

What bothered Phoebe most of all proved to be something so petty that she was ashamed of herself. If she had realized that she would wind up in jail that day, and if she had been told about the regulations for the dress of short-time prisoners, she would have been able to avoid the problem. As it was, she had chosen her clothes carefully. The navy-blue pants and matching jacket she usually wore for picketing had seemed appropriate, along with a pale blue sweater and a small silver peace symbol on a fine chain. But it hadn't occurred to Phoebe that there were still places where pants on a woman were considered immodest. "You can't wear that," the matron said before conducting her to her cell, and led her to a room which contained nothing but a vast pile of assorted clothes. Looking at them, Phoebe was amazed. Was it possible that this was where everything ended up that failed to

---

[3]The innocent hero of Alexandre Dumas's novel *The Count of Monte Cristo* spends nearly twenty years in a remote prison fortress. Nathaniel Hawthorne's novel *The Scarlet Letter* opens with the release of Hester Prynne, the protagonist, from a Puritan prison where she has been incarcerated for adultery. [Ed.]

sell at clothing exchanges and rummage sales or the Salvation Army and Morgan Memorial?

"See if you can find a dress that will fit," the matron said.

Phoebe began to sort reluctantly through the garments. Most of them were what her mother referred to as house dresses and what Phoebe had long ago promised herself she would never sink so low as to wear. She associated such dresses with colorlessness and drudgery. Not that the dresses themselves were colorless. Most of them were covered with large, unidentifiable flowers in yellow or red or purple or brown. The others were patterned in tartans which looked as if they belonged to clans that had been forced, like brand-new high schools, to design their uniforms after all the good colors had been used up. The thought of wearing one of these dresses for the next twenty days made Phoebe tremble. Some things simply hadn't been taken into account by the professors and clergymen who prepared people like her for facing jail. For the first time that day, she was afraid she might disgrace herself by shedding tears.

"I haven't got all day," the matron said, and Phoebe reached out blindly to search for something that she could bear to try on. The clothes weren't exactly dirty, but the cloth lacked body and clung to her fingers, and there was a faint smell of mildew. Finally she came to a skirt. If she chose that, she might be allowed to keep her sweater and jacket. She held the skirt against herself and saw that though the waist was probably the right size, it was much too short. Her knees and at least four inches of thigh would show. Prison regulations, if they were at all consistent, should certainly prohibit that. "That's fine. Come on," the matron said, and Phoebe surrendered her pants and put on the skirt, which was patterned in orange and red diagonal rows of flowers on a black background. It was gathered at the waist, where it bunched either under her sweater or over it, depending on whether or not she tried to tuck the sweater in.

Phoebe's morale, she realized, would be lower for the next few days than it might otherwise have been. Had any scholar studied seriously enough the effect on Joan of Arc when she was forced to change her clothes in prison?

The evening meal was served at three-thirty. Phoebe hadn't expected it to be good, and it wasn't. Leslie, whose spirits were wholesomely high in spite of her streaming eyes, made herself unpopular as soon as she sat down at the table. She inspected the enormous under-done potato, gristly ham, and spinach sitting in a pool of green water on her plate and then looked cheerfully around and said, "I don't know how long I can be with you ladies. My daughter has to play in a piano recital tomorrow."

There was a silence. "Fahn-cy that," someone said.

"She's only eight." Leslie still smiled, then wiped her nose.

Gayle was seated too far away to hear. She was trying to radicalize her fellow prisoners, she had said earlier, and she took their resentment as a hopeful sign. "It shows they have some spirit left," she said.

Leslie was gone the next morning. "Did your friend go home? The one with the musical daughter?" one of the other women asked Phoebe.

"Yes, I think she did." But Phoebe knew she wouldn't have stayed herself if it had been Louisa's recital.

(1981)

WAYNE KARLIN

Born in 1945 in Los Angeles, Wayne Karlin served in the U.S. Marines from 1963 to 1967, including a year (1966–1967) in Vietnam as a combat aircrew sergeant in the First Marine Air Wing, where he was awarded an Air Medal. In 1973, Karlin and two other Vietnam veterans, Basil Paquet and Larry Rottmann, collected and edited Free Fire Zone: Short Stories by Vietnam Veterans, *the first collection of its type.*

Karlin did not publish another book directly related to Vietnam until 1988, when his second novel, Lost Armies, *set in the marshlands of eastern Maryland, dramatized unhealed traumas of two Vietnam veterans and a settlement of Vietnamese refugees. Two other novels,* Crossover *(1984) and* The Extras *(1989), deal with conflicts involving Israel, where Karlin mainly lived between 1969 and 1976. The 1993 novel* US *returns to Southeast Asia, where Karlin, in a surreal mythic drama, interrelates the American MIA obsession with the opium armies of the Golden Triangle.*

Although he has published four novels with leading trade presses, Karlin's superb short fiction remains known only to a small audience. I had originally intended to include one of the five brilliant stories set in Vietnam that he contributed to Free Fire Zone, *but opted instead for two later tales set in America.*

"Moratorium" deals with a largely buried aspect of the antiwar movement: the extensive participation of Vietnam veterans. Contrary to the outlandish notion that antiwar activists went around spitting on veterans and calling them "baby killers," the civilian antiwar movement forged strong ties to the antiwar movement surging both among veterans and within the ranks of active military units. Set in 1969, "Moratorium" dramatizes aspects of the early phases of this coalescence. Soon many veterans were in the vanguard of the antiwar movement, as in the 1971 demonstration in Washington, when eight hundred combat veterans threw their medals, including many Purple Hearts, over a fence protecting the nation's Capitol building from them.

Moratorium

Mor*a*to*ri*um, n. 1. an authorization to delay payment due

Deborah asked, "Everything all right?"
"Just the early morning broods."

She watched his hands as he soaped them. "I'm still scared of how you're taking it."

"How am I taking it?"

"Too seriously. Like some momentous, ceremonial occasion. But it's just a party to most of the people. That's why I stopped going."

"I thought you stopped going because of me."

"That's what I mean."

They sat down on the bed, settling back against the pillow. She put her head on his chest.

"In our Operations tent," he said, "there was this gunny sergeant; he kept a framed photograph on his desk. Not the wife and kids, but this picture from the *New York Times*, a shot of one of the first demonstrations. He'd circled one marcher's head with a grease pencil he used on the flight status board to write in the names of the crews going on missions. Above the guy's head he wrote, 'Traitor—to be killed.' The circle was real thick and dark and you could see he'd pressed down very hard with rage because of the smudge where the tip of the pencil had broken off."

"Nobody's going to draw a halo around your head," Deborah said.

He got off the bed and walked over to the closet. The night before he'd hung up his jungle shirt and some jeans and hooked the hanger over the door, ready as if he were going on an early morning flight, a mission. He'd pinned his silver aircrew wings to the shirt. The gunny, he remembered suddenly, was the kind of NCO who would write people up for chickenshit, stateside offenses like being out of uniform, as if he felt he had a mission to maintain standards, standards that didn't apply in the circumstances of the war.

He put on the shirt, running the tip of his fingertips over the metal wings. A knock startled him. He waited until Deborah had pulled on a long shirt and then opened the door.

Barry was wearing a khaki shirt with his ribbons and Combat Infantry Badge on it. He grinned at Brian: their choice of clothing hadn't been planned.

"Green side out," he said. He touched Brian's shoulder. "How you feeling?"

"Traitor—to be killed."

"Absolutely."

They made a pit stop at Maryland House. He and Barry had a smoke while they waited for Deborah and Barry's girl Phyllis to get out of the rest room. Barry pumped gas, the cigarette dangling from his mouth. A silvergray Plymouth pulled up next to them. In the passenger seat was a blond woman with a beehive hairdo. She glanced at Brian, then patted her hair, as if his gaze had made her conscious of it. The driver was wearing a khaki uniform, Army class A's, like Barry's, a colored rectangle of ribbons on his chest. The woman tilted the mirror again and a rhomboid of light projected over the face of the soldier inside. The face looked vaguely accusing and pissed off. He'd been holding a kind of tension, Brian realized, since the day before, since he'd decided to go to the demonstration. Now something in the angle of light, in the blurred features of the face, allowed that tension to relax in a kind of internal collapse into the face of Jim Hardesty.

Hardesty was a boy who had died in Brian's place, flying gunner on a routine resupply mission to Hill 327 during what was to have been the last week of the war for both of them. The squadron was rotating to Okinawa to get new helicopters; it had lost five aircraft and the ships it had left were in bad shape after four solid months of operations along the DMZ. He and Jim Hardesty were in the last increment to leave. On nearly the last day Brian had drawn flight duty, but Hardesty had asked if he could take it instead. Brian couldn't even remember the reason for it, he didn't know Hardesty that well, they weren't really friends, just military acquaintances. Maybe Hardesty figured he'd be called to fly the next day anyway and wanted to get it over with; maybe he needed a mission for an air medal. There were enough stories of people killed in the last days of their tours. Outside the war, you told stories like that to prevent them from happening to you. But in the war telling them was more like calling something to life. If Hardesty wanted to take his place, that was fine with him. They'd gone to the operations sergeant, the one with the photograph on his desk, and made the switch. That night the helicopter in which Brian would have flown gunner went on a standard resupply flight to a company of grunts. It was on approach when it came under fire and a single bullet hit the helicopter and penetrated it and Hardesty's body, going through the gunner's seat where Brian would have been sitting, entering below the bottom edge of Hardesty's flak jacket instead of his, travelling perpendicularly through Hardesty's body instead of Brian's.

Now Brian stood alive in a gas station in Maryland watching the face of a soldier watching him from behind a windshield.

He wondered if the request to switch had been a last minute effort on Hardesty's part to deal with some perceived internal weakness while he still had the chance. There were people who came to the war for that. Perhaps many people. He remembered how scared Hardesty had been. In the old aviator's canard, he wasn't afraid of flying, only of coming down. The country itself filled Hardesty with terror; it was so unlike the flat Kansas plains he came from. It pulsed with the overlush greens of an evil Oz. The fragmented mirrors of its paddies held images of broken helicopters in their depths. Its jagged, broody cordilleras and secretive triple-canopied jungle randomly and maliciously spat fire upwards. The helicopters would only touch the land briefly to release men onto it, then touch briefly again soon after to pick up the bodies of the same men, torn as if they been gnawed by the country. What happened in the time between was unknown to the helicopter crews. One of the crew chiefs Hardesty flew with was a friend of Brian's; like all the good crew chiefs, he was a keen observer of changes in terrain. He'd confided his uneasiness about Hardesty—he'd seen how Hardesty's finger would tremble on the trigger even in cold L.Z.'s as if on some hair trigger inside himself that was wearing closer and closer to the sear. Brian understood; he was worn in the same places. On missions, the gunner was an impotent spectator except when shooting his gun. He sat in the same seat; he knew the feeling of helplessness. His helicopter had flown cover on one insert when Hardesty's helicopter had let off a squad of grunts and the crews had watched in horror, not frozen, but hovering, darting, hosing the treeline with fire, but all of it useless as the grunts ran in fire team rushes toward that treeline, falling, one fire team after another cut down and not one hesitating, just working, moving professionally toward the trees that were killing them; one man after another zigging and zagging and falling as if it were some well rehearsed, tactically planned process they were all following to get killed quickly. Then on Hardesty's next flight, his helicopter developed a hydraulic leak and had to autorotate down to a hard landing in a paddy, the ship spinning, the land sucking him down to itself. A clearly pregnant woman squatted among the rice shoots, watching him come into her life. She'd frozen, war wise, knowing that the helicopters shot anyone who ran, not knowing that Hardesty was in this one. That night he'd joked about getting two gooks with one round. The phrase became a standard with the aircrews, a measure of shooting proficiency. A joke.

The face behind the windshield mouthed silently at Brian. He saw the woman put a hand on the soldier's shoulder, as if restraining him.

The memories were coming faster, some compressed spring he'd lived with so long its tightness had become normal suddenly released in his mind. He remembered how he'd flown back to Travis Air Force Base in San Francisco on the same C-130 with about twenty other men from his squadron whose tours had finished while they were on Okinawa. It was the nearest thing the war had to the traditional coming back as a unit: the random mathematics of their time in country giving them an accidental parade, even if it only consisted of being herded up the ramp of the cargo plane together. For the first time they wore the class A khaki uniforms they hadn't seen for over a year, whitened crease lines on them where the cloth had been folded in their stored sea bags, new ribbons and silver combat aircrew wings bright on their chests. Perhaps noticing the wings, some of the Air Force crew brought them coffee; they had wings too; they were all birdmen, brothers of the air. How was it, the airmen had asked, and the marines told them sea stories, air stories, shot down stories, shoot up the village stories, toss the prisoners stories. Brian told how Hardesty had gotten two gooks with one round. But the airmen didn't laugh. They didn't get the joke. They looked at the marines, at the wings on their chests, strangely. Then the marines had fallen silent too. They blinked as if awakening from a dream in which the laws and customs of the world had been suspended. Brian could feel a silence folding around them and he knew that they, he, wouldn't talk about the war anymore, or if they did, they'd try to fit it into more expected and acceptable references. That nobody would get the joke.

"What are you men doing?"

The soldier had gotten out of the Plymouth. Focusing back, Brian realized that he hadn't even noticed the process; it played in his mind like a memory behind the memories of that flight home and Hardesty: the car door opening, the frowning face, the woman tugging the soldier's arm, trying to pull him back. There were silver first lieutenant's bars on the man's collar. Brian's eyes went automatically to the ribbons. The yellow and red Vietnam service ribbon was there, but there was no CIB, no wings, no purple heart, only the been-there ribbons.

"I said what are you men doing?" The lieutenant frowned at Brian.

"You men?" Barry said, squinting at him.

The lieutenant's face went red. "Let me see your i.d.'s."

Barry laughed. "Look L.T., we're not in the service anymore."

"Then you have no right to be wearing those uniforms. There's a law against impersonating a soldier." He glared at them. "I know where you're going. You're both disgraces. I want your names—both of you."

Brian looked, startled, at the lieutenant, then began laughing. "You want to write me up," he said in wonder. The lieutenant stared at him, still frowning. "You want to write me up now." He laughed more. "Hey, lieutenant, where the fuck were you?" Out of the corner of his eye, he saw Phyllis and Deborah coming back from the ladies room. "Why don't you just di-di the fuck out of here," he said. "You understand that term, lieutenant? Or you just impersonating a dick head?"

He saw Barry pull the nozzle out of the gas tank and screw on the cap, his shoulders stiff and high, his face tight. Barry spun around, arcing the gas nozzle close to the lieutenant's face. Some gas globbed from the end and the lieutenant stepped back slightly. Barry nodded and poked the nozzle forward, closer, and the lieutenant backed up. Gas dribbled onto his spit shine. Barry held his lit cigarette in his other hand, between thumb and forefinger. He flicked it. "Ever see a gook flambé, L.T., a crispy critter?" he asked. "Ever write one up? No? Where were you when that was going down? Like the man asked—where the fuck were you? Some office? Pointing your pointer at some map overlay, some grid I was on? Want a ciggie? Souvenir you Salem? Want a light? No? Then like my friend said, you better di-di. Don't let your alligator mouth overload your lizard ass and all that other kind of Vietnam talk."

The lieutenant tried a hard OCS stare at him. "You men will hear about this, I promise you. I have your license number."

The woman in the Plymouth stuck her head out of the window. "Leave them alone, Martin. We're late."

"You're late, Martin," Brian said, coming up next to Barry. "Move on, lieutenant pogue. You got my number—give me a call sometimes."

The lieutenant left. Brian saw that Deborah and Phyllis were staring at him and Barry in the same way Deborah had stared at his hands that morning.

The movement of the march trembled between the buildings and Brian felt an answering shudder in his chest. He couldn't see either end of the column. On the car radio they'd heard there were half a million people in the streets of Washington. The announcer had commented that this was the equivalent of the number of troops still in Vietnam. Similar numbers were reported from New York, San Francisco, Chicago.

He tried to hang onto a feeling of purposefulness in being part of the movement of so many people. But instead he found himself settling into the dullness he always assumed when marching in a column, an interior blankness that he moved in until he got where he was going. The people around him were linking arms, smiling at each other, chanting for peace now. He lip synched the words, feeling self-conscious. Deborah had been pushed a little ways from him and a woman hooked her arm with his and grinned at him. Her other arm was linked with a priest's. The priest smiled at him too. He saw the priest's gaze brush the wings on his chest, the man catching his eye, nodding in approval. Brothers of the air. He brought his hand up, covered the insignia. He had the wings, he needed the halo. I'm out of uniform, priest. Write me up. The chanting grew louder. Phyllis, Barry's arm draped over her shoulder, looked around at him; she was smiling also. I can't hear you, she mouthed. All of a sudden he was back in bootcamp. Get back and do it again. Get it right this time. I can't hear you. All the people around him were chanting and grinning as if they knew something about it, moving their signs and banners up and down in a cadence. They didn't know but they'd been told. "I can't hear you!" he yelled. He thought how they would look without the noise coming from their mouths, the way he would turn down the sound on the TV and watch the grotesque pantomimes of the news announcers, their inane smiles encompassing images of corpses and shooting men and burning hootches. When he'd first gotten back, before he'd met Deborah, he'd rented a small room and spent hours watching TV, as if he could plug himself back into the country, get back on some wavelength he was missing. On the screen, little gray figures ran across paddies, fell, rose; he was one of them, escaped right out of the box, loose in the streets. Out of uniform. Impersonating a human being. PEACE NOW! he yelled, and laughed. The woman and the priest laughed too, but he laughed louder, until they looked at him uneasily. He could get the two of them with one round. They were all bunched up with someplace to go. He couldn't see Deborah. Suddenly a truck pulled in front of him from a side street, breaking into the crowd. It was draped with VC and North Vietnamese flags and there was a rock band on its bed, playing very hard, the marching band for this parade. The music jerked the crowd. He could see one of the players' faces very clearly. It was pale and pimpled and the boy's eyes were blank as if all his emotions had been poured into the blurred motion of his fingers on the guitar strings. The boy had made a VC flag into a vest. He was bare-chested under it, his upper body white and skinny. He stared at the boy's face. He wanted to break it with his fist, knead expressions into it, give it to Jim Hardesty. But the face stayed blank. His feelings didn't particularly move it.

"Hey, man," he yelled at the boy. "Hey, you're out of uniform." The boy cupped one hand behind his ear and smiled at Brian helplessly. He didn't get the joke.

He looked away from the boy, searching for Deborah; she'd been squeezed a little further forward. He spotted Barry and Phyllis near her. They were looking up at the spectators in the windows of government office buildings, searching for anyone cheering them from behind the walls of legitimate authority. Some of the windows had jungly green plants behind them, as if screening another world that hid behind the facade of the building. Faces peered at him in silent disapproval. They had his number. The lieutenant's face mouthed angrily at him from behind the glass. It blurred and disappeared. Move on, lieutenant pogue.

He'd stopped to look up at the windows, letting the crowd break around him. When he looked back down, he couldn't see Deborah anywhere. He felt a sense of trapped panic. He began shoving through the marchers. The crowd was a pressure at his temples. He pushed through, feeling bodies like vines and roots, holding his passage for an instant then giving and slipping past him. He grasped with his hands in a swimming motion, taking people by the shoulders and parting them out of his way. They glared at him, but said nothing until he was past; then they'd start chanting again as if he'd never touched them. "Over here!" he heard Deborah yell. She was next to the priest. He made a final thrust and broke through, reaching out blindly, connecting with the priest's arm. He gripped the priest's arm. All those personnel wishing halos will assemble to the right and rear of the duty priest. Semper fi, sky pilot, you got yours, how'm I doing? The priest was staring at him. He released his arm.

You're late, sky pilot. Move on. Don't let your alligator intentions overload your lizard dimensions.

They were moving now through a gap in a row of parked school buses and into the Mall area. As the column broke and spread into the clearing, he could see for the first time the vastness of the crowd, gathered because of his war. It filled the center of the city, the white tower of the monument rising from its center. Half a million people, Deborah said into his ear, half a million was his number and he could see it unabstract, solidly filling space. He could see with his eyes what half a million was. He felt utterly outside them, on the other side of a hard, transparent screen. The half million were laughing and dancing and he tried to think about Jim Hardesty who'd died in his place and the woman and the future Hardesty had killed from his place and in their name, these people around him who wouldn't look at him and he looked at them and he could see how they would be dead, all dead and lying on the grass, silent and spilling into the earth. I can't hear you, he thought. He sat down where he was. He was waiting for something inside himself and when it finally came and he began crying it came in waves so hard he felt they had to move out of him, ripple through the hugeness of the crowd. But when he looked up he only saw a woman staring as if surprised at what he was doing. He couldn't stop it. There was no release in it. Deborah put a hand on his shoulder. He bowed his head back down, pressing his face against the cloth of his shirt and the noise faded again. It was as if he were alone in the cradle of his arms.

(1991)

THE VIETNAM WAR
AND AMERICAN SCIENCE FICTION

Science fiction fans who tried to escape from the Vietnam War by diving into their favorite magazines in the spring of 1968 instead found themselves plunged right back into the conflict—in two opposing advertisements about the war, each signed by scores of science fiction writers, artists, and editors. The June 1968 issue of *Galaxy Science Fiction* showcased the two ads on facing pages, followed by pages of anguish by editor Frederik Pohl, who chastised both groups for splitting what he had thought was a tight community by fomenting a "polarized debate," thus making "opponents of people who should be friends" and threatening to "endlessly" protract the national debate, and hence the war.

The rival advertisements dramatize the deep fissure splitting not only the science fiction community but also the American people and their culture. The prowar list reads like a roll call of champions of superscience and supermen, of manly and military virtue, indeed some of the very values that had helped shape the technowar being waged in Indochina. The antiwar list includes almost the entire vanguard of an emerging kind of science fiction, opposed to technocracy, militarism, and imperialism; originally called the "New Wave," it evolved into new forms prominent in the 1970s, 1980s, and 1990s. Editor Pohl's yearning for the vanished if not mythical community of science fiction also represented a wider national nostalgia. For the apparently unified, content, smiling-faced nation of the late 1950s seemed in the process of being torn asunder by the war in Vietnam.

Indeed, when writers Kate Wilhelm and Judith Merril began soliciting signatures for the antiwar statement, they had naively assumed that "95 percent" of the writers would sign because of the "global and anti-racist view" that supposedly guided science fiction. Merril was shocked when Robert Heinlein, known as "the Dean of American science fiction," responded with vociferous declarations of "America first" and the "U.S. must win."

Perhaps the very first literary science fiction or fantasy flowing from America's war in Vietnam was Heinlein's *Glory Road*, serialized way back in 1963. The hero of *Glory Road* is bitter about the Korean War because "we weren't allowed to win." So he goes off to fight as a "Military Adviser" in the jungles of Vietnam, where "the bushes are filled with insects and natives who shoot at you." Like Rambo, the hero of *Glory Road* (who is also a martial arts expert) is embittered by what he sees as government betrayal during the war and is thoroughly alienated from the domestic American society he finds when he returns.

The hero's lament that "we weren't allowed to win" the Korean War alludes to the decision not to use nuclear bombs. The U.S. government had already entertained such thoughts about Vietnam, envisioning nuclear weapons as a magical power that could reshape Indochinese reality.

As early as April 5, 1954, while France teetered on the brink of defeat, the National Security Council's plans for possible intervention stipulated: "Nuclear weapons will be available for use as required" (*Pentagon Papers*, Senator Gravel Edition, I, 466), and later that month Washington offered two nuclear bombs to be dropped on the forces besieging the French bastion of Dien Bien Phu. A decade later, U.S. policy makers considered the use of nuclear weapons to support its own forces in Vietnam, even though officially these troops weren't even there (*Pentagon Papers*, III, 65, 175). In 1968, with U.S. forces beleaguered throughout South Vietnam, their supreme commander, General William Westmoreland, suggested the use of nuclear weapons. These schemes never burst upon the world, thanks to political realities.

But reality had no such control over the fantasies of some of the signers of the 1968 prowar advertisement in the science fiction magazines. Some imagined a final solution to the Vietnam problem in the form of that ultimate technological fix: nuclear weapons.

For example, one of those signers was Joe Poyer, who back in 1966 had published "Challenge: The Insurgent vs. the Counterinsurgent" in *Analog* science fiction magazine, where he had confidently asserted that all guerrilla insurgencies were now doomed by the evolving technological wizardry commanded by counterinsurgent forces—such as spy satellites and people sniffers (electronic devices to detect the chemicals exuded by guerrillas). In July 1968, Poyer published a story titled "Null Zone" in *Analog*. This tale combines two dominant American images of what wins wars: superwarriors and superweapons. Its hero is a Rambo-like Green Beret who, stalking alone deep in the jungles of Indochina, ambushes and slays innumerable North Vietnamese soldiers who are tracking him, while taking pictures with an infrared camera to augment the computer-generated holograph map back at his base in

We the undersigned believe the United States must remain in Vietnam to fulfill its responsibilities to the people of that country.

Thailand. He wins the war by clearing the way for a "Null Zone" formed by air drops of "deadly radioactive waste."

Another signer of the 1968 prowar ad was Jerry Pournelle, who was to emerge in the 1970s and 1980s as the loudest voice in science fiction exalting militarism, superweapons, and mercenary warriors. In 1970, Pournelle coauthored with Stefan Possony a technowar apologia, *The Strategy of Technology*, which argues that the only thing necessary to win the Vietnam War would be "3 megatons of small nuclear bombs with a strong neutron flux." (In mid-1995 Pournelle was coauthoring with Speaker of the House Newt Gingrich a science-fiction novel about a future war based on weaponry proposed in *The Strategy of Technology*.)

If the technowarriors of the Pentagon, White House, and *Analog* were possessed by such fantasies, New Wave science fiction sought to exorcise them through alternative visions. For example, Norman Spinrad, who signed the antiwar ad, in his 1969 story "The Big Flash" imagines a demonic rock group called "The Four Horsemen" who seem to offer the perfect solution to those who believed that they could win the war with nuclear weapons if it were not for public opinion. Since the band's repertoire consists of orgiastic numbers that mesmerize their audience into lust for "the big flash," the Administration, Pentagon, and aerospace companies sponsor their huge televised concerts to win over "precisely that element of the population which was most adamantly opposed to nuclear weapons." The campaign succeeds— although far beyond the dreams of the sponsors, for the resulting nuclear holocaust initiates the annihilation of the human species.

Besides the enticement of technowar and Special Forces was yet another official U.S. vision, one glowing with liberal ideological colors. This was epitomized in the slogan "Winning Hearts and Minds."

"Winning Hearts and Minds" reached its climax in 1968 and 1969, when the CIA conducted a gigantic carrot-and-stick campaign aimed at reestablishing control in the countryside lost during the Tet Offensive. The stick was Operation Phoenix, a program that relied on torture and assassination to root out the NLF infrastructure. U.S. intelligence officers subsequently testified to Congress that not one of the many "Viet Cong suspects" whose arrest they witnessed ever survived interrogation; the death toll from Phoenix was at least twenty thousand. The carrot was a "land reform" program that coopted Lenin's slogan, "Land to the Tiller." It was designed and run by University of Washington law professor Roy L. Prosterman, who also drew up the document that asserted a legal basis for Operation Phoenix. In 1980, Prosterman, again functioning in a CIA operation, was given the job of implementing his "Land to the Tiller" program in El Salvador. Between these two projects, in 1970, Prosterman wrote the science fiction story "Peace Probe" (published in the July 1973 *Analog*).

Prosterman's tale expresses the overarching vision that was being frustrated in Vietnam: a world entirely subservient to American intentions, which, of course, are always benign. After two unnamed nations convulse the world in a 1978 nuclear and bacteriological war, the U.S. president, being "a very good and a very wise man," issues a Unilateral Declaration stipulating that "any nation, entity or person other than the United States" found to possess any "weapons of mass destruction" or "such other weapons, armies and armaments as the President of the United States shall from time to time designate" shall be utterly annihilated by the United States. To enforce this decree, he establishes the Unilateral Declaration Agency (UDA), which is authorized to use drugs and "other techniques" to "probe" the minds of "officials and citizens" throughout the world, "without limitation as to persons, times or places" so as to guarantee that the world will remain perpetually under the sway of this Pax Americana. This vision of a global Operation Phoenix is narrated by a heroic UDA agent who ferrets out a plot by some renegade Argentines to force the United States to deal with other nations "as 'equals.'" By using chemical interrogation to unmask the conspirators, he spares the entire population of Argentina in the nick of time from righteous thermonuclear incineration by the UDA.

Just as Prosterman's "Peace Probe" reveals in the form of science fiction the interchangeability of "very good" intentions with genocidal practices, events in post-Tet Vietnam displayed to much of the American people how the benign appearance of "Winning Hearts and Minds" translated into wholesale terror and slaughter. The most infamous example occurred in the province of Quang Ngai, an NLF stronghold, where, by late 1967, U.S. forces had already destroyed 70 percent of the villages. In the aftermath of Tet, units of the Americal Division went on a rampage of arson, rape, and murder through the remaining rural settlements of Quang Ngai, including the village of My Lai. Because photographs of the My Lai massacre were sold to *Life* and because some U.S. soldiers testified to the atrocities, the American public learned that American soldiers had gone through the village murdering some five hundred unarmed civilians while raping and sodomizing the women and girls, butchering the animals, and using babies and small children for target practice.

Perhaps the finest work of art memorializing My Lai—and similar scenes that appeared on American television—is Kate Wilhelm's story "The Village" (page 124). Comparable in ways to Picasso's *Guernica* mural, which also used nonrealistic conventions to portray a reality too atrocious for realism, "The Village" uses the science fiction convention of transposing realistic surfaces into an unfamiliar time-space zone. The village of the title exists simultaneously in Vietnam and America, where an old man finds himself futilely shouting at American soldiers that they are brutalizing "the wrong town."

Wilhelm's fantasy of a time-space zone where America and Vietnam merge poignantly expresses a growing consciousness that America's war against Vietnam was coming home. Science fiction stories projecting the effects of the Vietnam War on America deepened in the 1980s, as projected in Lewis Shiner's "The War at Home" (page 178), where America itself is transformed into a surrealist Vietnam. One of the most incisive visions of what America's war against Vietnam was doing to America is the poem "And what would you do, ma" (page 258), by Steve Hassett, who served as an infantryman and intelligence analyst in Vietnam; here the fantasy of American soldiers stepping out of the television set to threaten ma and apple pie turns out to be the reality, which can be denied only by switching to fantasies on other channels.

The most popular novel about the Vietnam War, with well over a million copies sold, is *The Forever War*, by wounded Vietnam combat engineer Joe Haldeman. It extrapolates both kinds of extreme alienation experienced by U.S. veterans—first as alien invaders of a foreign land, then as aliens returning to what seems no longer their own society — into the experience of becoming both extraterrestrial invaders of alien planets and exiles in time and space from planet Earth. *The Forever War* fantasizes and extrapolates America's longest war into an 1,143-year intergalactic combat instigated by generals and politicians, waged for profits, and conducted as a devastating fiasco from beginning to end.

KATE WILHELM

With dozens of volumes of fiction published since the early 1960s, Kate Wilhelm has won an ever-widening audience and ever-increasing admiration. She has long been a preeminent figure in science fiction, where she has won the top awards given in the field: Hugo, Jupiter, and Nebula. But her mainstream fiction, such as her 1976 novel The Clewiston Test, *has also been acclaimed for the same qualities that distinguish her science fiction: a profound moral sensibility, splendid characterization, and storytelling so deftly crafted that even the most bizarre situations become fully believable.*

From 1963 to 1976, Wilhelm was codirector of the Milford Science Fiction Writers Conference, a seminal institution cofounded by her husband, Damon Knight, himself a distinguished writer, editor, and critic. It was at the 1967 Milford Conference, where many established as well as aspiring science fiction writers and editors were gathered, that Wilhelm and Judith Merril decided to organize a petition against the Vietnam War. Wilhelm revealed much about these traumatic times, and about her own engagement, in a recent letter:

> I recall perhaps too vividly the night we discussed and worded our protest over the Vietnam war. We planned for our discussion to take place after the Milford Conference was officially ended on Saturday night. We announced . . . that it had nothing to do with the writing conference, and we stated precisely that it was to discuss the wording of a protest against the war. Most of the attendees of the conference came, and it was clear that the whole thing would degenerate into yet another debate about the pros and cons of the war. I took the floor and repeated what we had stated earlier. This was not a meeting to debate the war, it was to form a nucleus of protesters who would sign a statement of protest and circulate it. I invited those who opposed such a statement to leave.

> It was the first time I ever had asked anyone to leave my house, and there was shock and dismay among those in opposition. I remember Doris Buck, a dear friend, who was very upset and said she supported the war effort; after all, she had a son in Vietnam. I said so did I.

Asked about the genesis of "The Village," one of the true literary masterpieces to emerge from the war, Wilhelm told me this:

When I heard the report on My Lai on the radio, I was so upset I couldn't sleep. I had an infant then. I paced the floor until near dawn. I vowed that the next day I would write something about this. Then I finally fell asleep. When I awoke, the story was just there. I wrote it in a passion, a white heat. I didn't edit it at all.

Although Wilhelm wrote "The Village" in 1969, it was not published until 1973, when Tom Disch included it in his anthology Bad Moon Rising. *Wilhelm explained:*

I couldn't get it published. I sent it around to everyone I could think of. The last one was an editor who said that the story certainly should *be published but that he *not do it.*

The Village

Mildred Carey decided to walk to the post office early, before the sun turned the two blocks into a furnace. "They've done something to the weather," she said to her husband, packing his three sandwiches and thermos of lemonade. "Never used to be this hot this early."

"It'll get cooler again. Always does."

She followed him to the door and waved as he backed out of the drive. The tomato plants she had set out the day before were wilted. She watered them, then started to walk slowly to town. With a feeling of satisfaction she noticed that Mrs. Mareno's roses had black spot. Forcing the blooms with too much fertilizer just wasn't good for them.

Mike Donatti dozed as he awaited orders to regroup and start the search-and-clear maneuver. Stilwell nudged him. "Hey, Mike, you been over here before?"

"Nope. One fuckin' village is just like the others. Mud or dust. That's the only fuckin' difference."

Stilwell was so new that he was sunburned red. Everyone else in the company was burned black. "Man, could we pass," they liked to say to Latimore, who couldn't.

Mr. Peters was sweeping the sidewalk before the market. "Got some good fresh salami," he said. "Ed made it over the weekend."

"You sure Ed made it, not Buz? When Buz makes it, he uses too much garlic. What's he covering up is what I want to know."

"Now, Miz Carey, you know he's not covering up. Some folks like it hot and strong."

"I'll stop back by after I get the mail."

The four Henry children were already out in the street, filthy, chasing each other randomly. Their mother was not in sight. Mildred Carey pursed her lips. Her Mark never had played in the street in his life.

She dropped in the five-and-dime, not to buy anything but to look over the flats of annuals—petunias, marigolds, nasturtiums. "They sure don't look healthy," she said to Doris Offinger.

"They're fine, Miz Carey. Brother bought them fresh this morning from Connor's down at Midbury. You know Connor's has good stock."

"How's Larry getting along? Still in the veterans' hospital at Lakeview?"

"Yes. He'll be out in a couple of weeks, I guess." Doris' pretty face remained untroubled. "They've got such good doctors down there, I hate to see him get so far from them all, but he wants to come home."

"How can these people stand this heat all the time?" Stilwell said after a moment. The sun wasn't up yet, but it was eighty-six degrees, humidity near one hundred percent.

"People, he says. Boy, ain't you even been briefed? People can't stand it, that's the first clue." Mike sighed and sat up. He lighted a cigarette. "Boy, back home in August. You know the hills where I come from are cold, even in August?"

"Where's that?"

"Vermont. I can remember plenty of times it snowed in August. Nights under a blanket."

"Well, he can help out here in the store. With his pension and the store and all, the two of you are set, aren't you? Isn't that Tessie Hetherton going in Peters' market?"

"I didn't notice her. Did you want one of those flats, Miz Carey?"

"No. They aren't healthy. Connor's must have culled the runts and set *them* out." She stood in the doorway squinting to see across the way to Peters' market. "I'm sure it was. And she told me she's too arthritic to do any more housework. I'll just go talk to her."

"I don't think she will, though. Miz Avery wanted her on Wednesdays and she said no. You know Mr. Hetherton's got a job? With the paper mill."

"Shtt. That won't last. They'll pay off a few of last winter's bills and then he'll start to complain about his liver or something and she'll be hustling for work. I know that man." She left the store without looking back, certain that Doris would be eyeing the price tags of the flats. "You take care of yourself, Doris. You're looking peaked. You should get out in the sun."

"Mrs. Hetherton, you're looking fit again," Mildred Carey said, cornering the woman as she emerged from the store.

"Warm weather's helped some."

"Look, can you possibly come over Thursday morning? You know the Garden Club meets this week, and I can't possibly get ready without some help."

"Well, I just don't know . . . Danny's dead set against my going out to work again."

"But they're going to have to close down the mill. And then where will he be?"

"Close it down? Why? Who says?"

"It's been in the papers for weeks now. All those dead fish, and the stink. You know that committee came up and took samples and said they're the ones responsible. And they can't afford to change over the whole process. They're going to move instead."

"Oh, that. Danny said don't hold your breath. They're making a study, and then they'll have to come up with a plan and have it studied, and all in all it's going to take five years or even more before it all comes to a head."

"Hm. Another big kill and the Department of Health . . ."

Mrs. Hetherton laughed and Mildred Carey had to smile too. "Well, anyway, can you come over just this time? For this one meeting?"

"Sure, Miz Carey. Thursday morning? But only half a day."

The school bus turned the corner and rolled noisily down the broad new street. The two women watched it out of sight. "Have you seen the Tomkins boys lately?" Mildred Carey asked. "Hair down to here."

"Winona says they're having someone in to talk about drugs. I asked her point blank if there are drugs around here and she said no, but you never can tell. The kids won't tell you nothing."

"Well, I just thank God that Mark is grown up and out of it all."

"He's due home soon now, isn't he?"

"Seven weeks. Then off to college in the fall. I told him that he's probably safer over there than at one of the universities right now." They laughed and moved apart. "See you Thursday."

"Listen Mike, when you get back, you'll go through New York, won't you? Give my mother a call, will you? Just tell her . . ."

"What? That you got jungle rot the first time out and it's gone to your brain?"

"Just call her. Say I'm fine. That's all. She'll want to have you over for dinner, or take you to a good restaurant, something. Say you don't have time. But it'd mean a lot to her to have you call."

"Sure. Sure. Come on, we're moving."

They walked for two hours without making contact. The men were straggling along in two uneven columns at the sides of the road. The dirt road was covered with recent growth, no mines. The temperature was going to hit one hundred any second. Sweat and dirt mixed on faces, arms, muddy sweat trickled down shirts.

The concrete street was a glare now. Heat rose in patterns that shifted and vanished and rose again. Mildred Carey wondered if it hadn't been a mistake to rebuild the street, take out the maples and make it wide enough for the traffic that they predicted would be here in another year or two. She shrugged and walked more briskly toward the post office. That wasn't her affair. Her husband, who should know, said it was necessary for the town to grow. After being in road construction for twenty-five years, he should know. Fran Marple and Dodie Wilson waved to her from outside the coffee shop. Fran looked overdue and miserable. Last thing she needed was to go in the coffee shop and have pastry. Mildred Carey smiled at them and went on.

Claud Emerson was weighing a box for Bill Stokes. Bill leaned against the counter smoking, flicking ashes on the floor. "Don't like it here, get out, that's what I say. Goddamn kids with their filthy clothes and dirty feet. Bet they had marijuana up there. Should have called the troopers, that's what I should have done."

"They was on state land, Bill. You had no call to run them off."

"They didn't know that. You think I'm going to let them plop themselves down right outside my front door? Let 'em find somewhere else to muck about."

Claud Emerson stamped the box. "One seventy-two."

Stilwell and Mike were following Laski, Berat, and Humboldt. Berat was talking.

"You let it stick out, see, and come at them with your M-16 and you know what they watch! Man, they never seen nothing like it! Scared shitless by it. Tight! Whooee! Tight and hot!"

Stilwell looked as if he saw a green monster. Mike laughed and lit another cigarette. The sun was almost straight up when the lieutenant called for a break. He and Sergeant Durkins consulted a map and Humboldt swore at great length. "They've got us lost, the bastards. This fuckin' road ain't even on their fuckin' map."

Mildred Carey looked through the bills and advertising in her box, saving the letter from Mark for last. She always read them twice, once very quickly to be sure that he was all right, then again, word for word, pausing to pronounce the strange syllables aloud. She scanned the scrawled page, then replaced it in its envelope to be reread at home with coffee.

Bill Stokes' jeep roared outside the door, down the street to screech to a halt outside the feed store.

Mildred shook her head. "He's a mean man."

"Yep," Claud Emerson said. "Always was, always will be, I reckon. Wonder where them kids spent the night after he chased them."

Durkins sent out two scouts and the rest of them waited, cursing and sweating. A helicopter throbbed over them, drowned out their voices, vanished. The scouts returned.

Durkins stood up. "Okay. About four miles. The gooks are there, all right. Or will be again tonight. It's a free-fire zone, and our orders are to clean it out. Let's go."

Loud voices drifted across the street and they both looked toward the sound. "Old Dave's at it again," Claud Emerson said, frowning. "He'll have himself another heart attack, that's what."

"What good does arguing do anyway? Everybody around here knows what everybody else thinks and nobody ever changes. Just what good does it do?" She stuffed her mail into her purse. "Just have to do the best you can. Do what's right and hope for the best." She waved good-bye.

She still had to pick up cottage cheese and milk. "Maybe I'll try that new salami," she said to Peters. "Just six slices. Don't like to keep it more than a day. Just look at those tomatoes! Sixty-nine a pound! Mr. Peters, that's a disgrace!"

"Field-grown, Miz Carey. Up from Georgia. Shipping costs go up and up, you know." He sliced the salami carefully, medium thick.

A new tension was in them now and the minesweepers walked gingerly on the road carpeted with green sprouts. Stilwell coughed again and again, a meaningless bark of nervousness. Durkins sent him to the rear, then sent Mike back with him. "Keep an eye on the fuckin' bastard," he said. Mike nodded and waited for the rear to catch up with him. The two brothers from Alabama looked at him expressionlessly as they passed. They didn't mind the heat either, he thought, then spat. Stilwell looked sick.

"Is it a trap?" he asked later.

"Who the fuck knows?"

"Company C walked into an ambush, didn't they?"

"They fucked up."

Mildred Carey put her milk on the checkout counter alongside the cottage cheese. Her blue housedress was wet with perspiration under her arms and she could feel a spot of wetness on her back when her dress touched her skin. That Janice Samuels, she thought, catching a glimpse of the girl across the street, with those shorts and no bra, pretending she was dressing to be comfortable. Always asking about Mark. And him, asking about her in his letters.

"That's a dollar five," Peters said.

They halted again less than a mile from the village. The lieutenant called for the helicopters to give cover and to close off the area. Durkins sent men around the village to cover the road leading from it. There was no more they could do until the helicopters arrived. There were fields under cultivation off to the left.

"What if they're still there?" Stilwell asked, waiting.

"You heard Durkins. This is a free-fire zone. They'll be gone."

"But what if they haven't?"

"We clear the area."

Stilwell wasn't satisfied, but he didn't want to ask the questions. He didn't want to hear the answers. Mike looked at him with hatred. Stilwell turned away and stared into the bushes at the side of the road.

"Let's go."

There was a deafening beating roar overhead and Mildred Carey and Peters went to the door to look. A green-and-brown helicopter hovered over the street, then moved down toward the post office, casting a grotesque shadow on the white concrete. Two more of the monstrous machines came over, making talk impossible. There was another helicopter to the north; their throb was everywhere, as if the clear blue sky had loosened a rain of them.

From the feed-store entrance Bill Stokes shouted something lost in the din. He raced to his jeep and fumbled for something under the seat. He straightened up holding binoculars and started to move to the center of the street, looking through them down the highway. One of the helicopters dipped, banked, and turned, and there was a spray of gunfire. Bill Stokes fell, jerked several times, then lay still. Now others began to run in the street, pointing and shouting and screaming. O'Neal and his hired hand ran to Bill Stokes and tried to lift him. Fran Marple and Dodie Wilson had left the coffee shop, were standing outside the door; they turned and ran back inside. A truck rounded the corner at the far end of the street and again the helicopter fired; the truck careened out of control into cars parked outside the bank. One of the cars was propelled through the bank windows. The thunder of the helicopters swallowed the sound of the crash and the breaking glass and the screams of the people who ran from the bank, some of them bleeding, clutching their heads or arms. Katharine Ormsby got to the side of the street, collapsed there. She crawled several more feet, then sprawled out and was still.

Mildred Carey backed into the store, her hands over her mouth. Suddenly she vomited. Peters was still on the sidewalk. She tried to close the door, but he flung it open, pushing her toward the rear of the store.

"Soldiers!" Peters yelled. "Soldiers coming!"

They went in low, on the sides of the road, ready for the explosion of gunfire, or the sudden eruption of a claymore. The helicopters' noise filled the world as they took up positions. The village was small, a hamlet. It had not been evacuated. The word passed through the company: slopes. They were there. A man ran into the street holding what could have been a grenade, or a bomb, or anything. One of the helicopters fired on him. There was a second burst of fire down the road and a vehicle burned. Now the company was entering the village warily. Mike cursed the slopes for their stupidity in staying.

Home was all Mildred Carey could think of. She had to get home. She ran to the back of the store and out to the alley that the delivery trucks used. She ran all the way home and, panting, with a pain in her chest, she rushed frantically through the house pulling down shades, locking doors. Then she went upstairs, where she could see the entire town. The soldiers were coming in crouched over, on both sides of the road, with their rifles out before them. She began to laugh suddenly; tears streaming, she ran downstairs again to fling open the door and shout.

"They're ours," she screamed toward the townspeople, laughing and crying all at once. "You fools, they're ours!"

Two of the khaki-clad GIs approached her, still pointing their guns at her. One of them said something, but she couldn't understand his words. "What are you doing here?" she cried. "You're American soldiers! What are you doing?"

The larger of the two grabbed her arm and twisted it behind her. She screamed and he pushed her toward the street. He spoke again, but the words were foreign to her. "I'm an American! For God's sake, this is America! What are you doing?" He hit her in the back with the rifle and she staggered and caught the fence to keep her balance. All down the street the people were being herded to the center of the highway. The soldier who had entered her house came out carrying her husband's hunting rifle, the shotgun, Mark's old .22. "Stop!" she shrieked at him. "Those are legal!" She was knocked down by the soldier behind her. He shouted at her and she opened her eyes to see him aiming the rifle at her head.

She scrambled to her feet and lurched forward to join the others in the street. She could taste blood and there was a stabbing pain in her jaw where teeth had been broken by her fall. A sergeant with a notebook was standing to one side. He kept making notations in it as more of the townspeople were forced from their houses and stores into the street.

Mike Donatti and Stilwell herded a raving old woman to the street; when she tried to grab a gun, Mike Donatti knocked her down and would have killed her then, but she was crying, obviously praying, and he simply motioned for her to join the others being rounded up.

The sun was high now, the heat relentless as the people were crowded closer together by each new addition. Some of the small children could be heard screaming even over the noise of the helicopters. Dodie Wilson ran past the crowd, naked from the waist down, naked and bleeding. A soldier caught her and he and another one carried her jerking and fighting into O'Neal's feed store. Her mouth was wide open in one long unheard scream. Old Dave ran toward the lieutenant, clutching at him, yelling at him in a high-pitched voice that it was the wrong town, damn fools, and other things that were lost. A smooth-faced boy hit him in the mouth, then again in the stomach, and when he fell moaning, he kicked him several times about the head. Then he shot him. Mildred Carey saw Janice Samuels being dragged by her wrists and she threw herself at the soldiers, who fought with her, their bodies hiding her from sight. They moved on, and she lay in a shining red pool that spread and spread. They tied Janice Samuels to the porch rail of Gordon's real-estate office, spread her legs open, and half a dozen men alternately raped and beat her. The sergeant yelled in the gibberish they spoke and the soldiers started to move the people as a lump toward the end of town.

Mike Donatti took up a post at the growing heap of weapons and watched the terrorized people. When the order came to move them out, he prodded and nudged, and when he had to, he clubbed them to make sure they moved as a unit. Some of them stumbled and fell, and if they didn't move again, they were shot where they lay.

The filthy Henry children were screaming for their mother. The biggest one, a girl with blond hair stringing down her back, darted away and ran down the empty street. The lieutenant motioned to the troops behind the group and after an appreciable pause there was a volley of shots and the child was lifted and for a moment flew. She rolled when she hit the ground again. Marjory Loomis threw herself down on top of her baby, and shots stilled both figures.

The people were driven to the edge of town, where the highway department had dug the ditch for a culvert that hadn't been laid yet. The sergeant closed his notebook and turned away. The firing started.

The men counted the weapons then, and searched the buildings methodically. Someone cut down a girl who had been tied to a rail. She fell in a heap. Fires were started. The lieutenant called for the helicopters to return to take them back to base camp.

Berat walked with his arm about Stilwell's shoulders, and they laughed a lot. Smoke from the fires began to spread horizontally, head high. Mike lighted another cigarette and thought about the cool green hills of Vermont and they waited to be picked up.

(1973)

KAREN JOY FOWLER

Born in 1950, Karen Joy Fowler leaped into prominence in science fiction with the publication of her first thirteen stories in 1985–1986. These were collected in Artificial Things *(1986), which won the John W. Campbell Award of 1987. Her first novel,* Sarah Canary *(1991), has been acclaimed as a major innovative work. She now lives in Davis, California, with her husband and two children.*

Fowler was involved in the antiwar movement while an undergraduate majoring in political science at the University of California, Berkeley, and later she received a master's degree in Asian studies from the University of California, Davis. "No one my age will ever get over Vietnam," she wrote in a recent letter, for, as she has said elsewhere, "those of us around my own age were defined by Vietnam in ways those much older and much younger will never understand."

Along with her 1987 story "Letters from Home," "The Lake Was Full of Artificial Things" (1985) is in part an attempt to complete a process of healing the psychological wounds of the war. It is also, like much of Fowler's other work, an exploration of the fiction-making process, as suggested by its title, taken from Wallace Stevens's poem "Notes Toward a Supreme Fiction."

The Lake Was Full of Artificial Things[1]

Daniel was older than Miranda had expected. In 1970, when they had said good-bye, he had been twenty-two. Two years later he was dead, but now, approaching her with the bouncing walk which had suited his personality so well, he appeared as a middle-aged man and quite gray, though solid and muscular.

Miranda noted with relief that he was smiling. "Randy!" he said. He laughed delightedly. "You look wonderful."

Miranda glanced down at herself, wondering what, in fact, she did look like or if she had any form at all. She saw the flesh of her arms firm again and the skin smooth and tight. So *she* was the twenty-year-

---

[1]Text revised by the author for her book *Artificial Things*. [Ed.]

old. Isn't that odd, she thought, turning her hands palms up to examine them. Then Daniel reached her. The sun was bright in the sky behind him, obscuring his face, giving him a halo. He put his arms around her. I feel him, she thought in astonishment. I smell him. She breathed in slowly. "Hello, Daniel," she said.

He squeezed her slightly, then dropped his arms and looked around. Miranda looked outward, too. They were on the college campus. Surely this was not the setting she would have chosen. It unsettled her, as if she had been sent backward in time and gifted with prescience, but remained powerless to make any changes, was doomed to see it all again, moving to its inevitable conclusion. Daniel, however, seemed pleased.

He pointed off to the right. "There's the creek," he said, and suddenly she could hear it. "Memories there, right?" and she remembered lying beneath him on the grass by the water. She put her hands on his shoulders now; his clothes were rough against her palms and military —like his hair.

He gestured to the round brick building behind her. "Tollman Hall," he said. "Am I right? God, this is great, Randy. I remember *everything*. Total recall. I had Physics 10 there with Dr. Fielding. Physics for nonmajors. I couldn't manage my vectors and I got a B." He laughed again, throwing an arm around Miranda. "It's great to be back."

They began to walk together toward the center of campus, slow walking with no destination, designed for conversation. They were all alone, Miranda noticed. The campus was deserted, then suddenly it wasn't. Students appeared on the pathways. Long-hairs with headbands and straights with slide rules. Just what she remembered. "Tell me what everyone's been doing," Daniel said. "It's been what? Thirty years? Don't leave out a thing."

Miranda stooped and picked a small daisy out of the grass. She twirled it absentmindedly in her fingers. It left a green stain on her thumb. Daniel stopped walking and waited beside her. "Well," Miranda said. "I've lost touch with most of them. Gail got a job on *Le Monde*. She went to Germany for the re-unification. I heard she was living there. The antinuclear movement was her permanent beat. She could still be there, I suppose."

"So she's still a radical," said Daniel. "What stamina."

"Margaret bought a bakery in San Francisco. Sixties cuisine.

Whole grains. Tofu brownies. Heaviest cookies west of the Rockies. We're in the same cable chapter so I keep up with her better. I saw her last marriage on TV. She's been married three times now, every one a loser."

"What about Allen?" Daniel asked.

"Allen," repeated Miranda. "Well, Allen had a promising career in jogging shoes. He was making great strides." She glanced at Daniel's face. "Sorry," she said. "Allen always brought out the worst in me. He lost his father in an air collision over Kennedy. Sued the airline and discovered he never had to work again. In short, Allen is rich. Last I heard, and this was maybe twenty years ago, he was headed to the Philippines to buy himself a submissive bride." She saw Daniel smile, the lines in his face deepening with his expression. "Oh, you'd like to blame me for Allen, wouldn't you?" she said. "But it wouldn't be fair. I dated him maybe three times, tops." Miranda shook her head. "Such an enthusiastic participant in the sexual revolution. And then it all turned to women's liberation on him. Poor Allen. We can only hope his tiny wife divorced him and won a large settlement when you could still get alimony."

Daniel moved closer to her and they began to walk again, passing under the shade of a redwood grove. The grass changed to needles under their feet. "You needn't be so hard on Allen," he said. "I never minded about him. I always knew you loved me."

"Did you?" asked Miranda anxiously. She looked at her feet, afraid to examine Daniel's face. My god, she was wearing moccasins. Had she ever worn moccasins? "I did get married, Daniel," she said. "I married a mathematician. His name was Michael." Miranda dropped her daisy, petals intact.

Daniel continued to walk, swinging his arms easily. "Well, you were always hot for mathematics. I didn't expect you to mourn me forever."

"So it's all right?"

Daniel stopped, turning to face her. He was still smiling, though it was not quite the smile she expected, not quite the easy, happy smile she remembered. "It's all right that you got married, Randy," he said softly. Something passed over his face and left it. "Hey!" he laughed again. "I remember something else from Physics 10. Zeno's paradox. You know what that is?"

"No," said Miranda.

"It's an argument. Zeno argued that motion was impossible because it required an object to pass through an infinite number of points in a finite amount of time." Daniel swung his arms energetically. "Think about it for a minute, Randy. Can you fault it? Then think about how far I came to be here with you."

"Miranda. Miranda." It was her mother's voice, rousing her for school. Only then it wasn't. It was Dr. Matsui who merely sounded maternal, despite the fact that she had no children of her own and was not yet thirty. Miranda felt her chair returning slowly to its upright position. "Are you back?" Dr. Matsui asked. "How did it go?"

"It was short," Miranda told her. She pulled the taped wires gently from her lids and opened her eyes. Dr. Matsui was seated beside her, reaching into Miranda's hair to detach the clips which touched her scalp.

"Perhaps we recalled you too early," she conceded. "Matthew spotted an apex so we pulled the plug. We just wanted a happy ending. It was happy, wasn't it?"

"Yes." Dr. Matsui's hair, parted on one side and curving smoothly under her chin, bobbed before Miranda's face. Miranda touched it briefly, then her own hair, her cheeks, and her nose. They felt solid under her hand, real, but no more so than Daniel had been. "Yes, it was," she repeated. "He was so happy to see me. So glad to be back. But, Anna, he was so real. I thought you said it would be like a dream."

"No," Dr. Matsui told her. "I said it *wouldn't* be. I said it was a memory of something that never happened and in that respect was like a dream. I wasn't speaking to the quality of the experience." She rolled her chair to the monitor and stripped the long feed-out sheet from it, tracing the curves quickly with one finger. Matthew, her technician, came to stand behind her. He leaned over her left shoulder, pointing. "There," he said. "That's Daniel. That's what I put in."

Dr. Matsui returned her chair to Miranda's side. "Here's the map," she said. "Maybe I can explain better."

Miranda tried to sit forward. One remaining clip pulled her hair and made her inhale sharply. She reached up to detach herself. "Sorry," said Dr. Matsui sheepishly. She held out the paper for Miranda to see. "The dark waves is the Daniel we recorded off your memories earlier. Happy memories, right? You can see the fainter echo here as you responded to it with the original memories. Think of it as memory squared. Naturally, it's going to be intense. Then, everything else here is the record of the additional activity you brought to this particular session. Look at these sharp peaks at the beginning. They indicate stress. You'll see that nowhere else do they recur. On paper it looks to have been an entirely successful session. Of course, only you know the content of the experience." Her dark eyes were searching and sympathetic. "Well," she said. "Do you feel better about him?"

"Yes," said Miranda. "I feel better."

"Wonderful." Dr. Matsui handed the feedback to Matthew. "Store it," she told him.

Miranda spoke hesitatingly. "I had other things I wanted to say to him," she said. "It doesn't feel resolved."

"I don't think the sessions ever resolve things," Dr. Matsui said. "The best they can do is open the mind to resolution. The resolution still has to be found in the real world."

"Can I see him again?" Miranda asked.

Dr. Matsui interlaced her fingers and pressed them to her chest. "A repeat would be less expensive, of course," she said. "Since we've already got Daniel. We could just run him through again. Still, I'm reluctant to advise it. I wonder what else we could possibly gain."

"Please, Anna," said Miranda. She was looking down at her arms, remembering how firmly fleshed they had seemed.

"Let's wait and see how you're feeling after our next couple of regular visits. If the old regrets persist and, more importantly, if they're still interfering with your ability to get on with things, then ask me again."

She was standing. Miranda swung her legs over the side of the chair and stood, too. Matthew walked with her to the door of the office. "We've got a goalie coming in next," he confided. "She stepped into the goal while holding the ball; she wants to remember it the way it didn't happen. Self-indulgent if you ask me. But then, athletes make the money, right?" He held the door open, his arm stretched in front of Miranda. "You feel better, don't you?" he asked.

"Yes," she reassured him.

She met Daniel for lunch at Frank Fats Café. They ordered fried clams and scallops, but the food never came. Daniel was twenty again and luminescent with youth. His hair was blond and his face was smooth. Had he really been so beautiful? Miranda wondered.

"I'd love a Coke," he said. "I haven't had one in thirty years."

"You're kidding," said Miranda. "They don't have the real thing in heaven?"

Daniel looked puzzled.

"Skip it," she told him. "I was just wondering what it was like being dead. You could tell me."

"It's classified," said Daniel. "On a need-to-know basis."

Miranda picked up her fork, which was heavy and cold. "This time it's you who looks wonderful. Positively beatific. Last time you looked so—" she started to say *old*, but amended it. After all, he had looked no older than she did these days. Such things were relative. "Tired," she finished.

"No, I wasn't tired," Daniel told her. "It was the war."

"The war's over now," Miranda said and this time his smile was decidedly unpleasant.

"Is it?" he asked. "Just because you don't read about it in the paper now? Just because you watch the evening news and there's no body count in the corner of the screen?"

"Television's not like that now," Miranda began, but Daniel hadn't stopped talking.

"What's really going on in Southeast Asia? Do you even know?" Daniel shook his head. "Wars never end," he said. He leaned threateningly over the table. "Do you imagine for one minute that it's over for me?"

Miranda slammed her fork down. "Don't do that," she said. "Don't try to make me guilty of that, too. You didn't have to go. I begged you not to. Jesus, you knew what the war was. If you'd gone off to save the world from communist aggression, I would have disagreed, but I could have understood. But you knew better than that. I never forgave you for going."

"It was so easy for you to see what was right," Daniel responded angrily. "You were completely safe. You women could graduate without losing your deferment. Your goddamn birthday wasn't drawn twelfth in the draft lottery and if it had been you wouldn't have cared. When was your birthday drawn? You don't even know." Daniel leaned back and looked out the window. People appeared on the street. A woman in a red miniskirt got into a blue car. Then Daniel faced her again, large before Miranda. She couldn't shut him out. "'Go to Canada,' you said. 'That's what I'd do.' I wonder. Could you have married your mathematician in Canada? I can just picture you saying good-bye to your mother forever."

"My mother's dead now," said Miranda. A knot of tears tightened about her throat.

"And so the hell am I." Daniel reached for her wrists, holding them too hard, hurting her deliberately. "But you're not, are you? You're just fine."

There was a voice behind Daniel. "Miranda. Miranda," it called.

"Mother," cried Miranda. But, of course it wasn't, it was Anna Matsui, gripping her wrists, bringing her back. Miranda gasped for breath and Dr. Matsui let go of her. "It was awful," said Miranda. She began to cry. "He accused me . . ." She pulled the wires from her eyes recklessly. Tears spilled out of them. Miranda ached all over.

"He accused you of nothing." Dr. Matsui's voice was sharp and disappointed. "You accused yourself. The same old accusations. We made Daniel out of you, remember?" She rolled her chair backward, moved to the monitor for the feedback. Matthew handed it to her and she read it, shaking her head. Her short black hair flew against her cheeks. "It shouldn't have happened," she said. "We used only the memories that made you happy. And with your gift for lucid dreaming —well, I didn't think there was a risk." Her face was apologetic as she handed Miranda a tissue and waited for the crying to stop. "Matthew wanted to recall you earlier," she confessed, "but I didn't want it to end this way."

"No!" said Miranda. "We can't stop now. I never answered him."

"You only need to answer yourself. It's your memory and imagination confronting you. He speaks only with your voice, he behaves only as you expect him to." Dr. Matsui examined the feedback map again. "I should never have agreed to a repeat. I certainly won't send you back." She looked at Miranda and softened her voice. "Lie still. Lie still until you feel better."

"Like in another thirty years?" asked Miranda. She closed her eyes; her head hurt from the crying and the wires. She reached up to detach one close to her ear. "Everything he said to me was true," she added tonelessly.

"Many things he didn't say are bound to be true as well," Dr. Matsui pointed out. "Therapy is not really concerned with truth, which is almost always merely a matter of perspective. Therapy is concerned with adjustment—adjustment to an unchangeable situation or to a changing truth." She lifted a pen from her collar, clicking the point in and out absentmindedly. "In any given case," she continued, "we face a number of elements within our control and a far greater number beyond it. In a case such as yours, where the patient has felt profoundly and morbidly guilty over an extended period of time, it is because she is focusing almost exclusively on her own behavior. 'If only I hadn't done x,' she thinks, 'then y would never have happened.' Do you understand what I'm saying, Miranda?"

"No."

"In these sessions we try to show you what might have happened if the elements you couldn't control were changed. In your case we let you experience a continued relationship with Daniel. You see that you bore him no malice. You wished him nothing ill. If he had come back the bitterness of your last meeting would have been unimportant."

"He asked me to marry him," said Miranda. "He asked me to wait for him. I told you that. And I said that I was seeing Allen. Allen! I said as far as I was concerned he was already gone."

"You wish you could change that, of course. But what you really want to change is his death and that was beyond your control." Dr. Matsui's face was sweet and intense.

Miranda shook her head. "You're not listening to me, Anna. I told you what happened, but I lied about why it happened. I pretended we had political differences. I thought my behavior would be palatable if it looked like a matter of conscience. But really I dated Allen for the first time before Daniel had even been drafted. Because I knew what was coming. I saw that his life was about to get complicated and messy. And I saw a way out of it. For me, of course. Not for him." Miranda began to pick unhappily at the loose skin around her nails. "What do you think of that?" she asked. "What do you think of me now?"

"What do *you* think?" Dr. Matsui said and Miranda responded in disgust.

"I know what *I* think. I think I'm sick of talking to myself. Is that the best you therapists can manage? I think I'll stay home and talk to the mirrors." She pulled off the remaining connections to her scalp and sat up. "Matthew," she said. "Matthew!"

Matthew came to the side of her chair. He looked thin, concerned, and awkward. What a baby he was, really, she thought. He couldn't be more than twenty-five. "How old are you, Matthew?" she asked.

"Twenty-seven."

"Be a hell of a time to die, wouldn't it?" She watched Matthew put a nervous hand on his short brown hair and run it backward. "I want your opinion about something, Matthew. A hypothetical case. I'm trusting you to answer honestly."

Matthew glanced at Dr. Matsui, who gestured with her pen for him to go ahead. He turned back to Miranda. "What would you think of a woman who deserted her lover, a man she really claimed to love, because he got sick and she didn't want to face the unpleasantness of it?"

Matthew spoke carefully. "I would imagine that it was motivated by cowardice rather than cruelty," he said. "I think we should always forgive sins of cowardice. Even our own." He stood looking at Miranda with his earnest, innocent face.

"All right, Matthew," she said. "Thank you." She lay back down in the chair and listened to the hum of the idle machines. "Anna," she said. "He didn't behave as I expected. I mean, sometimes he did and sometimes he didn't. Even the first time."

"Tell me about it," said Dr. Matsui.

"The first session he was older than I expected. Like he hadn't died; but had continued to age along with me."

"Wish fulfillment."

"Yes, but I was *surprised* by it. And I was surprised by the setting. And he said something very odd right at the end. He quoted me Zeno's paradox and it really exists, but I never heard it before. It didn't sound like something Daniel would say, either. It sounded more like my husband, Michael. Where did it come from?"

"Probably from just where you said," Dr. Matsui told her. "Michael. You don't think you remember it, but obviously you did. And husbands and lovers are bound to resemble each other, don't you think? We often get bits of overlap. Our parents show up one way or another in almost all our memories." Dr. Matsui stood. "Come in Tuesday," she said. "We'll talk some more."

"I'd like to see him one more time," said Miranda.

"Absolutely not," Dr. Matsui answered, returning Miranda's chair to its upright position.

"Where are we, Daniel?" Miranda asked. She couldn't see anything.

"Camp Pendleton," he answered. "On the beach. I used to run here mornings. Guys would bring their girlfriends. Not me, of course."

Miranda watched the landscape fill in as he spoke. Fog remained. It was early and overcast. She heard the ocean and felt the wet, heavy air begin to curl her hair. She was barefoot on the sand and a little cold. "I'm so sorry, Daniel," she said. "That's all I ever really wanted to tell you. I loved you."

"I know you did." He put his arm around her. She leaned against him. I must look like his mother, she thought; in fact, her own son was older than Daniel now. She looked up at him carefully. He must have just arrived at camp. The hair had been all but shaved from his head.

"Maybe you were right, anyway," Daniel told her. "Maybe I just shouldn't have gone. I was so angry at you by then I didn't care anymore. I even thought about dying with some sense of anticipation. Petulant, you know, like a little kid. I'll go and get killed and *then* she'll be sorry."

"And she was," said Miranda. "God, was she." She turned to face him, pressed her lined cheek against his chest, smelled his clothes. He must have started smoking again. Daniel put both arms around her. She heard a gull cry out ecstatically.

"But when the time came I really didn't want to die," Daniel's voice took on an unfamiliar edge, frightened, slightly hoarse. "When the time came I was willing to do *anything* rather than die." He hid his face in her neck. "Do you have kids?" he asked. "Did you and Michael ever?"

"A son," she said.

"How old? About six?"

Miranda wasn't sure how old Jeremy was now. It changed every year. But she told him, wonderingly, "Of course not, Daniel. He's all grown up. He owns a pizza franchise, can you believe it? He thinks I'm a bore."

"Because I killed a kid during the war. A kid about six years old. I figured it was him or me. I shot him." Miranda pushed back from Daniel, trying to get a good look at his face. "They used kids, you know," he said. "They counted on us not being able to kill them. I saw this little boy coming for me with his hands behind his back. I told him to stop. I shouted at him to stop. I pointed my rifle and said I was going to kill him. But he kept coming."

"Oh, Daniel," said Miranda. "Maybe he didn't speak English."

"A pointed rifle is universal. He walked into the bullet."

"What was he carrying?"

"Nothing," said Daniel. "How could I know?"

"Daniel," Miranda said. "I don't believe you. You wouldn't do that." Her words unsettled her even more. "Not the way I remember you," she said. "This is not the way I remember you."

"It's so easy for you to see what's right," said Daniel.

I'm going back, thought Miranda. Where am I really? I must be with Anna, but then she remembered that she was not. She was in her own study. She worked to feel the study chair beneath her, the ache in her back as she curved over her desk. Her feet dangled by the wheels; she concentrated until she could feel them. She saw her own hand, still holding the pencil, and she put it down. Things seemed very clear to her. She walked to the bedroom and summoned Dr. Matsui over the console. The doctor was with a patient. She waited perhaps fifteen minutes before Anna appeared.

"Daniel's the one with the problem," Miranda said. "It's not me, after all."

"There is no Daniel." Dr. Matsui's voice betrayed a startled concern. "Except in your mind and on my tapes. Apart from you, no Daniel."

"No. He came for me again. Just like in our sessions. Just as intense. Do you understand? Not a dream." She cut off Dr. Matsui's protest. "It was not a dream, because I wasn't asleep. I was working and then I was with him. I could feel him. I could smell him. He told me an absolutely horrible story about killing a child during the war. Where would I have gotten that? Not the sort of thing they send home in their letters to the bereaved."

"There were a thousand ugly stories out of Vietnam," said Dr. Matsui. "I know some and I wasn't even born yet. Or just barely born. Remember My Lai?" Miranda watched her image clasp its hands. "You heard this story somewhere. It became part of your concept of the war. So you put it together now with Daniel." Dr. Matsui's voice took on its professional patina. "I'd like you to come in, Miranda. Immediately. I'd like to take a complete read-out and keep you monitored a while. Maybe overnight. I don't like the turn this is taking."

"All right," said Miranda. "I don't want to be alone anyway. Because he's going to come again."

"No," said Dr. Matsui firmly. "He's not."

Miranda took the elevator to the garage and unlocked her bicycle. She was not frightened and wondered why not. She felt unhappy and uncertain, but in complete control of herself. She pushed out into the bike lane.

When the helicopter appeared overhead, Miranda knew immediately where she was. A banana tree sketched itself in on her right. There was a smell in the air which was strange to her. Old diesel engines, which she recognized, but also something organic. A lushness almost turned to rot. In the distance the breathtaking green of rice growing. But the dirt at her feet was bare.

Miranda had never imagined a war could be so quiet. Then she heard the chopper. And she heard Daniel. He was screaming. He stood right next to her, beside a pile of sandbags, his rifle stretched out before him. A small, delicately featured child was just walking into Miranda's view, his arms held behind him. All Miranda had to do was lift her hand.

"No, Daniel," she said. "His hands are empty."

Daniel didn't move. The war stopped. "I killed him, Randy," said Daniel. "You can't change that."

Miranda looked at the boy. His eyes were dark, a streak of dust ran all the way up one shoulder and onto his face. He was barefoot. "I know," she said. "I can't help him." The child faded and disappeared. "I'm trying to help you."

The boy reappeared again, back further, at the very edge of her vision. He was beautiful, unbearably young. He began to walk to them once more.

"*Can* you help me?" Daniel asked.

Miranda pressed her palm into his back. He wore no shirt and was slick and sweaty. "I don't know," she said. "Was it a crime of cowardice or of cruelty? I'm told you can be forgiven the one, but not the other."

Daniel dropped his rifle into the dirt. The landscape turned slowly about them, became mountainous. The air smelled cleaner and was cold.

A bird flew over them in a beautiful arc, and then it became a baseball and began to fall in slow motion, and then it became death and she could plot its trajectory. It was aimed at Daniel, whose rifle had reappeared in his hands.

Now, Miranda thought. She could stay and die with Daniel the way she'd always believed she should. Death moved so slowly in the sky. She could see its progress moment to moment. It descended like a series of scarcely differentiated still frames. "Look, Daniel," she said, but he refused to look up. "It's Zeno's paradox in reverse. Finite points. Infinite time." How long did she have to make this decision? A lifetime. Her lifetime.

Daniel reached out his hand to touch her hair. Gray, she knew. Her gray hair under his young hand. He was twenty-four. "Don't stay," he said. "Do you think I would have wanted you to? I would never have wanted that."

So Miranda moved from his hand and found she was glad to do so. She began to think her way out, tried to feel the bicycle between her legs, the pedaling movement of her feet, her hands gripping too hard. "I always loved you," she said as if it mattered to Daniel, who dimmed before her eyes. He looked through her as though she were already gone. She just glimpsed the soldiers who materialized beside him and death which grew to accommodate them. But they wouldn't all die. Some of them would survive in pieces. She remembered this. And some would survive whole. Wouldn't they?

(1985)

AFTERMATHS

"Post-Vietnam" America is so different from "pre-Vietnam" America that time travelers from the earlier period to the later might think they had arrived in some other continuum. Indeed, during the war the rate of change was so rapid that many veterans returning from Vietnam after only a year's absence felt just like time travelers, and some have written that it was like landing on a different planet.

It is logically impossible to determine how much of this mutation was due directly to the war. Furthermore, there is hardly any agreement even about the nature of the changes. Debate about the differences between America before and after the Vietnam War is as intense and unresolved as debate about the war itself.

Some differences can be measured and quantified. For example, during the decade from 1965 to 1975, the value of the dollar was cut almost in half, the murder rate doubled, the rate of robbery tripled, and the annual value of illegal drugs seized at the nation's borders went from $394,000 to over $45,000,000. People's opinions also can be measured, although with iffy reliability. One of the more revealing surveys, conducted each national election year by the Center for Political Studies of the University of Michigan, asked "Would you say the government is pretty much run by a few big interests looking out for themselves or that it is run for the benefit of all the people?" Here are the results for the surveys during the three key election years:

	1964	1968	1972
For benefit of all	64.0%	51.2%	37.7%
Few big interests	28.6%	39.5%	53.3%

More subjective and impressionistic are people's senses of changes in styles and culture, not to mention their significance. Beards and long hair are certainly no longer emblems of rebellion. Or take blue denim. The bib overalls adopted by the civil rights movement in the 1950s as a symbol of identification with the black underclass evolved into the ragged jeans of the 1960s counterculture, and by the late 1970s had been transformed into fashionable and expensive designer jeans.

There does seem to be some consensus that the Vietnam War divided and still divides the nation, that "no more Vietnams" is a slogan commanding wide agreement despite wildly different interpretations of what it means, and that President George Bush was premature when he jubilantly announced in March 1991, "By God, we've kicked the Vietnam syndrome once and for all!" As relations between Vietnam and the United States finally normalize, the legacies and effects of the war will no doubt continue to shift.

Some consequences of the war are undeniable. There are millions of Vietnam veterans in American society, from the tens of thousands homeless on the streets to the dozens sitting as senators and representatives in Congress. There are hundreds of thousands of surviving family members of the fifty-eight thousand Americans killed in Vietnam. The POW/MIA issue continues to roil as an undercurrent, helping to propel H. Ross Perot into a presidential candidate first in 1992. Hundreds of thousands of ethnic Vietnamese live in communities from Louisiana to California and Massachusetts. There are trophies and archives of news films and official documents, missing limbs and scars both physical and psychological, memories and myths. And there is that vast and growing literature, from which this book draws its samples.

The five stories chosen here as explorations of the aftermaths of the war all have in common an implicit recognition of the complexity, profundity, and irresolvable nature of their subject. This is brought out explicitly by Ronald Anthony Cross in "The Heavenly Blue Answer." All five stories suggest that the legacies of the war, whether confronted directly or not, remain inescapably part of American society. Stephanie Vaughn chooses an all-too-common war trophy as an emblem of the nation's inability to resolve what is to be done with its Vietnam legacies. The strange cult of the veteran, which has generated in the 1980s and 1990s numerous examples of phony veterans, is taken into another dimension by Lewis Shiner's "The War at Home," where America becomes what it envisioned as its nemesis. In Robert Olen Butler's "A Good Scent from a Strange Mountain," Vietnamese exiles weave the history of Vietnam into America's present and possible future. Wayne Karlin's "The Last VC" is a living legacy, one embodiment of what America engendered and heralded in its contact with Vietnam.

RONALD ANTHONY CROSS

Ronald Anthony Cross, who describes himself as "just a writer," was born in 1937. His stories have been featured in a wide variety of anthologies and magazines in this country, England, Germany, Canada, and Japan. In 1988 he published his first novel, Prisoners of Paradise. The Fourth Guardian *(1994) and* The Lost Guardian *(1995) are the first two volumes in his planned quartet of occult thrillers. Cross lives in Santa Monica, California, with his wife and child.*

Cross has written in a recent letter that those who see the soldiers who fought in Vietnam as "any less heroic—or more heroic, for that matter" than any other soldiers "fail to grasp the extent of misery involved": "To live a life without hurting anyone is what's heroic." "The Heavenly Blue Answer," written for In the Field of Fire, *a 1987 collection of science fiction and fantasy about the Vietnam War, dramatizes one of Cross's main themes, a "melting of the borders" necessary to apprehend reality.*

The Heavenly Blue Answer

I

He tried not to think of it at all. He wasn't interested in trying to come to terms with it. Just forget it. But sometimes they wouldn't let you forget it. Like when he opened the papers to the movie section, just going to a movie, and there is this ridiculous stud with muscles popping out all over him holding some kind of fancy gun with a big knobby head on it, from which was spraying—you guess. Talk about phallic. This dude had been pumping up until his muscles were like iron. Only they weren't iron, no, looks were deceiving, and one little piece of metal from one of those fucking AK-47s would deflate him like a balloon, forever. Big, tough, musclebound stud punches out Cong, right?

Only that wasn't the way it was at all. Nobody gave a shit about muscle, or manliness, and it was the little ones you worried about, not the big ones. The skinny little ones who could scurry into cracks in the walls like cockroaches, or hide in trees like snakes.

Which is one reason that the Cong were so fucking bad, because they were all the right size for fighting in a jungle.

Shit. He didn't want to think about it, but there it was. It sprang forth fully grown from his mind, like Athena from the mind of Zeus.

The same scene. Always the same, over and over again. Always happening now.

Edge of a deserted jungle village. Side of a river. They have spent the night here. There is argument as to whether they should wade out downriver to evade snipers (might be mined), or go out along the bank to evade the mines and run into sniper fire.

Meanwhile, Little Jim was seated on an oil drum, smoking a jay, watching Oogie fiddling around with one of his crazy Rube Goldberg traps. It wasn't that Little Jimmy was so little, but Big Jimmy was so big, right? So Little Jimmy he was.

And the argument about the river versus the riverbank didn't involve them. Let the brass fight it out. Fuck it. Whatever they chose was bound to be wrong. Because we're never getting out, right? It had dawned on him about a week ago (or was that only yesterday?), and it did not come from reason, or from anything at all. It was just some sort of goddamn wonderful divine revelation. It came along with its twin realization. This is real. Really real! All these guys are really dead. The bullets really kill you. Everything else is a dream. In the cruel light of this reality, "you ain't getting out" is another reality you simply live. It doesn't matter if it's true or not. You just ain't getting out. Fuck it. Fuck everything.

He sucked on the joint, strong grass. Like everything in 'Nam, too strong, too weird.

Like Oogie here, building his weird little booby trap. Well—big booby trap. Happy as could be, working away like a busy little beaver. Whistling. What kind of reality was he living?

As far as Little Jim could tell, the plan was this—or something like it.

Fu-gas. First Oogie had mixed the gasoline and soap together, sort of creating his own version of napalm. Stirring it and stirring it to get just the right consistency. There's a thermite grenade in front of the gas barrel, and a stick of dynamite underneath.

Oogie maintained that you had to use a No. 2 cap on the thermite and No. 4 on the dynamite. Little Jim had heard many arguments over that one. The dynamite is supposed to push the gas up and the thermite ignites it. Everything in a big circle is burnt to a crisp.

"Oogie, you crazy little bastard, one of these days you're going to blow yourself away." Little Jim got up and nervously moved back another fifty yards (out of range?).

Oogie looks up and grins his crazy grin. "Better me than them," he shouts. Laughs insanely. Turns back to his work.

Little Jim is trying to figure out what stage Oogie is working at, when it all happens. All at once. No matter how many times he has to live it all over again, he can't ever sort it out into a logical chain of events. Newton's laws don't work in 'Nam.

There is a popping noise: that came first. Of that he is certain. Almost certain. Sniper!

Then either the sniper hits Oogie and he accidentally somehow sets off the trap, or the sniper's bullets set it off, or even possibly, Oogie—crazy to start with—hears the sniper fire and flips out and deliberately just says fuck it and blows himself up. Maybe that's the reality he was living.

And Little Jim can dig that. Why not? Maybe there's just so much you can take, and—what was it Oogie had shouted? "Better me than them"? Famous last words. Had he really said that or was Little Jim's munged-up mind just making it up? Working overtime to bring Newton's laws to the jungle.

Anyhow. *Pop. Pop. Pop.* Oogie is hit (pretty sure of that). Then Oogie's booby trap goes off. Even at over fifty yards away, Little Jim is too close to this incredible homemade bomb to emerge unscathed. He is, in fact, both mentally and physically scathed.

For a moment, loud, loud noise and a blaze of light and heat that obliterates thought. Then silence and hot burning sensations on his cheeks and arms. Then ears ringing and his thoughts squirming around like fucking worms, and suddenly he can hear.

Everyone is shouting, including himself. For some reason he hears himself shouting "Oogie, you little fart, I'll kill your ass for this," while others are shouting about the sniper. "He's here, no, no, there, no—those trees over there," like a fucking silly magic trick.

And now all of a sudden everyone is firing everything they've got at once, all directions.

It is not so much that they are shooting at Charlie, as it is that they are responding to Oogie's crazy explosion in some kind of primitive ritual. It's the Fu-gas bomb that's thrown them over the edge. And here, in the middle of it all, this is clear to him, though later logic will enter in and confuse the issue. ("You were shooting at a sniper, Corporal? One sniper? All that ammo for one sniper?")

Because now everyone was firing off everything they had, in all directions at once, and shouting at the same time.

Little Jim was popping away with his M-16 into the nearest trees, and of course most everyone was blowing away the treetops with M-16s, but also machine guns were rattling away, grenade launchers were launching, and now — mortar fire.

For a long time everyone just fired away, using up, he guessed, maybe thousands of good old U.S. dollars' worth of ammunition on one little Cong tree snake—poisonous variety.

Then, gradually, everyone pulled themselves back into the area of consciousness we call control, until finally only one M-16 was still coughing. It stopped.

They all waited there in silence, sweating. Some were now in the river, some sharing the village foxholes with the corpses (Cong or whatever) which had been there since who knows when, and some were in huts. Some, like Little Jim, were just standing around.

"We must have blown away half the fuckin' jungle," someone shouts. Somebody laughs at that, but it is not fun laughter.

"Shit, we must have got him," someone else shouts.

Silence. Nobody moves. Then, *pop—pop—pop*. From somewhere. Anywhere. From little guy in trees, AK-47 sends message: Hello American pig. Find me if you can. Ha ha.

Everyone is firing into the trees again, and Little Jim notices a strange thing now. Several guys are down. Hit hard. And one of them is Big Jim. No longer Little Jim, he thinks insanely, now I'm just plain Jim. This thought fills him with weird brief elation. Which is here. Gone.

But there is no more room for fear. This is what flipped out means, he is saying to himself, when he sees something, someone coming out of one of the huts.

He aims the M-16 at the old man's belly. Vietnamese? Viet Cong? Outer space? Siamese if you please? his crazy mind is singing.

And the old man, empty hands (who cares at this point?), long scraggly grey beard and big, big brown eyes (the better to see you with), holding out empty hands (empty, full, who cares now?). Says, in English. In fucking English says, "I . . . am . . ." And just as he is saying this, holding out his hands, empty hands. Just as he is getting to the good part. The part that Little Jim (now just plain Jim) has got to hear, Jim's finger, independent of Jim's mind and body and philosophy and morality, just sort of squeezes off the trigger and blows him away. Then and there. Now. Always now.

But there is another kind of now. And in that less immediate yet coexistent now, Little Jim, who was no longer Little Jim or even Jim, but a man who worked away the days as a computer programmer everyone called James, closed the movie section of the newspaper with the macho stud super Vietnam vet fearlessly blowing away the Cong or whoever it was nowadays, and thought, No, it wasn't like that.

II

And so he lived in two nows—the one which was always right there, always the same, and the other one, which while being the reality that everyone else had agreed upon, was nevertheless somehow more distant and less realistic than the one frozen in his mind. There was not a day that went by without his asking himself, what had the old man been trying to say? "I am"—what?

In fact, now that he thought of it, perhaps he could make a case for three worlds. Because the America he left to go fight in Vietnam was not at all the America he came back to. Had it been the dream of his youth he had left behind, or an actual place? He could no longer be quite certain of anything.

In his memories it was bright and clean and simple. The bad guys wore duck-butt haircuts so you could distinguish them. There were good girls and bad ones, and you could tell them at a glance. No problem. Everything was like that. Simple. Straightforward.

Then there was the America he had come back to. Whoever it was said you can't go home again, James understood what he meant. It just plain wasn't there.

What was there was some strange cross between the America he had left and—surprise—Vietnam. America had become, in his absence, somehow Orientalized. Weird kids in orange robes danced in the streets chanting Hindu mantras, and everywhere he looked, restaurants advertised food from China, Japan—sure—but now India, Thailand, Korea, and yes—Vietnam. Every neighborhood was littered with karate and kung fu and Thai boxing schools. Schoolkids fought like Japanese soldiers, and his brother's wife, Jeanie, now served occasional (once a week) vegetarian meals, strangely Oriental in their nature.

Oriental concepts like guru, mantra, karma, and sushi were commonplace knowledge in every household. But even more alarming than that, and at the same time more subtle, was a sort of melting of the borders, of all the borders, so that everything ran together. Yes, that was it.

That was what, to him, was the essence of Orientalism. This was all brought home to him, in a grand tragic style, by a trip to Disneyland.

James had been coerced into a family outing with his brother and his wife and their two kids.

For the family, it had been a success. His brother, Bob, felt that they had succeeded in cheering James up. But this was because James, who really could not bear to let the family down, knew enough to behave in a more manic manner. Crack more jokes, talk more, smile more often: he was aware of his brother and his sister-in-law constantly monitoring his expressions, and he could feel them both begin to relax as the day wore on. A family success.

"See, I know it's corny, James, but it's true," Bob told him. "It's the simple things that make life livable. A job. Kids. A wife. But mainly kids. It's through kids that you really get the most out of everything. They're like—like somehow being born again. Hell, I can't explain it, but I know it. It's what you've got to do, Jimmy, believe me." To James's surprise, upon staring into his brother Bob's eyes, he had found there tears. He really wanted to help. The whole family did. How had James ever managed to misunderstand this simple fact?

"I believe you, Bobbie, but I can't," he had said. "Not yet."

Bob seemed satisfied with the answer. Jeanie seemed satisfied. The kids were satisfied.

But for James the whole trip was a disaster. He remembered a visit to Disneyland when he was a kid: the first time.

It had gleamed. It had been so clear and clean and fresh and new. The sidewalks, in his memory, were clean enough to eat off of, for who would have thought of throwing trash on the ground in California in those days, let alone on the hallowed ground of Disneyland?

But, most important of all, the people were as clean as the park. And there was a certain uniformity about the dress, the hairstyles, that added—what was it?—a sense of style to the overall picture.

All of that was gone forever. Now the streets and sidewalks of the park were liberally sprinkled with trash and spilled food and drink. James had watched small children throw dirty napkins on the ground under the approving glances of their parents. He had watched the parents throw empty cartons on the sidewalks under the approving glances of their children. It seemed to James that everything in the park had faded, diminished, and become tainted.

And worst of all, the people. My God, there was no sense of style left in America anymore. But more than that: there was a flaunting, screaming insanity; people actually deliberately dressed like lunatics. Fully grown men with dazed marijuana expressions, dressed in crazy hats, some wearing loud garish shirts, some wearing undershirts— some not bothering to wear any shirts at all. Fully grown men wearing earrings and shorts. Older, grey-haired men in blaring, striped track costumes. And the women. Jesus, he didn't even want to think about that.

But when he contrasted all this in his mind with the pictures of the Disneyland he had visited when it was new, he had been more than merely shocked. He had been horrified. Because it was obviously not just Disneyland. No, it was his whole world. He had noticed it, of course, but it had taken this trip to Disneyland, the sanctuary of his ordered youth, to drive it home to him in its entirety: America's psyche was disintegrating, rather along the lines of one gigantic hebephrenic breakdown.

Suddenly he had to break away from his brother. Be alone with whatever it was that was throbbing and pounding inside his head.

"Bathroom," he mumbled. "Meet you at Peter Pan's in a few minutes."

And coming out of the bathroom and around the corner of the building, suddenly, impossibly, there it was. Again. Now.

The clearing. Crazy Oogie was working on his booby trap, humming, whistling to himself.

"Well, well, Little Jimmy, you can't bring America to 'Nam, but you bring 'Nam to America, am I right, man? I mean, who's invading who, here? Ha ha."

His laughter, as always, was totally manic. And he looked ridiculous, as always, in that stupid cowboy hat he was wearing.

"Should wear a helmet," Little Jim muttered, for what must have been the thousandth time.

Oogie laughed again. "Don't make no matter," he said. "Ain't going to make it. Ain't none of us going to make it out of here, Jimmy."

"But I made it."

"Wrong." Oogie laughed. "Here you is."

And he was, of course, right. Here Jim was.

I'll never get out, James thought, as he looked around him, not without terror, but yet not without—what?—interest, no, stronger than that.

Because, it was different from what he would have thought insanity would be like. More lucid. More simple.

It wasn't that Disneyland wasn't here. It was. And it wasn't as if the world of his mind had taken the place of his objective world. No, they were both sort of blended together. And he was aware, for instance, that he was not actually talking to Oogie. And he was aware of the tourists sporting mouse ears whom he almost bumped into, and he was quite aware that he was flipping out. The beginning of the end, he thought, not without terror, but then again, not without relief.

And then, just as suddenly as the vision had come, it was gone. No 'Nam, just Disneyland, but a Disneyland that was not so different from 'Nam as it once had been, and would never be again.

The beginning of the end. The trip was followed by such a fit of depression that he simply could not return to work: he called in sick. The beginning of the end, because, of course, he knew that now that the 'Nam in his mind had got out and mixed with the real world, it would do so again. And again. Until?

That night in bed, far from sleep, but so, so weary, he listened to Oogie babbling to him from the corner of his room, still working away, as always.

"I think it's the old man, you know? An ancient curse, right?" Laughs his crazy laugh. "The Vietnamese disease, right?" Laughs again. Suddenly turns serious and looks down into the Fu-gas he's stirring. "I still can't figure what went wrong, you know? It all happened so fast. Maybe I used the wrong-sized caps after all, or maybe I just flipped out and set the fuckin' thing off. Who the fuck knows? It all happened so fast."

And James finally dropped off to sleep to the sound of Oogie crying into his barrel of Fu-gas, stirring away. Working on his trap.

And dreamed. The old man. "I am"—squeezed the trigger. "I am" —squeezed the trigger. "What?" James shouts, "I am what?"

"I am," the old man says in English, and again James tries, but cannot keep from squeezing that trigger.

III

James has not been outside for two days, knows he must go outside, and so he manages to do so.

Vietnam is in the streets. Oh, it's L.A., all right. But Vietnam is here, too. And, here, he sees a flash of jungle. The clearing over there. He is fighting hard to get his mind back inside of his head, and out of the streets, but even as he is fighting to do it, he wonders if it really is the thing to do. All day long he wanders up and down the sidewalks, going nowhere. Just struggling, looking, and he is well aware that he is now talking to Oogie out loud. Mumbling to himself and stumbling along.

And what is so amazing is that he is not alone. Not even close to alone! The streets of L.A. are full of mumbling, stumbling burnouts, living out the lives from inside their heads out there on the sidewalks. Dirty. Crazy. Falling down un-drunks. Way beyond him. Experts at insanity.

Jesus Christ, he thought, it couldn't ever have been like this. What the fuck is this, anyway?

"Get a shopping cart from a grocery store," an old lady was telling him. "They're magic. They're what make me so beautiful. . . . Hell, look at that bitch. She used to be as big as a house. Now look at her. And that little fart used to be . . ."

A slender man whose age would have been impossible to guess, bolted by them in running shorts and shoes, obviously running home from work like James used to run home from school when he was a little kid. The runner paid no attention to the old lady's story, or curse or whatever it was, and James's consciousness followed him as he darted across the street, expertly dodging cars, the angry drivers of which seemed to James to be deliberately aiming at him. In a few moments he was gone, but somehow the incident had left James feeling a little better.

James wandered on, leaving the old lady cursing and mumbling, and next passed through the territory of a skinny black man who wore his hair in long intricately woven strings, Rastafarian style.

They each seemed to have staked out their own little plot of sidewalk, and somehow each lunatic operated within his or her own territory and respected the boundaries. Home, sweet home!

And late that night, James found his way home, through the L.A. streets and the Vietnam jungle, to his apartment. Where he spent the night talking to Oogie and dozing off, from time to time. When he slept, he dreamed of the old man.

The next day was a warm smoggy day in the jungle. James was out on the sidewalks early, laughing and mumbling to himself with the best of them.

Yes, the jungle was here to stay now. He was sure of that. He would never force it all back into his head again. It was too big for that.

And at the same time, there was a kind of ecstasy to it. Once he stopped struggling with it, and just let go—why, hell—all that clutter and trash and weirdness had its own beauty.

He sat down on the curb and just looked at things for a while.

Objects glowed in the blazing sunlight. Broken glass was particularly ornamental. "Everything is God," the crazy Rastafarian had shouted at him. Sure. Why not?

As he sat there, an old man with a white beard wandered over and, seemingly reading his mind, stumbled and fell off the curb onto his hands and knees. "Shit!" he shouted. "But what a beauty."

James saw that he was alluding to a Coke bottle in the gutter.

Now the old man turned to James, his face transfixed with joy.

"See," he held out the bottle. "Blue heaven. Goddamn." He tilted the bottle up to the sun and peered directly into the mouth of it. A sticky syrup ran down out of it, into his eye, and down his cheek.

In spite of his revulsion, James was intrigued. "What do you see in there?" he said.

"I see everything in there," the old man said. "It's my blue heaven. I see every answer to every question. I see God. I see myself. Here, have a look."

James swallowed and held the bottle up to the sun and peered into it.

Blue fractured and sparkled into other blues, and there was something he could almost see . . . but couldn't quite, and yet . . . Suddenly he was looking through dazzling blue light, and shimmering heat waves, into the dark cool interior of the hut. The old Vietnamese was holding out his hands. "I," he said. James's finger tried to squeeze on the trigger at the same time as James was struggling against that. "Am," the old man said. James fought desperately to hold himself back, but couldn't, and then, from the sky, like the voice of God, he heard the voice of another old man, from another world. "It's the answer to everything. Just everything. You can do it," the voice said.

And suddenly it was true. This time he did not have to squeeze the trigger, and at last the old Vietnamese man was able to finish his sentence:

"You. I am you."

James dropped the Coke bottle in the street, and began to weep.

"See, it didn't break," the old man sitting next to him on the curb said. "It's a miracle. They almost never break."

James was weeping in huge gasping sobs. Holding nothing back now. And was it his imagination, or did the old burnout actually pat him on the back and mumble, "The war is over, son," before he wandered off, shouting to himself?

And now emotion was pouring out of James, blasting out of his body like Oogie's fucking booby-trap explosion, and he wasn't even crying so much anymore as just plain howling, releasing everything all at once, clouds of pain and confusion and remorse and . . . just everything.

Later, when he came out of it, it was afternoon again. He felt so empty that for a moment he couldn't even remember who he was. But that was okay. Then he looked down, and there the blue Coke bottle lay in the street, near the curb. Still glittering. Still unbroken. A miracle. James smiled, but it was a weary smile.

I've got to get some sleep, he thought, if I'm going to make it to work tomorrow. And so he stood up, and began to thread his way methodically through the incredible crazy late afternoon L.A. pedestrian traffic. Back home.

(1987)

STEPHANIE VAUGHN

Born in Millersburg, Ohio, Stephanie Vaughn grew up as the daughter of a career army officer, living in upstate New York, Oklahoma, the Philippines, and Italy. She studied at Ohio State University and in the writing programs of the University of Iowa and Stanford. She now lives in Ithaca, New York, and teaches writing at Cornell.

Vaughn's short stories began appearing in the late 1970s in the New Yorker *and other magazines, and soon gained acclaim, winning both the Pushcart and O. Henry awards. "Kid MacArthur," first published in the* New Yorker *in 1984, was reprinted in* Prize Stories, 1986: The O. Henry Awards. *Most of the stories in her 1990 collection* Sweet Talk, *including "Kid MacArthur," are interlinked tales narrated by Gemma, who shares much of Vaughn's own background.*

Kid MacArthur

I grew up in the Army. About the only kind of dove I ever saw was a dead dove resting small-boned upon a dinner plate. Even though we were Protestants and Bible readers, no one regarded the dove sentimentally as a symbol of peace—the bird who had flown back to Noah carrying the olive branch, as if to say, "The land is green again, come back to the land." When I was thirteen, my family moved to Fort Sill, Oklahoma, only a few weeks before the dove-hunting season opened. My father, who liked to tinker with guns on weekends, sat down at the dining-room table one Saturday and unwrapped a metal device called the Lombreglia Self-Loader. The Self-Loader was a crimping mechanism that enabled a person to assemble shotgun ammunition at home. "Save Money and Earn Pleasure," the box label said. "For the Self-Reliant Sportsman Who Wants to Do the Job Right!"

"If you can learn to handle this," my father said, "you can load my shells for me when the hunting season arrives." He was addressing my brother, MacArthur, who was ten years old. We pulled up chairs to the table, while my mother and grandmother remained near the light of the kitchen door. My father delivered a little lecture on the percussive action of the firing pin as he set out the rest of the loading equipment — empty red cartridges, cardboard wads, brass caps, a bowl of gunpowder, and several bowls of lead shot. He spoke in his officer's briefing-room voice—a voice that seemed to say, "This will be a difficult mission, soldier, but I know you are up to the mark." MacArthur seemed to grow taller listening to that voice, his spine perfectly erect as he helped align the equipment in the center of the table. My father finished the lecture by explaining that the smallest-size shot was best for dove or quail, the medium size was best for duck or rabbit, and the largest size was best for goose or wild turkey.

"And which size shot is best for humans?" my grandmother said. She did not disapprove of guns, but she could rarely pass up a chance to say something sharp to my father. My grandmother was a member of the WCTU, and he was conducting this lesson in between sips of a scotch-and-soda.

"It depends," my father said. "It depends on whether you want to eat the person afterward."

"Well, ha, ha," my grandmother said.

"It is a lot of work trying to prize small shot out of a large body," my father said.

"Very funny," my grandmother said.

My father turned to MacArthur and grew serious. "Never forget that a gun is always loaded."

MacArthur nodded.

"And what else?" my father said to MacArthur.

"Never point a gun at someone unless you mean to kill him," MacArthur said.

"Excuse me," my mother said, moving near the table. "Are you sure all of this is quite safe?" Her hands wavered above the bowl of gunpowder.

"That's right," my grandmother said. "Couldn't something blow up here?"

My father and MacArthur seemed to have been hoping for this question. They led us outside for a demonstration, MacArthur following behind my father with the bowl of powder and a box of matches. "Gunpowder is not like gasoline in a tank," my father said. He tipped a line of powder onto the sidewalk.

"It's not like wheat in a silo, either," MacArthur said, handing the matches to my father.

"Everybody stand back," my father said as he touched a match to the powder. It flared up with a hiss and gave off a stream of pungent smoke.

We watched the white smoke curl into the branches of our pecan tree, and then my grandmother said, "Well, it surely is a pleasure to learn that the house can burn down without blowing up."

Even my father laughed. On the way back into the house, he grew magnanimous and said to me, "You can learn to load shells, too, you know."

"No, thanks," I said. "My destiny is with the baton." I was practicing to be a majorette. It was the white tasseled boots I was after, and the pink lipstick. Years later, a woman friend, seeing a snapshot of me in the white-braided costume, a sort of paramilitary outfit with ruffles, said, "What a waste of your youth, what a corruption of your womanhood." Today, when I contemplate my wasted youth and corrupted womanhood, I recall that when I left high school I went to college. When MacArthur left high school, he went to war.

It is nine years after the gunpowder lesson, and I am a graduate student teaching a section of freshman composition at a large university. On a bright June day, at the end of the school year, one of my students, a Vietnam veteran, offers to give me a present of a human ear. We are walking under a long row of trees after the last class of the term and moving into the dark, brilliant shadows of the trees, then again into the swimming light of the afternoon. We are two weeks short of the solstice, and the sun has never seemed so bright. The student slides his book bag from his shoulder and says, "I would like to give you a present for the end of the course."

Ahead of us, the plane trees are so uniformly spaced, so beautifully arched that they form a green arcaded cloister along the stone walk. A soft, easing wind passes through the boughs with the sound of falling water. "Don't get me wrong," he says. "But I'd like to give you an ear."

Did he know that I came from a military family? Did he know that I had a nineteen-year-old brother in Vietnam? Did he know that my sense of the war derived largely from the color snapshots MacArthur had sent of happy young men posed before the Army's largest movable artillery weapon, their boots heavy with red dust, the jungle rising like a green temple behind them? There were two things MacArthur asked me to send him during his thirteen-month tour—marinated artichoke hearts and Rolling Stones tapes. The only artichoke hearts I could find came in glass jars and were not permitted in the Army's mailbags. The first Stones tapes I sent were washed away in a monsoon flood. I sent more tapes. These were stolen by an old man who wanted to sell them on the black market. I sent more Stones tapes. These MacArthur gave to a wounded boy who was being airlifted to a hospital in Tokyo.

It has been said that the war in Vietnam was so fully photographed that it was the one war we learned the truth about. Which truth did we learn, and who learned it? One of the most famous pictures to come out of the war was the videotape of the South Vietnam chief of police firing a bullet into the head of a prisoner, a man who stood before the chief in shorts and a loose plaid shirt. He looked the chief in the eye, looked with fear and no hope, and was still looking with fear and no hope in that moment when he was already dead but had not yet fallen like a rag into the Saigon street. There were other memorable pictures like that. There were also ones like the picture of the blond, blue-eyed soldier, his head wrapped becomingly in a narrow bandage ("Just a flesh wound, sir"), reaching toward the camera as if to summon help for his wounded comrade. This photograph, with its depiction of handsome, capable, white middle-class goodwill, was so popular that it appeared in every major American news source and has been republished many times since, whenever a news agency wants to do a story on the Vietnam era.

That picture always reminds me of my student, a man in his late twenties who had served three tours of duty in Vietnam and was being put through college by the Army so that he could return to active duty as an officer—the student who stood before me pulling a canvas sack from his book bag on that dazzling June day at the end of my first year as a teacher.

"Don't get me wrong," the student said. "But I would like to give you an ear."

"What would you want to do that for?"

"I want to give you a present. I want to give you something for the end of the course." He withdrew his hand from the sack and opened it, palm up.

You probably have heard about the ears they brought back with them from Vietnam. You may have heard how the ears were carried in pouches or worn like necklaces, the lobes perforated so that they could be threaded on a leather thong. You may have heard that the ears looked like dried fruit, or like seashells, or like leaves curling beneath an oak tree. The mind will often make a metaphor when it cannot make anything else.

A human ear, though, still looks like a human ear. It is only after you have stared at it for a long while, at its curving ridges and shallow basins, that you begin to see: here is the dry bed of a wide river valley, here is the tiny village, the bright paddy, the water buffalo. Here is the world so green you could taste that greenness on your tongue even from an altitude of ten thousand feet in a jet bomber.

As the student and I looked at each other in the sunlight, two young women strolling along the walk separated in order to pass us— parted like river water moving around an island. They were laughing and did not notice what the student held in his hand. "So," said one of the women, "my mother calls me back to say they had to put the poor dog to sleep, and you know what she says?" The student and I turned to hear what the mother had said. "She says, 'And you know, Anita, that dog's mind was still good. He wasn't even senile.'"

When the student turned back to me, he was smiling. "What a world," he said. He extended his hand.

"Thank you," I said. "But I do not want that present."

We had begun to move again. I was walking slowly, trying to show with my easy pace that I was not afraid. Perhaps he was angry with me for something I had said in class. Perhaps he was on drugs.

"It's okay," he said, "I have lots more."

"Really," I said. "No, but thank you."

"If you don't want this one, I can give you a better one." He reached into the bag again.

"How can you tell which is which?" I said calmly, as if I were inquiring about fishing lures or nuts and bolts or types of flower seed.

"I can tell," he said. "I've got this one memorized. This one's a girl." The girl, he told me, was thirteen. At first, the men in his outfit had taken pity on her and given her food and cigarettes. Then they learned that she was the one who planted mines around their encampment in the night.

It took us a long time to cross the campus and shake hands and say good-bye. Two days later, the student left a bottle of vodka on my desk while I was out. Apparently he had been sincere in wanting to give me a present. I never saw the student again. I did not see another war souvenir of that kind until after my brother returned from Vietnam.

The autumn we lived at Fort Sill, our family ate five hundred doves. There was a fifty-day dove season, a ten-dove limit each day. Every night, my mother brought the birds to the table in a different guise. They were baked and braised and broiled. They were basted and stuffed, olive-oiled and gravied. But there were too many of them, each tiny and heart-shaped, the breastbone prominent in outline even under a sauce. Finally, a platter of doves was set before us and MacArthur said, "I am now helping myself to a tuna casserole. There is cheese in this casserole, and some cracker crumbs." He passed the platter to me. "And what are you having, Gemma?"

"I am having jumbo shrimps," I said. "And some lemon."

In this way, the platter moved around the table. My mother was having lamb. My grandmother was having pork chops. My father hesitated before he took the meat fork. All his life, he had been shooting game for the dinner table. He believed he was teaching his family a lesson in economy and his son a lesson in wilderness survival. No one had ever made a joke about these meals. He looked at MacArthur. Although my father had never said it, MacArthur was exactly the kind of son he had hoped to have—tall and good-natured, smart and obedient, a boy who could hit a bull's-eye on a paper target with his .22 rifle. "All right," my father said at last. "I'm having a steak."

However, after dinner he said, "If you want to play a game, let's play a real game. Let's play twenty questions." He took a pen from his pocket and flattened a paper napkin to use as a scorecard. He looked at MacArthur. "I am thinking of something. What is it?" We were all going to play this game, but my father's look implied that MacArthur was the principal opponent.

MacArthur tried to assume the gamesman's bland expression. "Is it animal?" he said.

My father appeared to think for a while. He mused at the candles. He considered the ceiling. This was part of the game, trying to throw the opponents off the trail. "Yes, it is animal."

"Is it a toad?" my grandmother said.

"No, no," MacArthur said. "It's too soon to ask that."

"It certainly is not a toad," my father said. He made a great show of entering a mark against us on the napkin. This was another part of the game, trying to rattle the opponents by gloating.

"Is it bigger than a breadbox?" my mother said.

"Yes."

"Is it bigger than a car?" I said.

"Yes."

"Is it bigger than a house?" MacArthur said.

"Yes."

"Is it the Eiffel Tower?" my grandmother said.

Again my father used exaggerated motions to record the mark. MacArthur dropped his head into his arms. This was an unmanly response.

"Settle down," my father said. "Think."

"Can't we play some other game?" my grandmother said. "This game is never any fun."

"We are not trying to have fun," my father said. "We are trying to use our minds."

So the game went, until we had used up our twenty no answers, and my father revealed the thing he had been thinking of. The thing was "the rocket's red glare"—the light from exploded gunpowder. Gunpowder, if you analyzed its ingredients, was actually animal, vegetable, *and* mineral—providing you agreed that the carbon component could be derived from animal sources. He poured a drink and leaned back to tell us a story. The first time he had played the game he was a soldier on a ship going to England. The ship was in one of the largest convoys ever to cross the Atlantic during the Second World War. The sea was rough. German submarines were nearby. Some men got seasick, and everyone was nervous. They began to play games, and they played one game of twenty questions for two days. That was the game whose answer was "the rocket's red glare." My father had thought that one up.

That was as close as he ever came to telling us a war story. He had gone from England to Normandy Beach and later to the Battle of the Bulge, but when he remembered the war for us he remembered brave, high-spirited men not yet under attack. When he had finished speaking, he looked at his glass of scotch as the true drinker will—as if it contains a prophecy.

The spring following the season in which we ate whole generations of doves, MacArthur acquired two live chicks. A Woolworth's in the town near the post was giving chicks away to the first hundred customers in the door the Saturday before Palm Sunday. MacArthur was the first customer through the door and also the fifty-seventh. He named the chicks Harold and Georgette. He made big plans for Harold and Georgette. He was going to teach them how to walk a tightrope made of string and ride a chicken-sized Ferris wheel.

A week later, Harold and Georgette were eaten by our cat while we were at church. The chicks had been living in an open cardboard box on top of the refrigerator. No one imagined that a cat as fat and slothful as Al Bear would hurl himself that high to get an extra meal.

Looking at the few pale feathers left in the box, MacArthur said, "He ate them whole. He even ate the beaks."

"Poor chicks," my mother said.

"They were making an awful lot of noise up there," my grandmother said. "They should have kept those beaks shut."

Everyone looked to see if MacArthur was crying. In our family,
people believed that getting through a hardship intact was its own re-
ward. "This is nothing to be upset about," my father said. "This is the
way nature works." It was in the natural order of things for cats to eat
birds, he told us. Even some birds ate other birds. Some animals ate
cats. Everything we ate had once been alive. Wasn't a steak part of a
steer? MacArthur looked away just long enough to roll his eyes at me.
My father began to gesture and to project his voice. Now he was lec-
turing on the principles of Darwinian selection. He used the phrase
"nature red in tooth and claw." He seemed to like that phrase, and used
it again. The third time he said, "nature red in tooth and claw," Al Bear
walked up behind him and threw up on the floor, all the little bird parts
of Harold and Georgette still recognizable on the linoleum.

MacArthur never became a hunter of birds. By the time he turned
twelve, and was given a shotgun for his birthday, we were stationed in
Italy. The Italians, always a poor people, would shoot a bird out of a
tree or blast one on the ground to get a meal. They had gone through
entire species of game birds this way and were now working on the
German songbirds that flew south for the winter. Thus, the misfor-
tunes of the Italian economy allowed my brother to turn from real
birds to imitation ones. Soon after his birthday, he was taken to the
skeet range at Camp Darby, where he was permitted to shoot fifty
rounds at black-and-yellow disks, called pigeons. Fifty recoils of a large
gun are a lot for a boy, even one big for his age, like MacArthur. By the
time he got home that day, there were bruises beginning to bloom
across his shoulder.

"Maybe he should wait until he's older," my mother said.

"What ever happened to the all-American sports?" my grandmother said. "Couldn't he learn to throw or kick something?"

Months later, when we all drove into the post to see him shoot in
his first tournament, MacArthur kept saying, "See Kid MacArthur forget to load the gun. Watch fake birds fall whole to the earth." "Kid
MacArthur" was what he called himself when something went wrong.
He did not like the general whose name he bore. He did not admire
him, as my parents did, for being the man who said, "I shall return."
MacArthur was not one of those ordinary names, like John or Joan,
which you could look up in my grandmother's *Dictionary of Christian*

Appellations. MacArthur was a name my brother had to research. General MacArthur, he decided, had talked a big game but then allowed his entire air force to be bombed on the ground the day after Pearl Harbor. General MacArthur had sent his troops into Bataan but had not sent along the trucks that carried food for the battalions. The general had fled to Australia, uttering his famous words, leaving his men to perish in the Death March.

"You'll be fine if you don't look out any windows," my father said. "Looking out the window" was his expression for allowing the mind to wander. "I'm pulling down all the shades on my windows," MacArthur said. "I'm battening all the hatches in my head."

Something overtook MacArthur when the tournament got under way and he finally stepped onto the range, the only boy among the shooters. The bones of his face grew prominent. His eyes became opaque, like the eyes of a man who can keep a secret. By the second time around the stations, he was third among the five shooters. No one spoke, except a man named Mr. Dimple, who was an engineer working for the American government in Italy, and the only civilian on the skeet range.

"That gosh-damned sun," Mr. Dimple said. "Those gosh-damned trees." It was a hot, bright day, and the angle of the sun made it difficult to see the disks as they sailed in front of a pine forest at the back of the range.

"Maybe we need a fence in front of those trees," Mr. Dimple said. After his next two shots, he said, "Damned if the wind didn't get to those birds before I did." It was clear that Mr. Dimple was disgracing himself before the cream of the American Army. When he spoke, the other men looked at the grass. The women, seated behind the semicircular range, looked at each other. Their eyes seemed to say, "Our men are not going to complain about any trees. Our men are not going to complain about the wind or the sun."

"I'm not wearing the right sunglasses," Mr. Dimple said.

MacArthur stepped up to the station just in front of the viewing area and called for the pigeons. "Pull!" Swinging to his right, he aimed just ahead of the flying, spinning disk. He pulled the first trigger and began the swing back to his left to get the second sailing bird before it touched the ground. The first bird exploded in a star of fragments and fell to the earth with the sound of raining gravel. The second bird fell untouched and landed on the ground with a *clack* as it struck another unexploded bird. Perhaps because his swing back had seemed so sure, so exactly timed, MacArthur could not believe he had missed. He shook his head as he stepped away from the station.

My father looked over at him and said within hearing of everyone on the range, "Whenever you step back from that peg, you step back the same way, hit or miss. You do not shake your head."

Mr. Dimple put his hand on his hip and sighed at his gun. Colonel McGrath and Major Solman looked away.

"Do you understand?"

MacArthur did understand. He was embarrassed. "Yes, sir," he said. As the group moved to the next station, the other men nodded at my father and gave MacArthur friendly punches on the arm. He was not going to grow up to be a Mr. Dimple.

The next year, MacArthur won a place on the championship team my father took to Naples. For years, my father liked to tell about MacArthur's first day on the range. "He was black-and-blue all over," my father said. "But he never spoke a word of complaint."

Two years later, we returned to the States to live on a post on Governors Island, which was in the middle of New York Harbor and so close to the Statue of Liberty that we could see her torchlight from our bedroom windows. It was on Governors Island that my father received a letter from the government that seemed to imply that MacArthur might not be an American citizen, because he had been born in the Philippines. He was not quite a foreigner, either, because his parents had been born in Ohio.

"He's a juvenile delinquent, is what he is," my grandmother said one day when my father was trying to explain the citizenship difficulty. She had slipped into MacArthur's room and found a cache of cigarette lighters. "Where does a fourteen-year-old boy get enough money to buy these things?" she said. "What does he do with them, anyway?"

"He doesn't smoke," I said, although I knew that with my father the health issue would not be the central one.

My mother beheld the lighters with great sadness. "I'll have a talk with him tonight."

"No one will speak to him yet," my father said. He was troubled because the evidence of MacArthur's criminality had been gathered in a kind of illegal search and seizure.

"Does this mean that MacArthur can never become president of the United States?" I said. In our family, we had been taught that if children were scrupulously honest, and also rose from their seats when strangers entered the room, and said "Yes, sir" and "No, sir" at the appropriate moments, and then went on to get a college education, they could grow up to be anything, including president of the United States. Even a woman could be president, if she kept her record clean and also went to college.

No one smiled at my joke.

The document my father held seemed to suggest that even though MacArthur was the son of patriots, someone somewhere might question the quality of his citizenship. It was a great blow to learn that he might be a thief as well as a quasi foreigner.

The document was a letter from the judge advocate of the post advising that foreign-born children be interviewed by the Department of Naturalization and Immigration. It also advised that they attend a ceremony in which they would raise their right hands, like ordinary immigrants, and renounce any residual loyalty to the countries of their births. It did not "require" that they do these things but it did "strongly recommend" that they do so. We never learned why the government made its strong recommendation, but there was something in the language of the letter that allowed one to think that foreign birth was like a genetic defect that could be surgically altered—it was like an extra brain that could be lopped off. (A communist brain! A socialist brain! The brain that would tell the hand to raise the gun against American democracy.)

"What were you doing in his chest of drawers?" my father said.

"I was dusting," my grandmother said.

"You were dusting the contents of a brown sack?"

"This would never have happened in Ohio," my grandmother said. "If we lived in Ohio, he would already be a citizen and would not have to hang around that neighborhood after school."

"In this house, we do not take other people's possessions without asking."

"That's the point." My grandmother picked up a lighter with each hand. "These *are* other people's possessions."

It was dark when I slipped out to intercept MacArthur. At night, it was always a surprise to ascend the slope of the post golf course and come upon a vision of New York City standing above the harbor, the lights of Wall Street rising like fire into the sky, all the glory and fearfulness of the city casting its spangled image back across the water to our becalmed and languorous island. If you looked away from the light of the city, you looked back into the darkness of the last three centuries, across roofs of brick buildings built by the British and the Dutch. The post was a Colonial retreat, an administrative headquarters, where soldiers strolled to work under the boughs of hardwood trees, and the trumpetings of the recorded bugle drifted through the leaves like a mist. It was a green, antique island, giving its last year of service to the United States Army.

My grandmother never boarded the ferry for Manhattan without believing that her life or, at the very least, the quality of her character was in peril. She did not like New Yorkers. They were grim and anxious. They had bad teeth. They did not live in a place where parents told their children that if they bit into an apple and found a worm, they would know that they were just getting a little extra protein.

"About how many do you think she took?" MacArthur said to me.

"She took about exactly all of them."

His face went slack. He still did not have that implacable expression that was supposed to help you through any crisis. "I was going to hock those on Monday to get some more cash for Christmas."

"By Monday, you will be restricted to quarters. By Monday, you will be calling your friends to tell them you can't go to any movies or parties over the holidays." I handed him a lighter. "I don't think they've got them counted," I said. The others were still lying on the dining table.

He was grateful for that lighter. "Thanks," he said. "This is the best one."

"How about a light?" I said. I opened a pack of my father's cigarettes and took one out.

He snapped open the lighter and ignited it so deftly that the whole movement looked like a magic trick. "This is what we learn to do at P.S. 104," he said.

Neither of us smoked, but we inflicted the cigarette upon ourselves with relish, exhaling fiercely into the raw night air. "I'm not asking where you got them, of course," I said.

He smiled. "I won almost every one of them throwing dice and playing cards. At lunch everybody goes out to steal, and after school everybody plays for the loot. Remember me? Kid Competition. I'm great at games."

"That's a story you could probably tell them," I said.

He ground the cigarette out under his foot. "Look at me," he said. "I'm littering Army property." Then he said, "I did steal a couple of them. Either you steal, and you're one of the guys, or you don't steal, and you're a sleazo and everybody wants to fight."

He was very tall by then. The bones close to his skin—his wrist bones, knees, shoulder bones—looked as though they had been borrowed from a piece of farm machinery. If you were as big as he was and also the new kid at school, someone would always want to fight you. We had started walking and were now on the dark side of Governors Island, standing by the seawall that looked toward the small lights of Brooklyn. The wind was blowing at our backs from the west, bringing the sharp, oily smell from the New Jersey refineries, but we could also smell the salt and fish taste of the ocean, and for a moment I could imagine us far away from every city and every Army post and every rural town we had ever known. He leaned across the railing of the seawall and looked tired. He had posed for himself an even more demanding ideal than the family had, and he was humiliated to perceive himself as a thief.

"Look," I said. "Just tell them you bought a couple of lighters with your lunch money to get the stake for the gambling." He nodded toward the water without conviction. "Don't ruin Christmas for yourself."

"Okay, I won't."

The next day he volunteered the truth to my father and was not only restricted to quarters but also made to go uptown to meet the victims of the crimes. My father wore his uniform, with the brass artilleryman's insignia, two cannons crossed under a missile. MacArthur wore the puffy green jacket and the green hat that had inspired his friends to call him the Jolly Green Giant. They were a gift from my mother and grandmother, so he had to wear them. They made him look like a lumbering asparagus stalk, a huge vegetable king, who could be spotted on any subway platform or down any length of city blocks. At each store, he removed his green hat and made a speech of apology, then returned one or several of the lighters. Since the lighters were now used, he also paid for them out of his Christmas-shopping money. It hurt him to be the one who had nothing to give on Christmas morning. And at school he was an outcast.

"I am now Kid Scum," he said. "The Jolly Green Creep."

He got a Certificate of Citizenship, though, and when he entered the Army, four years later, he went in as a real American.

On MacArthur's last day of leave before he left for Vietnam, we drove him to the Cleveland airport and then stood like potted palms behind the plate-glass window of the terminal building. My father had retired from the Army by then, and the family had returned to Ohio.

"He ought to love the heat," my grandmother said. "He was born in the heat."

"He's a smart soldier," my father said. "It's the smart men who are most likely to get through any war." My father had always believed in smartness as other people believe in amulets.

The plane began to move, and we strained to find MacArthur's face in one of the small windows. "There he is," my mother said. "I see his hand in the window."

A woman standing next to her said, "No, that's our son. See how big that hand is?"

The woman's husband said, "Our son was a linebacker at Ohio State. He weighs two hundred and sixty-five pounds."

"He's a good boy," the woman said, and we all nodded, as if it were obvious that physical size could be a measure of a person's character.

After we left the turnpike and drove south to the fertile, rolling land of the Killbuck Valley, which had never produced a war protester, my grandmother said, "I believe in Vietnam." She emphasized the word *believe*, as if Vietnam were a denomination of the Christian faith. In the 1950s, she had been a member of something called the Ground Observer Corps. Members of the Corps scanned the skies with binoculars, looking for Russian aircraft. At that time she lived in a small Ohio town whose major industries were a bus-seat factory and an egg-noodle plant. Twice a month she stood on the roof of the high school to keep these vital industries safe from a communist air attack.

"I believe in luck," I said. "I believe the Jolly Green Giant's luck will get him through. Remember how he always won at bingo?"

"We took care of the Japs and the Jerries," my grandmother said. "We held off the pinkos in Korea."

"I do not think that any pinkos are planning to invade the United States," I said.

"You've got a lot to learn," my mother said. "They're already here."

"When you get back to school, I do not want to hear that you are marching in those protests," my father said.

I was already marching, but that was a secret. "Isn't this the place where we notice the grass?" I said.

When my father was still in the Army, we spent all of his leave time going back to the Killbuck Valley. As we crossed the state line and drew closer to the valley where the Killbuck River ran and all of our relatives lived, my father would say, "Doesn't anyone notice that the grass is getting greener?" We used to say, "Naw, this grass looks like any other grass." We made a joke of the grass, but we all did love the look of that land. On some level, the grasses of the Killbuck Valley, the clover, timothy, alfalfa, the corn, wheat, and oats, the dense woods of the hills, the freshwater springs, and the shivering stream—all of this was connected with the necessity of a standing Army. It was as if my father had said, "This is what we will fight for."

MacArthur had been out of the Army for a year, and his life seemed defined by negatives—no job, no college, no telephone, no meat. He lived alone in a rented farmhouse deep in the Killbuck Valley, about twenty miles from the town where the family had settled.

"He comes every other Sunday and all he eats is the salad or the string beans," my grandmother said to me. The soul of our family life always hovered over the dinner table, where we renewed the bond of our kinship over game and steaks and chops and meatloaf. My parents and grandmother perceived MacArthur's new diet both as a disease and as a mark of failing character. When they went to visit, they took along a roast or a ten-pound bag of hamburger.

"See what you can find out," my mother said. I was home for Christmas week and on my way out to see him. "Talk to him. See if he has any plans."

He did not have any plans. What he had was a souvenir of the war just like the one my student had tried to give me on that June day under the trees. This one was tucked into a small padded envelope lying on the kitchen table. The envelope made me curious, and I kept reaching out to finger the ragged edges of brown paper as we drank a pot of tea. MacArthur, sitting on the kitchen counter because there was only one chair, finally said, "Go ahead. Look." I opened the envelope and looked. There was a moment then when the winter sun was like heavy metal in the room, like something that could achieve critical mass if a question mark sparked the air. For some reason, I thought of the young woman reporting what her mother had said about the dead dog—"And you know, that dog's mind was still good. He wasn't even senile." I thought of what I had wanted to say to my student that day: "I didn't think that something like this could look exactly like itself so much later and so far away."

"That's not mine," MacArthur said. "That belongs to Dixon." His face was as flat as pond ice, and I saw that at last he had achieved the gamesman's implacable expression. Even in the long curves of his body there was something that said that nothing could startle or move him.

"Who's Dixon?" I said.

"Oh, you know who he is. My friend the space cadet. The one in the V.A. hospital."

"The one from Oklahoma." Now I remembered Dixon from the snapshots. He was the one who glued chicken feathers to his helmet.

"This is his idea of a great Christmas present," MacArthur said.

His eyes were so still and wide I could see the gold flecks in them. He looked away, looked down at his legs dangling from the counter, and I suddenly felt the solitariness of that rented farmhouse in the Killbuck Valley, the hills and fields hardened under snow, the vegetable garden rutted with ice. When I stood up to touch his arm, he did not move or speak. He seemed to have escaped from me in an evaporation of heat. Even in my imagination, I could not go where he had gone. All I knew was that somewhere in the jungle had been a boy named Dixon, a boy from Oklahoma, who had grown up on land just like the land my father used to hunt while MacArthur trailed behind with bright-red boxes of homemade ammunition. But now Dixon was a nut who sent ears through the mail, and MacArthur was unemployed and living alone in the country.

Suddenly the ear was back in the envelope Dixon had sent it in, and MacArthur was saying, "I'm sorry, but I don't have much around here you'd like to eat."

Later, we stood out back where the garden was and looked at the corn stubble and broken vines. MacArthur paced the rows and said, "These are my snap beans. These are my pumpkins." He proceeded past carrots, beets, onions, turnips, cabbages, and summer squash, looking at each old furrow with a stalwart affection, as if the plants he named would bloom in snow when they heard him speak.

"They asked me to find out what you plan for the future," I said.

"Oh, great." He kicked a hump of snow. "Did you ever notice how with the family your life is always a prospective event? 'When you're a little older, when you grow up, when you get old just like me'?" He relaxed again and dropped an arm across my shoulders. "I'm just a carpenter now. Let me show you my lights." I thought he meant lamps, since most of his rooms were empty except for secondhand lamps standing in corners. He was restoring the house for its owner, to work off the rent. In the front room, he said, "Now we are going to play a game. Tell me what you see. All right? Do you get it? Tell me what you see."

"I see an old iron floor lamp."

"No, tell me about the *light*. What kind of light do you see?" The walls were freshly painted white, but the sun had moved around the house, so the room was growing dark. I fumbled for a proper answer.

"Eggshell light?" I said.

He made a great show of entering an imaginary mark on an imaginary napkin in his hand. "Nooooo," he said. "It certainly is not eggshell light."

Then I understood, and I laughed. "Is it animal light?"

"Settle down, now. Use your head."

"Is it vegetable light?"

He surveyed the room, its greens, and blue-greens and ochers, the pale colors of a northern room at the end of the day. "Yes, I think you could call this vegetable light. Maybe *eggplant* light." He laughed and wadded up the imaginary napkin.

We moved through the house then, making up ridiculous names for the light we saw. We found moose light, and hippopotamus light, and potato-chip light. We found a violet light we named after our cousin Neilon's purple car, and an orange light we called Aunt Sheila's Hair, and a silver light we called Uncle Dave, after the silver dollars he used to send us on our birthdays. We returned to the kitchen, with its wide reach of western windows, and saw the red light of the sunset splayed across the cabinets. "Oh, yes," MacArthur said. "And here we have another light. Here we have a light just like the light of the rocket's red glare."

The sun had dropped below the tree line when he went to turn on his lamps, and I put on my coat. "Well, I have to go," I said. "I'll keep writing. I'll come see you the next time I'm back."

He walked me to the car, holding my arm as I slipped over the pebbly snow. We stopped to look at the western sky, now furrowed with that fierce red you see at that time of year when there are ice crystals in the air. All the things nearby had become brilliant black silhouettes — the stand of trees to our right, the boarded-up barn, the spiky fragments of the garden. The sky grew fiercer and gave off a light I could not name.

"The shortest day of the year," MacArthur said. He reached into his jacket and withdrew the brown envelope. "Take this," he said.

He held it out, and this time, because he was my brother, I said, "All right," and took it. I hugged him and got in the car. I knew he was not going to be home for Christmas. "You're going all the way to Ok-lahoma to see Dixon, aren't you?"

He had already started back to the house and had to turn to face me with his surprise.

"Remember me?" I said. "I'm the Kid's sister. I'll think of some-thing to tell them at home."

"Thanks," he said.

When I got to the bottom of the lane, I stopped the car to wave. He had come back through the house and was standing on the dark porch, legs evenly spaced, like a soldier at ease, the gold light of his house swooning in every window. Before I drove off, I slipped the en-velope under the front seat with the road maps, thinking that someday I would remove it and decide what to do.

It was still there five years later, when I sold the car. During those five years, my father, always a weekend drinker, began to drink during the week. My grandmother broke her hip in a fall. My mother, a quiet woman, was now helped through her quiet by Valium. MacArthur fin-ished restoring his rooms and moved to another farmhouse, in a differ-ent county. Finally, he took a job as a cook—a breakfast cook, doing mostly eggs and pancakes—and in this way continued to be a person without plans.

The boy I sold the car to was just eighteen years old and wanted to go west to California. He was tall, like my brother, and happy to be managing his own life at last. The cuffs of his plaid flannel shirt had shrunk past his wrists, and, seeing his large wrist bones exposed to the cold bright air, I liked him immediately.

"Are you sure you're charging me enough for this?" Leaning under the hood, he looked like a construction crane. "This is one of the best engines Ford ever made," he said. "Whooee!"

"Believe me. I'm charging you a good price."

He wanted to celebrate the purchase and buy me a drink. "I bet this old Betsy has some stories to tell." He winked at me. He could not believe his good luck, and he was flirting. The cold spring air seemed to take the shape of a promise, but then there was still the problem of the envelope under the front seat. In five years, I had removed it sev-eral times. I had thought of bureau drawers and safe-deposit boxes. I had even thought of getting Dixon's address and sending it back. Again and again, I slid it under the seat once more unopened.

"Come on," the boy said. "Let's have a drink and tell some stories."

"Really, I can't," I said. "I have to go somewhere." I didn't want to get to know him. I had meant to retrieve the envelope before I turned over the car, but, standing on the curb, signing the pink slip, I discovered it would be easier just to leave it there.

"Hey," the boy said. "Look what you did. You made a sheep."

"What?" I said.

"You made a sheep with your breath. Hey — there, you did it again." Now I tried to see what he had seen in the frosty air, but it was gone. He gave me the money, we shook hands, and he got in the car. "Not many people can make a whole sheep," he said. He turned the key. "Most folks just puff out a part of a sheep."

"Wait," I said.

He put the car back in neutral and leaned out the window. "You change your mind? You hop in and I'll take you to Mr. Mike's Rock-and-Roll Heaven."

"No," I said. "I have to tell you something. There's something I didn't tell you about the car."

He stopped smiling, because he must have thought I hadn't given him a good price after all—that there was a crack in the engine block or a dogleg in the frame.

"Well, what the heck is it? Just lay me out then. The last car I had broke down on me in three weeks." He was remorseful now and disappointed in both of us.

I paused a long time. "I just think I should tell you that this car takes premium gas."

He was happy again. "Shoot, I knew that," he said. He put the car back into gear.

"You be careful," I said. "You have a good trip."

He gave me the thumbs-up sign and edged away from the curb, looking both ways, in case there was traffic.

I liked that boy. I wanted him to get safely to California and find a good life and fall in love and father a large brood of cheerful people who would try to give you too much for a used car and would always wear their shirtsleeves too short. I watched him drive away and around the corner. I started back to the house but then turned to look at the cloud of exhaust that hung in the air. I wanted to see what figure it made. I wanted to see if it would be a sheep or a part of a sheep or a person or something else, and what I saw instead, before it unfurled into the maple trees, was a thin banner of pale smoke.

(1985)

LEWIS SHINER

Although Lewis Shiner's fiction was once lumped together with what was known in the 1980s as cyberpunk, his writings are too original for categorization, especially since he never repeats himself. Only his first novel, Frontera *(1984), which is set on Mars, fits neatly into the genre of science fiction. If his magnificent second novel,* Deserted Cities of the Heart *(1988), had been authored by a Latin American, it would be called "magic realism."* Slam *(1990) makes skateboarding its dominant metaphor; as one young character says, "Concrete is the future. You don't cry about it, man, you skate on it."* Glimpses *(1993), which won the 1994 World Fantasy Award for best novel of the year, is both a celebration and piercing critique of rock culture, brought about by time travel into the past that reconfigures the rock and roll of the 1960s.*

Yet Shiner's fiction is unified by his quest for what he has called "a new literature of idealism and compassion that is contemporary not only on the technological level but also the emotional." And central to that quest are the effects of the Vietnam War on his life, which he narrates in his introduction to When the Music's Over, *his anthology of antiwar science fiction stories. Born in 1950 and increasingly revolted by the war, especially after the killing of college students at Kent State and Jackson State in 1970, he dropped out of college intending to play full-time with his rock-and-roll band. His father was an ardent Nixon supporter who once ripped a love-bead necklace off Shiner's neck because to him "beads equals hippy equals protest equals traitor." Yet when Shiner apprehensively called to tell him he had flunked his draft physical (intentionally), his father, rather than being angry, "was happy, and almost—proud. He said, 'This is not a war I want to send you to.'"*

"The War at Home" displaces the nexus between Vietnam and America into a surreal dimension. Published in 1985, it suggests how America had reimaged the war and what the war was doing to reimage America.

The War at Home

Ten of us in the back of a Huey, assholes clenched like fists, C-rations turned to sno-cones in our bellies. Tracers float up at us, swollen, sizzling with orange light, like one dud firecracker after another. Ahead of us the gunships pound Landing Zone Dog with everything they have, flex guns, rockets, and 50-calibers, while the artillery screams overhead and the Air Force A1-Es strafe the clearing into kindling.

We hover over the LZ in the sudden phosphorus dawn of a flare, screaming, "Land, you fucker, land!" while the tracers close in, the shell of the copter ticking like a clock as the thumb-sized rounds go through her, ripping the steel like paper, spattering somebody's brains across the aft bulkhead.

Then falling into the knee-high grass, the air humming with bullets and stinking of swamp ooze and gasoline and human shit and blood. Spinning wildly, my finger jamming down the trigger of the M-16, not caring anymore where the bullets go.

And waking up in my own bed, Clare beside me, shaking me, hissing, "Wake up, wake up for Christ's sake."

I sat up, the taste of it still in my lungs, hands twitching with berserker frenzy. "M okay," I mumbled. "Nightmare. I was back in Nam."

"What?"

"Flashback," I said. "The war."

"What are you talking about? You weren't in the war."

I looked at my hands and remembered. It was true. I'd never even been in the Army, never set foot in Vietnam.

Three months earlier we'd been shooting an *Eyewitness News* series on Vietnamese refugees. His name was Nguyen Ky Duk, former ARVN colonel, now a fry cook at Jack in the Box. "You killed my country," he said. "All of you. Americans, French, Japanese. Like you would kill a dog because you thought it might have, you know, rabies. Just kill it and throw it in a ditch. It was a living thing, and now it is dead."

The afternoon of the massacre we got raw footage over the wire. About a dozen of us crowded the monitor and stared at the shattered windows of the Safeway, the mounds of cartridges, the bloodstains and the puddles of congealing food.

"What was it he said?"

"Something about 'gooks.' 'You're all fucking gooks, just like the others, and now I'll kill you too,' something like that."

"But he wasn't in Nam. They talked to his wife."

"So why'd he do it?"

"He was a gun nut. Black market shit, like that M-16 he had. Camo clothes, the whole nine yards. A nut."

I walked down the hall, past the lines of potted ferns and bamboo, and bought a Coke from the machine. I could still remember the dream, the feel of the M-16 in my hands, the rage, the fear.

"Like it?" Clare asked. She turned slowly, the loose folds of her black cotton pajamas fluttering, her face hidden by the conical straw hat.

"No," I said. "I don't know. It makes me feel weird."

"It's fashion," she said. "Fashion's supposed to make you feel weird."

I walked away from her, through the sliding glass door and into the back yard. The grass had grown a foot or more without my noticing, and strange plants had come up between the flowers, suffocating them in sharp fronds and broad green leaves.

"Did you go?"

"No," I said. "I was 1-Y. Underweight, if you can believe that." But in fact I was losing weight again, the muscles turning stringy under sallow skin.

"Me either. My dad got a shrink to write me a letter. I did the marches, Washington and all that. But you know something? I feel weird about not going. Kind of guilty, somehow. Even though we shouldn't ever have been there, even though we were burning villages and fragging our own guys. I feel like . . . I don't know. Like I missed something. Something important."

"Maybe not," I said. Through cracked glass I could see the sunset thickening the trees.

"What do you mean?"

I shrugged. I wasn't sure myself. "Maybe it's not too late," I said.

I walk through the haunted streets of my town, sweltering in the January heat. The jungle arches over me; children's voices in the distance chatter in their weird pidgin Vietnamese. The TV station is a crumbling ruin and none of us feel comfortable there any longer. We work now in a thatched hut with a mimeo machine.

The air is humid, fragrant with anticipation. Soon the planes will come and it will begin in earnest.

(1985)

ROBERT OLEN BUTLER

Born in Illinois in 1945, Robert Olen Butler spent three years (1969–1972) in the U.S. Army. In Vietnam he used his command of the Vietnamese language in army intelligence and as an interpreter for the U.S. adviser to the mayor of Saigon.

Complex relations between American and Vietnamese cultures have been a recurring theme in his work since his first novel, Alleys of Eden *(1981), centering on an American deserter and a Vietnamese prostitute who live together first in Saigon and then in the United States. He has published five subsequent novels:* Sun Dogs *(1982), whose protagonist is a former U.S. prisoner of war in Vietnam turned private investigator;* Countrymen of Bones *(1983);* Wabash *(1987);* The Deuce *(1989); and* They Whisper *(1994), whose main character is a Vietnam veteran who had been used in intelligence work because of his command of Vietnamese. Butler now teaches creative writing at McNeese State University in Lake Charles, Louisiana.*

Butler's familiarity with Vietnamese language, culture, and the exile community in Louisiana is central to his short stories collected in A Good Scent from a Strange Mountain, *which won the 1993 Pulitzer Prize for fiction. For each of these stories, he creates a distinctive Vietnamese narrator. In the title story, reprinted here, Butler evokes the ghost of a Vietnamese as fascinated with America and American culture as he himself is with Vietnam and Vietnamese culture: Ho Chi Minh, who, beginning in 1919, attempted over and over again to convince the United States to support the independence of his country. Butler's details about Ho's early life are based on careful research.*

A Good Scent from a Strange Mountain

Hô Chí Minh came to me again last night, his hands covered with confectioners' sugar. This was something of a surprise to me, the first time I saw him beside my bed, in the dim light from the open shade. My oldest daughter leaves my shades open, I think so that I will not forget that the sun has risen again in the morning. I am a very old man. She seems to expect that one morning I will simply forget to keep living. This is very foolish. I will one night rise up from my bed and slip into her room and open the shade there. Let her see the sun in the morning. She is sixty-four years old and she should worry for herself. I could never die from forgetting.

But the light from the street was enough to let me recognize Hô when I woke, and he said to me, "Đạo, my old friend, I have heard it is time to visit you." Already on that first night there was a sweet smell about him, very strong in the dark, even before I could see his hands. I said nothing, but I stretched to the nightstand beside me and I turned on the light to see if he would go away. And he did not. He stood there beside the bed—I could even see him reflected in the window—and I knew it was real because he did not appear as he was when I'd known him but as he was when he'd died. This was Uncle Hô before me, the thin old man with the dewlap beard wearing the dark clothes of a peasant and the rubber sandals, just like in the news pictures I studied with such a strange feeling for all those years. Strange because when I knew him, he was not yet Hô Chí Minh. It was 1917 and he was Nguyễn Aí Quốc and we were both young men with clean-shaven faces, the best of friends, and we worked at the Carlton Hotel in London, where I was a dishwasher and he was a pastry cook under the great Escoffier. We were the best of friends and we saw snow for the first time together. This was before we began to work at the hotel. We shoveled snow and Hô would stop for a moment and blow his breath out before him and it would make him smile, to see what was inside him, as if it was the casting of bones to tell the future.

On that first night when he came to me in my house in New Orleans, I finally saw what it was that smelled so sweet and I said to him, "Your hands are covered with sugar."

He looked at them with a kind of sadness.

I have received that look myself in the past week. It is time now for me to see my family, and the friends I have made who are still alive. This is our custom from Vietnam. When you are very old, you put aside a week or two to receive the people of your life so that you can tell one another your feelings, or try at last to understand one another, or simply say good-bye. It is a formal leave-taking, and with good luck you can do this before you have your final illness. I have lived almost a century and perhaps I should have called them all to me sooner, but at last I felt a deep weariness and I said to my oldest daughter that it was time.

They look at me with sadness, some of them. Usually the dull-witted ones, or the insincere ones. But Hô's look was, of course, not dull-witted or insincere. He considered his hands and said, "The glaze. Maestro's glaze."

There was the soft edge of yearning in his voice and I had the thought that perhaps he had come to me for some sort of help. I said to him, "I don't remember. I only washed dishes." As soon as the words were out of my mouth, I decided it was foolish for me to think he had come to ask me about the glaze.

But Hô did not treat me as foolish. He looked at me and shook his head. "It's all right," he said. "I remember the temperature now. Two hundred and thirty degrees, when the sugar is between the large thread stage and the small orb stage. The Maestro was very clear about that and I remember." I knew from his eyes, however, that there was much more that still eluded him. His eyes did not seem to move at all from my face, but there was some little shifting of them, a restlessness that perhaps only I could see, since I was his close friend from the days when the world did not know him.

I am nearly one hundred years old, but I can still read a man's face. Perhaps better than I ever have. I sit in the overstuffed chair in my living room and I receive my visitors and I want these people, even the dull-witted and insincere ones—please excuse an old man's ill temper for calling them that—I want them all to be good with one another. A Vietnamese family is extended as far as the bloodline strings us together, like so many paper lanterns around a village square. And we all give off light together. That's the way it has always been in our culture. But these people who come to visit me have been in America for a long time and there are very strange things going on that I can see in their faces.

None stranger than this morning. I was in my overstuffed chair and with me there were four of the many members of my family: my son-in-law Thắng, a former colonel in the Army of the Republic of Vietnam and one of the insincere ones, sitting on my Castro convertible couch; his youngest son, Lợi, who had come in late, just a few minutes earlier, and had thrown himself down on the couch as well, youngest but a man old enough to have served as a lieutenant under his father as our country fell to the communists more than a decade ago; my daughter Lâm, who is Thắng's wife, hovering behind the both of them and refusing all invitations to sit down; and my oldest daughter, leaning against the door frame, having no doubt just returned from my room, where she had opened the shade that I had closed when I awoke.

It was Thắng who gave me the sad look I have grown accustomed to, and I perhaps seemed to him at that moment a little weak, a little distant. I had stopped listening to the small talk of these people and I had let my eyes half close, though I could still see them clearly and I was very alert. Thắng has a steady face and the quick eyes of a man who is ready to come under fire, but I have always read much more there, in spite of his efforts to show nothing. So after he thought I'd faded from the room, it was with slow eyes, not quick, that he moved to his son and began to speak of the killing.

You should understand that Mr. Nguyễn Bích Lê had been shot dead in our community here in New Orleans just last week. There are many of us Vietnamese living in New Orleans and one man, Mr. Lê, published a little newspaper for all of us. He had recently made the fatal error—though it should not be that in America—of writing that it was time to accept the reality of the communist government in Vietnam and begin to talk with them. We had to work now with those who controlled our country. He said that he remained a patriot to the Republic of Vietnam, and I believed him. If anyone had asked an old man's opinion on this whole matter, I would not have been afraid to say that Mr. Lê was right.

But he was shot dead last week. He was forty-five years old and he had a wife and three children and he was shot as he sat behind the wheel of his Chevrolet pickup truck. I find a detail like that especially moving, that this man was killed in his Chevrolet, which I understand is a strongly American thing. We knew this in Saigon. In Saigon it was very American to own a Chevrolet, just as it was French to own a Citroën.

And Mr. Lê had taken one more step in his trusting embrace of this new culture. He had bought not only a Chevrolet but a Chevrolet pickup truck, which made him not only American but also a man of Louisiana, where there are many pickup trucks. He did not, however, also purchase a gun rack for the back window, another sign of this place. Perhaps it would have been well if he had, for it was through the back window that the bullet was fired. Someone had hidden in the bed of his truck and had killed him from behind in his Chevrolet and the reason for this act was made very clear in a phone call to the newspaper office by a nameless representative of the Vietnamese Party for the Annihilation of Communism and for the National Restoration.

And Thắng, my son-in-law, said to his youngest son, Lợi, "There is no murder weapon." What I saw was a faint lift of his eyebrows as he said this, like he was inviting his son to listen beneath his words. Then he said it again, more slowly, like it was code. "There is no *weapon*." My grandson nodded his head once, a crisp little snap. Then my daughter Lâm said in a very loud voice, with her eyes on me, "That was a terrible thing, the death of Mr. Lê." She nudged her husband and son, and both men turned their faces sharply to me and they looked at me squarely and said, also in very loud voices, "Yes, it was terrible."

I am not deaf, and I closed my eyes further, having seen enough and wanting them to think that their loud talk had not only failed to awake me but had put me more completely to sleep. I did not like to deceive them, however, even though I have already spoken critically of these members of my family. I am a Hòa Hảo Buddhist and I believe in harmony among all living things, especially the members of a Vietnamese family.

After Hô had reassured me, on that first visit, about the temperature needed to heat Maestro Escoffier's glaze, he said, "Đạo, my old friend, do you still follow the path you chose in Paris?"

He meant by this my religion. It was in Paris that I embraced the Buddha and disappointed Hô. We went to France in early 1918, with the war still on, and we lived in the poorest street of the poorest part of the Seventeenth Arrondissement. Number nine, Impasse Compoint, a blind alley with a few crumbling Houses, all but ours rented out for storage. The cobblestones were littered with fallen roof tiles and Quôc and I each had a tiny single room with only an iron bedstead and a crate to sit on. I could see my friend Quôc in the light of the tallow candle and he was dressed in a dark suit and a bowler hat and he looked very foolish. I did not say so, but he knew it himself and he kept seating and reseating the hat and shaking his head very slowly, with a loudly silent anger. This was near the end of our time together, for I was visiting daily with a Buddhist monk and he was drawing me back to the religion of my father. I had run from my father, gone to sea, and that was where I had met Nguyễn Aí Quôc and we had gone to London and to Paris and now my father was calling me back, through a Vietnamese monk I met in the Tuileries.

Quôc, on the other hand, was being called not from his past but from his future. He had rented the dark suit and bowler and he would spend the following weeks in Versailles, walking up and down the mirrored corridors of the Palace trying to gain an audience with Woodrow Wilson. Quôc had eight requests for the Western world concerning Indochina. Simple things. Equal rights, freedom of assembly, freedom of the press.[1] The essential things that he knew Wilson would understand, based as they were on Wilson's own Fourteen Points. And Quôc did not even intend to ask for independence. He wanted Vietnamese representatives in the French Parliament. That was all he would ask. But his bowler made him angry. He wrenched out of the puddle of candlelight, both his hands clutching the bowler, and I heard him muttering in the darkness and I felt that this was a bad sign already, even before he had set foot in Versailles. And as it turned out, he never saw Wilson, or Lloyd George either, or even Clemenceau.[2] But somehow his frustration with his hat was what made me sad, even now, and I reached out from my bedside and said, "Uncle Hô, it's all right."

He was still beside me. This was not an awakening, as you might expect, this was not a dream ending with the bowler in Paris and I awaking to find that Hô was never there. He was still beside my bed, though he was just beyond my outstretched hand and he did not move to me. He smiled on one side of his mouth, a smile full of irony, as if he, too, was thinking about the night he'd tried on his rented clothes. He said, "Do you remember how I worked in Paris?"

I thought about this and I did remember, with the words of his advertisement in the newspaper "La Vie Ouvrière": "If you would like a lifelong memento of your family, have your photos retouched at Nguyễn Aí Quôc's." This was his work in Paris; he retouched photos with a very delicate hand, the same fine hand that Monsieur Escoffier had admired in London. I said, "Yes, I remember."

Hô nodded gravely. "I painted the blush into the cheeks of Frenchmen."

I said, "A lovely portrait in a lovely frame for forty francs," another phrase from his advertisement.

"Forty-five," Hô said.

I thought now of his question that I had not answered. I motioned to the far corner of the room where the prayer table stood. "I still follow the path."

---

[1]These eight requests are spelled out in Nguyễn Aí Quôc's letter and memorandum of June 18, 1919, to the U.S. Secretary of State. Written in French, the original is still preserved in the National Archives in Washington. A translation of the document is available in *Vietnam and America: A Documented History*, edited by Marvin Gettleman, Jane Franklin, Marilyn Young, and H. Bruce Franklin (New York: Grove Atlantic, 1984; 1995), 19–20. [Ed.]

[2]David Lloyd George was then the British prime minister; Georges Clemenceau was the French premier. [Ed.]

He looked and said, "At least you became a Hòa Hảo."

He could tell this from the simplicity of the table. There was only a red cloth upon it and four Chinese characters: Bao Sơ´n Kỳ Hươ´ng. This is the saying of the Hòa Hảos. We follow the teachings of a monk who broke away from the fancy rituals of the other Buddhists. We do not need elaborate pagodas or rituals. The Hôa Hảo believes that the maintenance of our spirits is very simple, and the mystery of joy is simple, too. The four characters mean "A good scent from a strange mountain."

I had always admired the sense of humor of my friend Quôc, so I said, "You never did stop painting the blush into the faces of Westerners."

Hô looked back to me but he did not smile. I was surprised at this but more surprised at my little joke seeming to remind him of his hands. He raised them and studied them and said, "After the heating, what was the surface for the glaze?"

"My old friend," I said, "you worry me now."

But Hô did not seem to hear. He turned away and crossed the room and I knew he was real because he did not vanish from my sight but opened the door and went out and closed the door behind him with a loud click.

I rang for my daughter. She had given me a porcelain bell, and after allowing Hô enough time to go down the stairs and out the front door, if that was where he was headed, I rang the bell, and my daughter, who is a very light sleeper, soon appeared.

"What is it, Father?" she asked with great patience in her voice. She is a good girl. She understands about Vietnamese families and she is a smart girl.

"Please feel the doorknob," I said.

She did so without the slightest hesitation and this was a lovely gesture on her part, a thing that made me wish to rise up and embrace her, though I was very tired and did not move.

"Yes?" she asked after touching the knob.

"Is it sticky?"

She touched it again. "Ever so slightly," she said. "Would you like for me to clean it?"

"In the morning," I said.

She smiled and crossed the room and kissed me on the forehead. She smelled of lavender and fresh bedclothes and there are so many who have gone on before me into the world of spirits and I yearn for them all, yearn to find them all together in a village square, my wife there smelling of lavender and our own sweat, like on a night in Saigon soon after the terrible fighting in 1968 when we finally opened the windows onto the night and there were sounds of bombs falling on the horizon and there was no breeze at all, just the heavy stillness of the time between the dry season and the wet, and Saigon smelled of tar and motorcycle exhaust and cordite but when I opened the window and turned to my wife, the room was full of a wonderful scent, a sweet smell that made her sit up, for she sensed it, too. This was a smell that had nothing to do with flowers but instead reminded us that flowers were always ready to fall into dust, while this smell was as if a gemstone had begun to give off a scent, as if a mountain of emerald had found its own scent. I crossed the room to my wife and we were already old, we had already buried children and grandchildren that we prayed waited for us in that village square at the foot of the strange mountain, but when I came near the bed, she lifted her silk gown and threw it aside and I pressed close to her and our own sweat smelled sweet on that night. I want to be with her in that square and with the rest of those we'd buried, the tiny limbs and the sullen eyes and the gray faces of the puzzled children and the surprised adults and the weary old people who have gone before us, who know the secrets now. And the sweet smell of the glaze on Hô's hands reminds me of others that I would want in the square, the people from the ship, too, the Vietnamese boy from a village near my own who died of a fever in the Indian Ocean and the natives in Dakar who were forced by colonial officials to swim out to our ship in shark-infested waters to secure the moorings and two were killed before our eyes without a French regret. Hô was very moved by this, and I want those men in our square and I want the Frenchman, too, who called Hô "monsieur" for the first time. A man on the dock in Marseilles. Hô spoke of him twice more during our years together and I want that Frenchman there. And, of course, Hô. Was he in the village square even now, waiting? Heating his glaze fondant? My daughter was smoothing my covers around me and the smell of lavender on her was still strong.

"He was in this room," I said to her to explain the sticky doorknob. "Who was?"

But I was very sleepy and I could say no more, though perhaps she would not have understood anyway, in spite of being the smart girl that she is.

The next night I left my light on to watch for Hô's arrival, but I dozed off and he had to wake me. He was sitting in a chair that he'd brought from across the room. He said to me, "Đạo. Wake up, my old friend."

I must have awakened when he pulled the chair near to me, for I heard each of these words. "I am awake," I said. "I was thinking of the poor men who had to swim out to our ship."

"They are already among those I have served," Hô said. "Before I forgot." And he raised his hands and they were still covered with sugar.

I said, "Wasn't it a marble slab?" I had a memory, strangely clear after these many years, as strange as my memory of Hô's Paris business card.

"A marble slab," Hô repeated, puzzled.

"That you poured the heated sugar on."

"Yes." Hô's sweet-smelling hands came forward but they did not quite touch me. I thought to reach out from beneath the covers and take them in my own hands, but Hô leaped up and paced about the room. "The marble slab, moderately oiled. Of course. I am to let the sugar half cool and then use the spatula to move it about in all directions, every bit of it, so that it doesn't harden and form lumps."

I asked, "Have you seen my wife?"

Hô had wandered to the far side of the room, but he turned and crossed back to me at this. "I'm sorry, my friend. I never knew her."

I must have shown some disappointment in my face, for Hô sat down and brought his own face near mine. "I'm sorry," he said. "There are many other people that I must find here."

"Are you very disappointed in me?" I asked. "For not having traveled the road with you?"

"It's very complicated," Hô said softly. "You felt that you'd taken action. I am no longer in a position to question another soul's choice."

"Are you at peace, where you are?" I asked this knowing of his worry over the recipe for the glaze, but I hoped that this was only a minor difficulty in the afterlife, like the natural anticipation of the good cook expecting guests when everything always turns out fine in the end.

But Hô said, "I am not at peace."

"Is Monsieur Escoffier over there?"

"I have not seen him. This has nothing to do with him, directly."

"What is it about?"

"I don't know."

"You won the country. You know that, don't you?"

Hô shrugged. "There are no countries here."

I should have remembered Hô's shrug when I began to see things in the faces of my son-in-law and grandson this morning. But something quickened in me, a suspicion. I kept my eyes shut and laid my head to the side, as if I was fast asleep, encouraging them to talk more.

My daughter said, "This is not the place to speak."

But the men did not regard her. "How?" Lợi asked his father, referring to the missing murder weapon.

"It's best not to know too much," Thắng said.

Then there was a silence. For all the quickness I'd felt at the first suspicion, I was very slow now. In fact, I did think of Hô from that second night. Not his shrug. He had fallen silent for a long time and I had closed my eyes, for the light seemed very bright. I listened to his silence just as I listened to the silence of these two conspirators before me.

And then Hô said, "They were fools, but I can't bring myself to grow angry anymore."

I opened my eyes in the bedroom and the light was off. Hô had turned it off, knowing that it was bothering me. "Who were fools?" I asked.

"We had fought together to throw out the Japanese. I had very good friends among them. I smoked their lovely Salem cigarettes. They had been repressed by colonialists themselves. Did they not know their own history?"

"Do you mean the Americans?"

"There are a million souls here with me, the young men of our country, and they are all dressed in black suits and bowler hats. In the mirrors they are made ten million, a hundred million."

"I chose my path, my dear friend Quốc, so that there might be harmony."

And even with that yearning for harmony I could not overlook what my mind made of what my ears had heard this morning. Thắng was telling Lợi that the murder weapon had been disposed of. Thắng and Lợi both knew the killers, were in sympathy with them, perhaps were part of the killing. The father and son had been airborne rangers and I had several times heard them talk bitterly of the exile of our people. We were fools for trusting the Americans all along, they said. We should have taken matters forward and disposed of the infinitely corrupt Thiệu[3] and done what needed to be done. Whenever they spoke like this in front of me, there was soon a quick exchange of sideways glances at me and then a turn and an apology. "We're sorry, Grandfather. Old times often bring old anger. We are happy our family is living a new life."

I would wave my hand at this, glad to have the peace of the family restored. Glad to turn my face and smell the dogwood tree or even smell the coffee plant across the highway. These things had come to be the new smells of our family. But then a weakness often came upon me. The others would drift away, the men, and perhaps one of my daughters would come to me and stroke my head and not say a word and none of them ever would ask why I was weeping. I would smell the rich blood smells of the afterbirth and I would hold our first son, still slippery in my arms, and there was the smell of dust from the square and the smell of the South China Sea just over the rise of the hill and there was the smell of the blood and of the inner flesh from my wife as my son's own private sea flowed from this woman that I loved, flowed and carried him into the life that would disappear from him so soon. In the afterlife would he stand before me on unsteady child's legs? Would I have to bend low to greet him or would he be a man now?

My grandson said, after the silence had nearly carried me into real sleep, troubled sleep, my grandson Lợi said to his father, "I would be a coward not to know."

Thắng laughed and said, "You have proved yourself no coward."

And I wished then to sleep, I wished to fall asleep and let go of life somewhere in my dreams and seek my village square. I have lived too long, I thought. My daughter was saying, "Are you both mad?" And then she changed her voice, making the words very precise. "Let Grandfather sleep."

So when Hô came tonight for the third time, I wanted to ask his advice. His hands were still covered with sugar and his mind was, as it had been for the past two nights, very much distracted. "There's something still wrong with the glaze," he said to me in the dark, and I pulled

---

[3]Nguyen Van Thieu, a Vietnamese officer in the French colonial army during the 1946–1954 war, was one of the generals who overthrew the Saigon government of Ngo Dinh Diem in 1963. The military junta that took power in 1965 made him chief of state, and he was elected president in 1967. He resigned in April 1975 and fled to Taiwan. [Ed.]

back the covers and swung my legs around to get up. He did not try to stop me, but he did draw back quietly into the shadows.

"I want to pace the room with you," I said. "As we did in Paris, those tiny rooms of ours. We would talk about Marx and about Buddha and I must pace with you now."

"Very well," he said. "Perhaps it will help me remember."

I slipped on my sandals and I stood up and Hô's shadow moved past me, through the spill of streetlight and into the dark near the door. I followed him, smelling the sugar on his hands, first before me and then moving past me as I went on into the darkness he'd just left. I stopped as I turned and I could see Hô outlined before the window and I said, "I believe my son-in-law and grandson are involved in the killing of a man. A political killing."

Hô stayed where he was, a dark shape against the light, and he said nothing and I could not smell his hands from across the room and I smelled only the sourness of Lợi as he laid his head on my shoulder. He was a baby and my daughter Lâm retreated to our balcony window after handing him to me and the boy turned his head and I turned mine to him and I could smell his mother's milk, sour on his breath, he had a sour smell and there was incense burning in the room, jasmine, the smoke of souls, and the boy sighed on my shoulder, and I turned my face away from the smell of him. Thắng was across the room and his eyes were quick to find his wife and he was waiting for her to take the child from me.

"You have never done the political thing," Hô said.

"Is this true?"

"Of course."

I asked, "Are there politics where you are now, my friend?"

I did not see him moving toward me, but the smell of the sugar on his hands grew stronger, very strong, and I felt Hô Chí Minh very close to me, though I could not see him. He was very close and the smell was strong and sweet and it was filling my lungs as if from the inside, as if Hô was passing through my very body, and I heard the door open behind me and then close softly shut.

I moved across the room to the bed. I turned to sit down but I was facing the window, the scattering of a streetlamp on the window like a nova in some far part of the universe. I stepped to the window and touched the reflected light there, wondering if there was a great smell when a star explodes, a great burning smell of gas and dust. Then I closed the shade and slipped into bed, quite gracefully, I felt, I was quite wonderfully graceful, and I lie here now waiting for sleep. Hô is right, of course. I will never say a word about my grandson. And perhaps I will be as restless as Hô when I join him. But that will be all right. He and I will be together again and perhaps we can help each other. I know now what it is that he has forgotten. He has used confectioners' sugar for his glaze fondant and he should be using granulated sugar. I was only a washer of dishes but I did listen carefully when Monsieur Escoffier spoke. I wanted to understand everything. His kitchen was full of such smells that you knew you had to understand everything or you would be incomplete forever.

(1991)

WAYNE KARLIN

For biographical notes on Wayne Karlin, see the introduction to "Moratorium" (page 107). This is the first printing of "The Last VC" as a first-person narrative (a third-person version appeared in Vietnam Generation *in 1991). Karlin's story projects sequels of the Vietnam War into the 1990s and beyond.*

The Last VC

"And what exotic isle d'ye hail from?" the Union soldier asks me.

"Florida, mothafucka," I answer. The other girls crack up. The Union soldier has his act, I have mine. He's black and wears blue. I wear black. Other people dressed in history clothes parade back and forth on the grass. Me there to see the Ghost Tour with the other girls from Ruth's House, daffies, Disturbed Adolescent Females, the counselors think we don't know that label. Our second History Trip. Last week we went to Historic Maryland, saw the Founder's Ship, you can go aboard but nothing happens on it like Pirates of the Caribbean or anything, you just look at the sailors' hammocks and some barrels and go uh-huh. There wasn't much else. Just a visitor center looks like a barn and an inn (the dumb daffies singing we in the inn) and a brick building suppose to be the first capital, only the people looked around and said oh shit, the boonies, and left. That's it. Except for some little roped off places with signs telling you to believe that buried under the dirt is a tavern or a plantation or slave house or whatever they want to say is there. One little sign says trash midden: this window set into the ground like the glass bottom boat, what you see through it is four hundred years of dirty oyster shells and smashed up plates and cups, old chewed on bones. This garbage under everything.

"A saucy wench," the soldier say, winking at me. I give him my hooded, cool look, V.C.W.A.: Viet Cong With an Attitude, then look away, staring around the area. Near the beach this big cannon, around it, on the lawn these pyramid tents, camp fires, a fence made from long sharptop logs, everything blinking into existence as I look like the Star Trek holodeck where you can have any scene you want. For a minute I play with the scene being different for each group or individual that comes in, fitting these holes in their minds. I did a theme park, that's what it would be.

"K-K no saw-see 'xotic eye," Tonetta says to the Union soldier, putting her palms on both sides of her head and pulling up the skin, tilting her eyes up, to show him what I am. "K-K jus a gook."

The other girls giggle, say gook, gook, like a flock of daffies, these disturbed dyslex-iac-assed ducks who fuck up their quack. Tonetta must of picked the gook up from the tape we saw last night, Platoon, Tonetta pushing me to start Physical Confrontation, so I'll lose my privilege level. I'm cool though, smile at her, while I flip Mario mushrooms out of the top of my head. They arc through the air, smack Tonetta, she puffs to nothing with a blip. On I float, to the next obstacle. Which is, Tonetta smiles back at me, rubs and pats her rounded tummy with lovely tenderness. Bam. King Koopa zaps Mario, all five lives blink out. Tonetta came into the program too late for an abortion and now she rubs her big black ripe melon belly in my face every chance she gets, whenever she can't get at me with words or hands. Every chance, all the time, knowing the counselors were giving me BC pills, standing over me and watching me swallow, knowing if they didn't I would swell, put another mutant out in the world.

"Ladies," Louise the counselor says, "Behave. No verbal abuse."

"K-K started it," Tonetta says.

"That's Kiet, please." Louise says.

"Shee-it, whatever," Tonetta says and the other girls laugh. I am pissed at Louise for bringing it up. My name. I was Keisha when I came to Ruth's House from Crownsville Detention, but Larry got hold of my exotic I-land papers and he found Kiet, drew that name up out of the muck at the bottom of the sea, this old bone-memory he wanted me to wrap my new skin around. I had to explain to him that name was all drowned, all shrivelled up and fish nibbling its eye sockets, so I tried being reasonable and said go with K-K, but he tells me no, you need to be proud of your heritage. Meaning the gook part I didn't know fuck-all about, this from Larry, he's black but he's a vet, which is like this other color, something between black and puke green. Anyway in my head I was and still am K-K. Half-a-dink, half-a-splib, my third foster dad used to call me, both his way of saying nigger.

But meanwhile the bana-gana bonana name game further pisses Tonetta off, Tonetta getting her name from the cat in the first or second whatever foster home had tried to keep her. The way she had left that place, Tonetta the kid had hung Tonetta the cat with a lamp cord to which I can relate, but still it wasn't the cat's idea. Animals get fucked over. Like, my last ex-foster father I'd run away from, in Florida? He let me go to Sea World once and I'd smoked some dope before I went and then watched the Flipper Show. Flipper this dolphin who did all of these kissy-ass doggy-type tricks for these people in wet suits that were suppose to be its TV family, though I never saw the sitcom, it was suppose to be famous. I watched and I started to identify and cry from the reefer opening me up to things, lighting up things it touched like a pinball game. Like what do you think that dolphin's real name was? Something like Glub-Click. Or Fuk Luck. Or Kiet. Swimming around. Thinking to itself: what's this Flipper shit?

"Come on, ladies," Larry says. "We'll be late for the Historical Reenactment."

We shuffle towards the tents and an open field. Prisoners in raggy gray and guards, most of them black, with guns, walk around like fools. Inside one tent they pretending to cut off people's arms and legs, white guys in blood-stained aprons, cutting them up so they'll fit into the scene: the daffies going gag and barf. We pass an old black mama wearing a white hood and an apron; she's sitting in front of a kind of small barrel, stirring a stick in it in hard circles. I stop to look, but really to let Larry get in front of me cause Larry's stare is on my skin like dirty spiderwebs, this scared kind of sideway interest in me he got, like always looking at me for something, booby traps, I don't know what.

Stir, stir, stir. Like last night, we were watching the Platoon tape and I have never been able to take this scene where the bad sergeant Tom Berenger blows away this mother and threatens to kill her kid. The other daffies going burn or giggling, they're so bone ignorant, while I'm wondering if this was some history they sucked out of my memory, wondering if that was how someone did my real mom. On the screen all the G.I.'s fighting with each other whether they should waste all the gooks or not and I don't know which side my real dad would have been on, some of the splib soldiers in the movie were on Berenger's side, some on the good sergeant's side, and I was Charlie Sheen, split in half, I could feel them all inside of me. Stir, stir, stir. Willem Dafoe, he played the good sergeant.

So I got out of the room and sat on the couch in the office upstairs, in the dark. And sure enough, Larry came up after me. He went to switch on the light. Leave it off, I told him.

"Bad movie," he said, sitting down next to me, big and heavy and kind of leaning into me, not in any kind of coming on way, but like he was really trying to see me, in the dark, moonlight coming in the window, splitting my face, Keisha blacked out, only the tipped up Kiet eyes showing, like the eyes of his enemy. Or maybe some woman he remembered, some lover he left swollen with a half-a-dink half-a-splib mutant to come swimming after him one day. When I'd run away from Florida to D.C. I ran to the Wall I'd seen on T.V. The Wall took the high yellow out of my face and gave it back to me black, black with the white names scrawled all over it. I had walked along it slowly, letting the names write themselves across my skin, if my daddy's name was there it would have stayed on my skin when I turned from it.

"Who cares?" I said.

Larry shifted his weight, a creaking black heaviness next to me, the sounds of the movie drifting to us in the dark like a Historical Reenactment, screams and explosions and voices from this place where we first become some kind of garbage under each other's life.

"Don't mean nothin'," he'd said, a saying from the war. I remembered Historic Maryland, how he and Louise had herded the daffies into a little room that said Sensurround Theatre over its door. The inside walls were covered with pictures that showed the inside of the old time Founders' Ship. We all sat on benches. The doors shut. The light went out. A voice started whispering, trickling into my brain like Larry's whisper. The movie played on all the walls around me. Creaking ropes. Waves. A voice said: "Hardship and Starvation." I saw flickering people packed into the thin space of a wooden boat, heard their screams and moans, smelled their sour puke, piss, the stink of nuoc mam fish sauce. Sensurround. "The New World," the voice said. The lights flashed on. The movie was over.

Now a park ranger in a Smokey the Bear hat stands in front of us, megaphone in one hand, little casette recorder in the other. Starts talking about how here on this ground under our feet blah-blah was one of the largest prisoner of war camps from the Civil War, thirty thousand Confederate prisoners kept here, exposed to weather and abuse in Maryland. Talks about payback. While he's going on, this ragged ass white prisoner runs away and the sharp black guard I saw before raises his gun, shoots him down. Right. Just like real life. But the prisoner is too ragged to look white. Smeared and gray. A dink. Other place, three soldier guards, black and white, pretend to beat on another prisoner. Smokey the Bear talks about how if you leave out recorders here at night, no one at all around, they pick up these ghost voices he's going to let us listen to. He turns on the recorder. Garble, garble, the voices say.

"They really get into it," I hear Louise whisper to Larry.

"And vice versa," he says.

We walk over to some white tents set up in a row, little fires and pyramids of three old time guns leaning against each other in front of each tent. "Muskets," Louise says, explaining the new world. People are taking pictures of other people, some in the tents. A man is stuffing a little boy into the mouth of the old cannon. The kid's mother is taking pictures.

"Look terrified, Jason," she says. "Stop grinning like a dork."

A group of Union soldiers march by us, led by this roostery old white man. The volunteers are all black and white and waddley, fat bellies pushing out their uniforms, fat old men daffies led by a rooster. They're too old to be soldiers. Or they're like soldiers kept forever in the army for a forever war.

Somebody beats a drum. The military gets into this kind of raggy line, facing me. They point their guns at me. Run, run, run, run, run, the voices on the tape say to me. The rooster pulls out a sword and yells readyaimfire. The flash and the noise split me in half. Blow Kiet away from Keisha. Dink from splib.

I look back at the soldiers. They load and fire again. If I worked here I'd play a VC, I'd squat down near the entrance to a reconstructed straw hootch, rocking my baby, waiting while the tourists, dressed as G.I.'s, came into the village. Then I'd rise up, reveal the weapon hidden under my baby and pretend to blow them away. Then one day I'd forget where I really was. I'd put real bullets in the gun. I'd have a flashback and shoot a tourist, thinking he was a G.I., come to rape and murder. Then, before anyone realized what happened, I'd run. I'd hide in the marshes. I'd be the last VC.

"Fire!" the rooster says.

The soldiers load and fire again.

"Fix bayonets," the rooster says.

The soldiers stick their bayonets on the end of their guns. They point them at me and charge, yelling, their faces twisted.

I back up a little bit from the faces and stumble into Tonetta. She cusses me under her breath and pushes me into the stacked muskets. They fall with a clatter. The military men stop a few feet from me and threaten with their bayonets. I pick up one of the fallen muskets.

"Look terrified, bitch," I say to Tonetta.

"Kiet, put it down," Larry says. He steps in front of me. I see myself reflected in his shades, black-clad, holding a weapon.

"We're here now," I tell him. I point the gun at him.

He looks at me and backs up, funny smile on his face.

"Don't mean nothin'," I tell him.

"For your own safety," the announcer on the P.A. says, "please do not handle the weapons."

The musket is heavier than I thought it would be. I wonder what will happen. Everybody is looking at me. You can't trust the gooks, I'd say. Then I'd pull the trigger. The flash would leap out and hit Larry's chest. Maybe he'd have a heart attack and die, his last sight: my face. Or maybe he'd jump at me. I'd club his hands and turn and run.

Even as I think this, I club down at his hands and I'm turning and then I am running, a part of me still running in my head, but my feet really pounding against the grass. I zig-zag in the direction of the parking lot, holding onto the musket. Behind me, I hear Louise and Larry calling K-K as if to please me, but I keep on running: what's this Flipper shit? If I look over my shoulder now, I know I'll see the two of them and the guards and the prisoners, all chasing me, guns in their hands, their faces red and angry. I know I'll see armies of mad old men, all dressed like soldiers, all chasing after me.

(1995)

The history of American popular music from the mid-1960s on is intertwined with the Vietnam War. As record sales tripled during the 1960s, music became still another battleground. Songs were a prominent feature of the antiwar movement and a shaping element of its associated counterculture, an inspiration for prowar sentiment, and an essential part of GI culture in Vietnam. In more subtle ways, the war exerted deep and lasting influences on the form and content of popular music.

The explicit meaning of the lyrics of antiwar and prowar songs is only the most obvious part of the story. Songs have varied meanings, which multiply as people relate them to their own lives. GIs in Vietnam turned Peter, Paul, and Mary's "Puff the Magic Dragon," an apparently innocent childhood fantasy sung by leading antiwar folksingers, into both the nickname of the deadliest of all gunships and a sly celebration of marijuana. Rock songs, with their often intentionally covert, oblique, ambiguous, and malleable meanings, acquired multiple layers of significance, often contradictory. American soldiers in Vietnam heard the Animals' "We Gotta Get Out of This Place," although it was released back in 1965 and was by a British group, as an expression of their deepest wish—thus inducing the Armed Forces

Vietnam Network to ban the song.[1] Filmmaker Oliver Stone tried to explain what Jim Morrison and the Doors had meant to him:

> I first heard Jim and the Doors when I was in Vietnam, in the infantry, in '67. I had never heard this kind of music before. There was a sense of liberation about it. "Break on Through" was to me an anthem. The lyrics of his songs spoke of life and death, fear and Eros, all those good things infantrymen want to be in touch with. Right away I identified with Jim. He became one of my heroes.[2]

But when Stone attempted to express this vision in his 1991 movie *The Doors*, it was greeted with a cacophony of dissenting voices arguing with him and each other about the significance of the group, its music, and its era.

Even more problematic is the "meaning" of music's nonverbal sounds. Antiwar messages were most explicit first in folk songs and later in rock, whereas prowar messages were most explicit in country and western. Yet the electronic technology intrinsic to the war's distinctive weaponry was the electronic technology intrinsic to rock, while the instruments of country and western were closest to those of folk music.

Some of the first organized activities against the Vietnam War centered on the singing of songs at concerts, in clubs, and on campuses. Phil Ochs was one of the earliest and most persistent antiwar folksingers, with "Talking Vietnam Blues" (1964), "Draft Dodger Rag" (1964), "I Ain't Marching Anymore" (1964), "White Boots Marching in a Yellow Land" (1965), and "The War Is Over" (1968). Pete Seeger, blacklisted from radio and television from 1950 to 1967 because of his refusal to testify before the House Un-American Activities Committee, relentlessly toured the country with his antiwar songs, such as "Waist Deep in the Big Muddy" (1963), "Bring Them Home" (1966), and "Ballad of the Fort Hood Three" (1966), one of the first songs to celebrate the war resisters inside the army. In 1967, Seeger was finally invited to make a TV appearance (on the *Smothers Brothers Comedy Hour*), but when he sang "Waist Deep in the Big Muddy" it was cut from the show by Columbia Broadcasting Systems executives. Like Seeger, Tom Paxton sang from the soldiers' point of view in songs such as "Lyndon Johnson Told the Nation" (1965) and "Talking Vietnam Pot Luck Blues" (1968).

Three of the most influential antiwar singers were Joan Baez, the most prominent vocalist of the pacifist wing of the movement; Malvina Reynolds, whose "Napalm" (1965) contributed to the antinapalm campaign; and Barbara Dane, who coordinated the September 1965 Sing-In for Peace at New York's Carnegie Hall, where sixty performers sang for hours and then led a predawn march against the war. Dane and Irwin Silber published *The Vietnam Songbook* (1969), a historic antiwar collection. Dane also toured the GI coffeehouses set up by the movement at army bases across the country, leading to her 1970 album *FTA! Songs of the GI Resistance Sung by Barbara Dane with Active-Duty GIs*, recorded with GI choruses at Fort Hood, Fort Benning, and Fort Bragg.

The virtual anthem of the antiwar movement was Country Joe McDonald's 1964 "I-Feel-Like-I'm-Fixin'-to-Die Rag," performed frequently at early rallies by his Berkeley group Country Joe and the Fish, which led half a million people in an exuberant rendition at Woodstock in 1969. Like no other song, it expressed the vitality of the movement, its core rebelliousness, and its sense of the Vietnam War as a national exercise in grotesque absurdity. The song also formed part of the transition from folk to rock.

Another element in this transition, flowing from the Beat movement of the 1950s, came from one of the first underground rock groups, the Fugs, led by Greenwich Village beatnik poets Ed Sanders and Tuli Kupferberg. The Fugs' 1965 "Kill for Peace" proclaimed that "the only Gook an American can trust" is one "what got his yellow head bust" and ended with shouts of "Kill kill kill!"

Prowar responses came swiftly, especially on country-and-western radio stations, which seemed to thrive on the war (by 1970 there were more than six hundred country music stations, compared with only about eighty in 1961).[3] Staples of the country stations in 1965 and 1966 were Kris Kristofferson's "Viet Nam Blues" sung by Dave Dudley, Johnny Wright's "Hello Vietnam," Maybelle Carter's "I Told Them What You're Fighting For," Stonewall Jackson's "The Minutemen Are Turning in Their Grave," Pat Boone's "Wish You Were Here, Buddy," and songs from *Country Music Goes to War*, a 1966 album by Charlie Moore and Bill Napier. By the time the two most memorable songs in this genre appeared, Merle Haggard's "Okie from Muskogee" (1969) and "The Fightin' Side of Me" (1970), support for the war had become so suspect that Haggard never mentioned it but restricted himself to attacking what middle America regarded as the more outré aspects of the antiwar movement—draft card burning, long hair, beads, and "runnin' down our country." The following year, however, came an unabashedly jingoist chant by C Company, featuring Terry Nelson, "Battle Hymn of Lt. Calley"—a celebration of the man courtmartialed for leading the 1968 mass rape and massacre at My Lai. It sold more than a million copies.

The most spectacular success among the prowar songs was "The Ballad of the Green Berets," a martial tune sung by Green Beret staff sergeant Barry Sadler, written by Sadler with assistance from Robin Moore, author of the best-selling novel *The Green Berets*. Top executives of RCA, a major military contractor, decided on all-out promotion of this first recording by Sadler, and they were soon aided by the Pentagon, other corporations, and prowar columnists.[4] With Sadler singing the song on many prime-time TV shows, "The Ballad of the Green Berets" was *Billboard*'s number-one hit for five weeks in early 1966, became the top-selling single record for the year, and ended up as the theme song for John Wayne's 1968 movie *The Green Berets*.

On the other hand, most radio and TV stations refused to air antiwar songs until 1968, when popular sentiment swung dramatically against the war after the Tet Offensive of late January and February. There was then also an instant proliferation of available records, as major recording companies began to see antiwar songs as commercial products with a big profit potential.[5] Explicit antiwar hit songs that year included Bob Seger's "2+2=?," the Byrds' "Draft Morning," the Doors' "Unknown Soldier," and "Sky Pilot," by the British group Eric Burdon and the Animals.

In 1969, John Lennon's "Give Peace a Chance" promoted the antiwar movement's pacifist wing, which was being challenged by more radical elements among the millions opposing the war. The anticapitalist politics of these forces were expressed in a 1969 song far more popular then and now—Creedence Clearwater Revival's "Fortunate Son," which sold over a million copies, as did their "Who'll Stop the Rain," released in 1970 along with still another anti-Vietnam War song, "Run Through the Jungle." Meanwhile, Lennon himself was shifting to the more radical positions, as shown in his 1971 hits "Power to the People" and "Imagine."

In 1970 and 1971, Motown/Tamla/Gordy Records joined in and cashed in with such black antiwar hits as Edwin Starr's powerful "War," which was the nation's best-selling single for three weeks in

1970 (and still airs on rock stations), and "Stop the War Now" (1971); the Temptations' "Ball of Confusion" (1970); and Marvin Gaye's "What's Going On" (1971). Freda Payne's hauntingly beautiful "Bring the Boys Home" (1971), which sold over a million copies, expressed the anguish of African Americans over the "soldiers that are dying/ trying to get home" and ended with a demand to know "What they doing over there now/When we need them over here now."[6]

The year 1970 also saw protesting students shot down and killed on campuses, by soldiers at Kent State University in Ohio and three days later by police at Jackson State, a black college in Mississippi. The Steve Miller Band commemorated these events in "Jackson-Kent Blues." But the song born from Kent State that was to endure for decades was "Ohio," by Crosby, Stills, Nash, and Young.

As the Vietnam War became part of cultural memory in the 1980s, it continued to bubble up in popular music. New songs emerged, often about veterans, such as Billy Joel's "Goodnight Saigon" (1982), Charlie Daniels's "Still in Saigon" (1982), the Grateful Dead's "My Brother Esau" (1985), and, most memorably, Bruce Springsteen's "Born in the U.S.A."

From this abundance of popular music, five songs have been chosen here as exemplars. The first two—"I-Feel-Like-I'm-Fixin'-to-Die Rag" and "The Ballad of the Green Berets"—are the most militant and popular songs on opposite sides of the musical war over the war. The other three—"Fortunate Son," "Ohio," and "Born in the U.S.A"—were selected because all, still popular and frequently played on classical rock and other stations, are part of how the Vietnam War lives in American culture in the dawn of the twenty-first century.

Notes

1. "Radio Was the Only Thing the GI's Had," *Newsweek* (January 4, 1988), 50.

2. Paul Chutkow, "Oliver Stone and 'The Doors': Obsession Meets the Obsessed," *New York Times*, February 24, 1991. On the multiple meanings of songs among the GIs, see David E. James, "The Vietnam War and American Music," in *The Vietnam War and American Culture*, edited by John Carlos Rowe and Rick Berg (New York: Columbia University Press, 1991), 226–254, and Philip Beidler, *American Literature and the Experience of Vietnam* (Athens, GA: University of Georgia Press, 1982), 13–15, 23–24. My analysis is indebted to James; Beidler; R. Serge Denisoff, *Songs of Protest, War & Peace* (Santa Barbara, CA: American Bibliographic Center—Clio Press, 1973), xv–xvi; Terry H. Anderson, "American Popular Music and the War in Vietnam," *Peace and Change*,

COUNTRY JOE McDONALD

After a three-year hitch in the U.S. Navy and a year at Los Angeles City College, twenty-one-year-old Joe McDonald moved to Berkeley in 1963 and soon began writing protest songs. He made his first record in 1964, when he wrote what was destined to become the song sometimes called the anthem of the antiwar movement, "I-Feel-Like-I'm-Fixin'-to-Die Rag." The following year he and guitarist Barry Melton formed Country Joe and the Fish, a jug band that went electric in 1966 and soon became an adored feature attraction at antiwar rallies. The song was recorded in 1967 (Vanguard 79266).

The Fish broke up in 1970 and briefly regrouped for their Reunion record in 1977. McDonald has continued to remain active in Vietnam veterans' and ecology causes.

I-Feel-Like-I'm-Fixin'-to-Die Rag

Come on all of you big strong men,
Uncle Sam needs your help again;
He's got himself in a terrible jam
Way down yonder in Viet Nam;
So put down your books and pick up a gun,
We're gonna have a whole lot of fun!

Chorus:

And it's one two three,
What are we fighting for?
Don't ask me, I don't give a damn,
Next stop is Vietnam.
And it's five six seven,
Open up the Pearly Gates;
There ain't no time to wonder why,
Whoopie—we're all gonna die!

Come on, generals, let's move fast,
Your big chance has come at last;
Now you can go out and get those Reds,
The only good Commie is one that's dead;

You know that peace can only be won,
When we've blown 'em all to kingdom come!

(Chorus)

Come on, Wall Street, don't be slow,
Why, man, this is war Au-go-go;
There's plenty good money to be made,
Supplying the army with tools of the trade;
Just hope and pray if they drop the Bomb,
They drop it on the Viet Cong!

(Chorus)

Come on, mothers, throughout the land,
Pack your boys off to Vietnam;
Come on, fathers, don't hesitate,
Send your sons off before it's too late;
You can be the first one on your block
To have your boy come home in a box.

(Chorus)

(1965)

BARRY SADLER with ROBIN MOORE

Born in Carlsbad, New Mexico, in 1940, Barry Sadler enlisted in the U.S. Air Force at the age of seventeen. After a few months of civilian life in 1962, he joined the army and won assignment to the Special Forces. In 1963 he composed the first version of "The Ballad of the Green Berets" and performed it in San Antonio clubs.

Sent to Vietnam in December 1964, Sadler participated in the unofficial conflict and the campaign to "Win the Hearts and Minds" of the Vietnamese in the countryside. In his 1967 autobiography, I'm a Lucky One, *he describes some of the action:*

> *Because they were shelters for the Viet Cong, we had to destroy some villages in South Vietnam in 1965. Snipers in Cam Re [sic], just two miles from the Da Nang air base, for example, shot so many Marines there that the village had to be burned (106).*

In May, Sadler was scraped by a punji stick and his leg became so seriously infected that he was sent back home.

Meanwhile, "The Ballad of the Green Berets" was already being used effectively by the army, while Sadler was trying to sell it commercially. After he posed for the cover of the paperback edition of Robin Moore's best-seller, The Green Berets, *which came out in November, Moore helped him rewrite the song and establish contact with RCA. When Sadler recorded the song in December, in attendance were top executives of RCA, which provided a fifteen-piece orchestra, a male chorus, and an all-out promotional blitz. Although this was Sadler's first record, articles about it appeared in* Time, Life, Newsweek, *and* Variety; *UPI and AP both did feature stories; and he was invited to sing the song on many TV and radio programs, including the* Ed Sullivan Show, *the* Jimmy Dean Show, *and* Martha Raye's Hollywood Palace. *"The Ballad of the Green Berets" thus became one of the most effective prowar vehicles of 1966 and ultimately sold more than seven million copies.*

Sadler had one other hit song, "The 'A' Team," also in 1966, and then faded into obscurity. He returned to the news briefly in 1978, when he was involved in the shooting death of songwriter Lee Emerson Bellamy in Nashville, and again in 1981, when he was charged with, but acquitted of, the nonfatal shooting of a former business associate. Meanwhile, Sadler had launched a successful second career as a novelist of military adventure with the publication of Casca: The Eternal Mercenary *in 1979, eventually selling over two million copies of a dozen such novels, including the Casca series. In 1988, while training Nicaraguan contras in Guatemala, he was shot in the head by an unknown assailant. After suffering paralysis and brain damage, he died from the wound a year later.*

The Ballad of the Green Berets

Fighting soldiers from the sky,
Fearless men who jump and die.
Men who mean just what they say,
The brave men of The Green Beret.

Silver wings upon their chests,
These are men, America's best.
One hundred men we'll test today,
But only three win The Green Beret.

Trained to live off nature's land,
Trained to combat, hand to hand.
Men who fight by night and day,
Courage take from The Green Beret.

Silver wings upon their chests,
These are men, America's best.
One hundred men we'll test today,
But only three win The Green Beret.

Back at home a young wife waits
Her Green Beret has met his fate.
He has died for those oppressed,
Leaving her this last request.

Put silver wings on my son's chest,
Make him one of America's best.
He'll be a man they'll test one day.
Have him win The Green Beret.

(1966)

CROSBY, STILLS, NASH and YOUNG /
NEIL YOUNG

In mid-1969, Neil Young, former songwriter, lead guitarist, and vocalist for Buffalo Springfield, joined the group of Crosby, Stills, and Nash, formed a few months earlier by three other prominent songwriters, guitarists, and singers (David Crosby from the Byrds; Steve Sills from Buffalo Springfield; and Graham Nash from the Hollies). In August 1969, the new quartet made a spectacular appearance at Woodstock.

On April 29, 1970, the nation began to learn that a massive U.S. invasion of Cambodia was in progress. Angry protest demonstrations erupted across the country, especially on college campuses, and steadily increased in size and militance. On May 1, President Richard Nixon denounced the protesters as "bums." On the night of May 3, police and Ohio National Guard troops arrested sixty-nine students at Kent State University and herded hundreds of others into their dormitories, bayonetting one young woman in the process. The following day, the soldiers, ordered to disperse a new demonstration, promiscuously fired M-1 rifles, .45 caliber pistols, and a shotgun into the crowd, killing four young people and wounding nine. President Nixon's own Commission on Campus Unrest later reported that the nation had been "driven to use the weapons of war upon its youth."

By July, Neil Young's song "Ohio," performed by Crosby, Stills, Nash, and Young, had become a national best-seller, staying in the top forty for seven weeks. No other cultural work has so enduringly memorialized the massacre at Kent State or so successfully expressed what millions of Americans felt at the time.

Ohio

Tin soldiers and Nixon's coming
We're finally on our own
This summer I hear the drumming
Four dead in Ohio.

Got to get down to it
Soldiers are gunning us down,
Should have been done long ago
What if you knew her and

Found her dead on the ground
How can you run when you know?

Repeat

Tin soldiers and Nixon's coming,
And we're finally on our own.
This summer I hear the drumming
Four dead in Ohio.
Four dead in Ohio.
Four dead in Ohio.
How many more?
Four dead in Ohio.

(1970)

CREEDENCE CLEARWATER REVIVAL / JOHN FOGERTY

Widely regarded as one of the great rock and roll groups, Creedence Clearwater Revival originated in 1959 when three fourteen-year-old junior high school students in El Cerrito, California—John Fogerty, Stu Cook, and Doug Clifford—formed the Three Velvets. After the addition of John's older brother Tom, the group took the name Creedence Clearwater Revival in early 1968. From then through 1970, they released one top hit album and single after another, including three extremely popular anti-Vietnam-War songs: "Fortunate Son," "Who'll Stop the Rain," and "Run Through the Jungle." John Fogerty was the group's songwriter, lead guitarist, and lead vocalist, played harmonica and keyboards, and also did production. Typical of Fogerty's songs, "Fortunate Son" expresses Creedence's working-class sensibility, an unusual feature in rock of that period.

Fortunate Son

Some folks are born made to wave the flag,
Ooh, they're red, white and blue.
And when the band plays "Hail to the chief,"
They point the cannon right at you.
 It ain't me, it ain't me—
 I ain't no senator's son.
 It ain't me, it ain't me;—
 I ain't no fortunate one.
Some folks are born silver spoon in hand,
Lord, don't they help themselves.
But when the tax man comes to the door,
Lord, the house looks like a rummage sale.
 It ain't me, it ain't me—
 I ain't no millionaire's son.
 It ain't me, it ain't me;—
 I ain't no fortunate one.
Some folks inherit star spangled eyes,
Ooh, they send you down to war.
And when you ask them, "How much should we give?"

They only answer More! more! more!
It ain't me, it ain't me—
I ain't no military son.
It ain't me, it ain't me;—
I ain't no fortunate one.
It ain't me, it ain't me;—
I ain't no fortunate one.

(1969)

BRUCE SPRINGSTEEN

Born in Freehold, New Jersey, Bruce Springsteen joined his first band in 1963 at the age of fourteen and was soon writing songs. For twelve years he sang, wrote, played, and toured tirelessly, gathering a devoted regional follow-ing, mainly in New Jersey. Although his first two albums, both released in 1973—Greetings from Asbury Park, New Jersey *and* The Wild, the Innocent and the E-Street Shuffle—*were commercial failures, several of his songs on these records became hits for other singers. Springsteen finally achieved national recognition with his best-selling 1975 album* Born to Run, *and since then he has become one of the most admired and popular stars of rock and roll.*

Springsteen's characteristic songs express both the plight and the vitality of urban and suburban American working-class youth, trapped in blighted towns and decaying social structures, seeking escape from an enveloping dark-ness on highways, in love, and in music. He has generously supported social causes, especially those of Vietnam veterans, the antinuclear movement, work-ers, and the poor. In 1994 he received the Academy Award for the best origi-nal song, "Streets of Philadelphia," his profoundly moving theme song of the 1993 movie Philadelphia, *about a victim of AIDS.*

"Born in the U.S.A.," title song of his 1984 album, was so immensely popular that both presidential candidates that year—Ronald Reagan and Walter Mondale—invoked the song in their speeches and tried to identify themselves with its populist creator. But Springsteen spurned the politics of both their parties, preferring to donate money at each stop on his 1984–1985 Born in the U.S.A. *tour to local homeless shelters, soup kitchens, and unions. The ballad itself dramatizes the working-class veteran during and after the Vietnam War as an embodiment of Springsteen's most characteristic themes and images.*

Born in the U.S.A.

Born down in a dead man's town
The first kick I took was when I hit the ground
You end up like a dog that's been beat too much
Till you spend half your life just covering up
    Born in the U.S.A.

I was born in the U.S.A.
I was born in the U.S.A.
Born in the U.S.A.
Got in a little hometown jam so they put a rifle in my hand
Sent me off to a foreign land to go and kill the yellow man
Born in the U.S.A.
I was born in the U.S.A.
I was born in the U.S.A.
I was born in the U.S.A.
Born in the U.S.A.
Come back home to the refinery
Hiring man says "son if it was up to me"
Went down to see my V.A. man
He said "son don't you understand now"

Had a brother at Khe Sanh fighting off the Viet Cong
They're still there, he's all gone
He had a woman he loved in Saigon
I got a picture of him in her arms now

Down in the shadow of the penitentiary
Out by the gas fires of the refinery
I'm ten years burning down the road
Nowhere to run ain't got nowhere to go
Born in the U.S.A.
I was born in the U.S.A.
Born in the U.S.A.
I'm a long gone Daddy in the U.S.A.
Born in the U.S.A.
Born in the U.S.A.
Born in the U.S.A.
I'm a cool rocking Daddy in the U.S.A.

(1984)

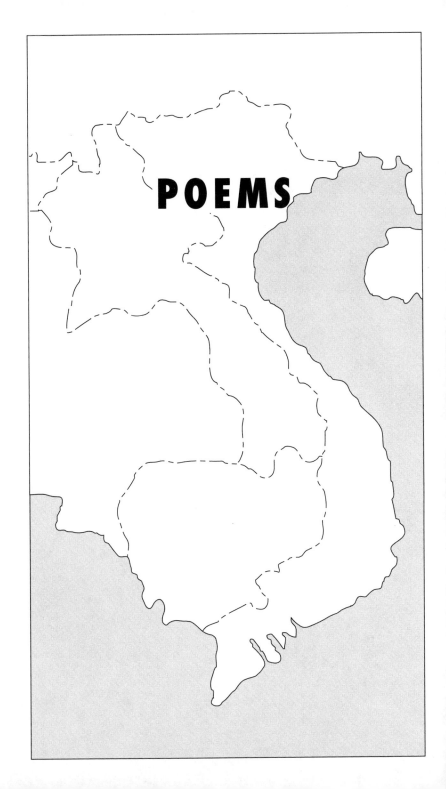

POEMS

Poetry is a universal human activity. All societies throughout the world—including preliterate tribes, agricultural colonies, industrial nation states, and financial empires—continually create poems. Moreover, in all societies the majority of people crave poetry, cherish it, and engage with it daily. If these statements do not seem to apply to modern America, that is because many Americans have come to accept a false dichotomy, inculcated throughout the educational system, between "poetry," which is presented as the property of a cultural elite, and the songs and other poems they enjoy, which are implicitly defined as cultural rubbish beneath notice. So when asked "Do you like poetry?" the great majority of American students will say no—and then later the same day turn on the radio or stereo to listen to poetry being sung, as most poetry usually has been.

Strangely, the Vietnam War has helped to erode the barriers between "poetry" as literature of the elite and poetry as relished by the masses. The songs discussed in the previous section have been a major source of this erosion. Another has been a most unforeseen product of the war: the written poetry created by its veterans, which has gradually come to public notice in the 1970s, 1980s, and 1990s.

During the war, written poetry played a role dramatically different from that in any other American war. Rather than bards celebrating the nation and some great national cause, eulogizing its heroes and the glories of combat, America's poets were almost unanimously anguished and angry protesters against the war. Their collective voice cried out in a historic 1967 anthology, *Where Is Vietnam? American Poets Respond,* edited by Walter Lowenfels, with antiwar poems by eighty-seven contributors, including many of the most distinguished figures in American poetry. Looking back on this volume, however, one can sense how radically the poetry by Vietnam veterans has since then transformed the sensibilities and expectations of Vietnam War poetry, shaping it into a more accessible art form.

When Jan Barry, one of the earliest of these veteran poets and a leading figure in promulgating veteran poetry, speaks to students in Vietnam courses, he describes his working-class youth in upstate New York when "the last thing I would ever think of being was a poet." What he wanted to be was a career man in the U.S. Army, and as for poetry, that was something just "for sissies." But what he, along with many others, discovered in Vietnam was that "poetry saved my life." He then explains how poetry, by expressing what seemed most inexpressible about the war, has led many to healing and "sanity."

The poetry of these veterans thus also has become part of American society's quest to comprehend the war and itself in the decades after the war. There is nothing especially unusual about a war producing poetry while combat rages. But certainly no other American war has generated poetry that keeps developing and intensifying, postwar decade after decade.

The two collections that introduced the achievement of the poet-veterans were *Winning Hearts and Minds: War Poems by Vietnam Veterans,* edited by Larry Rottmann, Jan Barry, and Basil T. Paquet (1972), and *Demilitarized Zones: Veterans after Vietnam,* edited by Jan Barry and W. D. Ehrhart (1976). W. D. Ehrhart's *Carrying the Darkness: The Poetry of the Vietnam War* has been the defining contemporary anthology since its original publication in 1985. The major omission in these three volumes, the poetry by women veterans, was corrected in 1991 by *Visions of War, Dreams of Peace: Writings of Women in the Vietnam War,* edited by Lynda Van Devanter and Joan A. Furey. Rottmann, Barry, Paquet, Ehrhart, Van Devanter, and Furey are among the poet-veterans represented in the following selections.

One of the startling discoveries made by some Americans serving in Vietnam was the universality of poetry among the Vietnamese people. John Balaban went back to Vietnam after his alternative service to wander around the countryside during the war collecting poems from common people. Combat veteran Bruce Weigl has recently edited and translated with Thanh T. Nguyen, *Poems from Captured Documents*, a bilingual compilation of poems found in diaries retrieved from dead or captured enemy soldiers. Larry Rottmann, almost killed in combat, has gone back to Vietnam to collect the stories of hundreds of Vietnamese on the other side, turning them into poems, many included in his multimedia show, *Voices from the Ho Chi Minh Trail*. It's almost as though poetry were a contagious Vietnamese disease infecting American veterans.

Perhaps the most piercing expression of this contact between American veterans and the role of poetry among the Vietnamese people they were warring against comes in Rottmann's poem "A Porter on the Trail," his rendition of a story told to him on a recent trip by a porter as familiar with Walt Whitman as he was with *Kim Van Kieu*, the classic Vietnamese epic.

A Porter on the Trail

In 1966,
when I started down the trail,
I carried a copy of
The Poems of Walt Whitman
in my rucksack.

I am not a learned man,
and I know only
two poems by heart:
"Kim Van Kieu,"[1] and
"Song of Myself."

I would read as I walked
from North to South, and back.
I could share "Kieu" with anyone,
but had less opportunity to discuss "Song"
with my comrades.

---

[1] "Kim Van Kieu"—the classic Vietnamese epic poem of selflessness. [Rottmann's note.]

Still, I drew strength from Whitman's poetry,
and optimism too. He wrote,
"All goes onward and outward . . ." and
"To die is different from what anyone supposed,
and luckier."

I wondered
how a nation
that gave birth to Walt Whitman
could also produce
napalm and Agent Orange.

He wrote,
"This is the grass that grows
wherever the land is and the water is,
This is the common air
that bathes the globe."

One day, near Khe Sanh, we captured a GI.
I was excited, and asked him about
"Song of Myself."
But the American said
he'd never heard of Walt Whitman.

(1990)

PHILIP APPLEMAN

Philip Appleman has had a distinguished career as a poet, novelist, and cultural historian. Born in 1926, he served during World War II in the U.S. Army Air Corps. In 1955 he began teaching at Indiana University, from which he is now Distinguished Professor of English Emeritus. He has published numerous volumes of poetry from Kites on a Windy Day *(1967) to* Let There Be Light *(1991) and several novels from the trenchant antiwar* In the Twelfth Year of the War *(1970) to* Apes and Angels *(1989). Appleman now lives on Long Island with his wife, Marjorie Appleman, a poet and playwright.*

Peace with Honor

Solitudinem faciunt, pacem appellant.[1]

1

The outer provinces are never secure:
our Legions hold the camps, their orders
do not embrace the minds
and hearts of barbarians. So, when the late-
late news reported the outlandish
screams in that distant temple,
the great bronze Victory toppled,
red stains in the sea, corpses
stranded by the ebb tide—all of that,
and only four hundred
armed men at the garrison—why,
of course it had to come, the massacre,
the plundering.

2

It was the decade's scandal at home,
the humiliation, the Eagles gone.
Senators put on grim faces
and gossiped over Bloody

---

[1]"They make a wasteland and call it peace." [Ed.]

Marys—what laureled head would roll for this?
Reports from the field
were cabled not to the Emperor but
to the Joint Chiefs, to filter
through at last, edited
and heavy with conclusions: the traitor,
they revealed, was not in uniform,
the treason was our own permissiveness;
in sterner times our Fathers would not
have suffered such dishonor.
We nodded: yes, they knew,
the Chiefs, what ancient virtue was.
The twilight shudders of matrons
seasoned our resolution. Somber, we took
a fourth martini, wandered to the couches,
the tables rich with peacocks' tongues,
and nodded,
nodded, waiting.

3

They sent our toughest
veterans, the Ninth Legion, the Fourteenth,
the Hundred-and-First, their orders un-
ambiguous: teach the barbarians respect.
Our marshals chose the spot: a steep defile
covering the rear, our regular troops drawn close,
light-armed auxiliaries at their flanks,
cavalry massed on the wings.
The enemy seethed everywhere, like a field
of wind-blown grasses.
There were the usual
harangues, the native leaders boasting
their vast numbers, screaming
freedom or death;
our generals, with that subtle sneer
they learn at the Academy,
pointing only to the Eagles on their tall shafts—
and every man remembered
the shame of Eagles fallen, comrades' bones

unburied: there was that curious thing,
men in bronze and steel, weeping.
And then the charge, the clash of arms,
cavalry with lances fixed, the glorious
victory: a hundred thousand tons of TNT
vaporized their villages, their forests were
defoliated, farmland poisoned forever,
the ditches full of screaming children,
target-practice for our infantry.
The land, once green and graceful,
running with pleasant streams in the rich brown earth,
was charred and gutted—not even a bird
would sing there again.

4

A glorious victory, of course,
but in a larger sense, a mandatory act
of justice: the general peace
was kept, the larger order held; peasants
for a thousand leagues around
are working their mules again.
Our prisoners and Eagles all returned,
we dine at the rich tables,
thinking of the Sunday games,
thinking of anything but rebellion—thinking
the honor of Empire
is saved.

                                                              (1976)

JOHN BALABAN

Born in Philadelphia in 1943, John Balaban became a Quaker at age sixteen. While a graduate student in English at Harvard, he voluntarily gave up his student deferment to become a conscientious objector in Vietnam, working first for the International Voluntary Services and then for the Committee of Responsibility to Save War-Injured Children from 1967 to 1969. He became fluent in Vietnamese, and returned to Vietnam in 1971, where, with the war still raging, he traveled alone around the countryside for a year collecting folk poems he later translated in Vietnamese Folk Poetry *(1974) and* Ca Dao Vietnam: A Bilingual Anthology of Vietnamese Folk Poetry *(1980). He describes his experiences in Vietnam in his own poetry, in his award-winning 1977 essay "Doing Good," and in his eloquent memoir,* Remembering Heaven's Face: A Moral Witness in Vietnam *(1991).*

Widely acknowledged as one of the finest poets of the war, Balaban is also the author of the well-received novel Coming Down Again, *set in Southeast Asia in 1974. He has won numerous fellowships and awards, including the Lamont Prize from the Academy of American Poets for* After Our War *(1974) and the Pushcart Prize for his poem "For the Missing in Action," collected in* Words for My Daughter *(1991). Balaban is currently a professor of English and the director of the master of fine arts program at the University of Miami.*

After Our War

After our war, the dismembered bits
—all those pierced eyes, ear slivers, jaw splinters,
gouged lips, odd tibias, skin flaps, and toes—
came squinting, wobbling, jabbering back.
The genitals, of course, were the most bizarre,
inching along roads like glowworms and slugs.
The living wanted them back but good as new.
The dead, of course, had no use for them.
And the ghosts, the tens of thousands of abandoned souls
who had appeared like swamp fog in the city streets,
on the evening altars, and on doorsills of cratered homes,
also had no use for the scraps and bits

because, in their opinion, they looked good without them.
Since all things naturally return to their source,
these snags and tatters arrived, with immigrant uncertainty,
in the United States. It was almost home.
So, now, one can sometimes see a friend or a famous man talking
with an extra pair of lips glued and yammering on his cheek,
and this is why handshakes are often unpleasant,
why it is better, sometimes, not to look another in the eye,
why, at your daughter's breast thickens a hard keloidal scar.
After the war, with such Cheshire cats grinning in our trees,
will the ancient tales still tell us new truths?
Will the myriad world surrender new metaphor?
After our war, how will love speak?

(1982)

Along the Mekong

1   CROSSING ON THE MEKONG FERRY, READING THE AUGUST 14 *NEW YORKER*

Near mud-tide mangrove swamps, under the drilling sun,
the glossy cover, styled green print, struck the eye:
trumpet-burst yellow blossoms, grapevine leaves,
—nasturtiums or pumpkin flowers? They twined
in tangles by our cottage in Pennsylvania.
Inside, another article by Thomas Whiteside.
2,4,5-T, teratogenicity in births;
South Vietnam 1/7th defoliated; residue
in rivers, foods, and mother's milk.
With a scientific turn of mind I can understand
that malformations in lab mice may not occur in children
but when, last week, I ushered hare-lipped, tusk-toothed kids
to surgery in Saigon, I wondered, what did they drink
that I have drunk. What dioxin, picloram, arsenic[1]

---

[1]Three chemical agents used to defoliate Vietnamese forests and crops were Agents Orange, White, and Blue. Fifty percent of Agent Orange was the herbicide 2,4,5-T, which contained dioxin, the chemical with the worst teratogenicity (causing birth defects) in laboratory animals. Picloram was a poisonous substance used as an active ingredient in Agent White. One of the main active ingredients in Agent Blue was a form of arsenic. [Ed.]

have knitted in my cells, in my wife now carrying
our first child. Pigs were squealing in a truck.
Through the slats, I saw one lather the foam in its mouth.

2   RIVER MARKET

Under the tattered umbrellas, piles of live eels
sliding in flat tin pans. Catfish flip for air.
Sunfish, gutted and gilled, cheek plates snipped.
Baskets of ginger roots, ginseng, and garlic cloves;
pails of shallots, chives, green citrons. Rice grain
in pyramids. Pig halves knotted with mushy fat.
Beef haunches hung from fist-size hooks. Sorcerers,
palmists, and, under a tarp: thick incense, candles.
Why, a reporter, or a cook, could write this poem
if he had learned dictation. But what if I said,
simply suggested, that all this blood fleck,
muscle rot, earth root and earth leaf, scraps
of glittery scales, fine white grains, fast talk,
gut grime, crab claws, bright light, sweetest smells
—Said: a human self; a mirror held up before.

3   WAITING FOR A BOAT TO CROSS BACK

Slouched on a bench under some shade,
I overhear that two men shot each other on the street,
and I watch turkey cocks drag cornstalk fans
like mad, rivaling kings in Kabuki
sweeping huge sleeve and brocaded train.
The drab hens huddle, beak to beak,
in queenly boredom of rhetoric and murder.
A mottled cur with a grease-paint grin
laps up fish scales and red, saw-toothed gills
gutted from panfish at the river's edge.

                                                      (1974)

In Celebration of Spring

Our Asian war is over; others have begun.
Our elders, who tried to mortgage lies,
are disgraced, or dead, and already
the brokers are picking their pockets
for the keys and the credit cards.

In delta swamp in a united Vietnam,
a Marine with a bullfrog for a face,
rots in equatorial heat. An eel
slides through the cage of his bared ribs.
At night, on the old battlefields, ghosts,
like patches of fog, lurk into villages
to maunder on doorsills of cratered homes,
while all across the U.S.A.
the wounded walk about and wonder where to go.

And today, in the simmer of lyric sunlight,
the chrysalis pulses in its mushy cocoon,
under the bark on a gnarled root of an elm.
In the brilliant creek, a minnow flashes
delirious with gnats. The turtle's heart
quickens its taps in the arm bank sludge.
As she chases a frisbee spinning in sunlight,
a girl's breasts bounce full and strong;
a boy's stomach, as he turns, is flat and strong.

Swear by the locust, by dragonflies on ferns,
by the minnow's flash, the tremble of a breast,
by the new earth spongy under our feet:
that as we grow old, we will not grow evil,
that although our garden seeps with sewage,
and our elders think it's up for auction—swear
by this dazzle that does not wish to leave us—
that we will be keepers of a garden, nonetheless.

(1976)

News Update

for Erhart, Gitelson, Flynn and Stone,
happily dead and gone.

Well, here I am in the *Centre Daily Times*
back to back with the page one refugees
fleeing the crossfire, pirates, starvation.
Familiar faces. We followed them
through defoliated forests, cratered fields,
past the blasted water buffalo,
the shredded tree lines, the human head
dropped on the dusty road, eyes open,
the dusty road which called you all to death.

One skims the memory like a moviola
editing out the candidate shots: Sean Flynn
dropping his camera and grabbing a gun
to muster the charge and retake the hill.
"That boy," the black corporal said,
"do in real life what his daddy do in movies."
Dana Stone, in an odd moment of mercy,
sneaking off from Green Beret assassins
to the boy they left for dead in the jungle.
Afraid of the pistol's report, Stone shut his eyes
and collapsed the kid's throat with a bayonet.
Or, Erhart, sitting on his motorcycle
smiling and stoned in the Free Strike Zone
as he filmed the ammo explosion at Lai Khe.
It wasn't just a macho game. Marie-Laure de Decker
photographed the man aflame on the public lawn.
She wept and shook and cranked her Pentax
until a cop smashed it to the street. Then
there was the girl returned from captivity
with a steel comb fashioned from a melted-down tank,
or some such cliché, and engraved: "To Sandra
From the People's Fifth Battalion, Best Wishes."

Christ, most of them are long dead. Tim Page
wobbles around with a steel plate in his head.
Gitelson roamed the Delta in cut-away blue jeans

like a hippy Johnny Appleseed with a burlap sack
full of seeds and mimeographed tips for farmers
until we pulled him from the canal. His brains
leaked on my hands and knee. Or me, yours truly,
agape in the Burn Ward in Danang, a quonset hut,
a half a garbage can that smelled like Burger King,
listening to whimpers and nitrate fizzing on flesh
in a silence that simmered like a fly in a wound.

And here I am, ten years later,
written up in the local small town press
for popping a loud-mouth punk in the choppers.
Oh, big sighs. Windy sighs. And ghostly laughter.

(1982)

For Mrs. Cam,
Whose Name Means "Printed Silk"

> *The ancients liked to write of natural beauty.*
> –Ho Chi Minh, "On Reading *The Ten Thousand Poets*"

In Vietnam, poets brushed on printed silk
those poems about clouds, mountains, and love.
But now their poems are cased in steel.

You lived beyond the Pass of Clouds
along the Perfume River, in Hué,
whose name means "lily."

The war has blown away your past.
No poems can call it back.
How does one start over?

You raise your kids in southern California;
run a key punch from 9:00 to 5:00,
and walk the beach each evening,

marveling at curls broken bare in crushed shells,
at the sheen and cracks of laved, salted wood,
at the pearling blues of rock-stuck mussels

all broken, all beautiful, accidents
which remind you of your life, lost friends
and pieces of poems which made you whole.

In tidal pools, the pipers wade
on twiggy legs, stabbing for starfish
with scissoring, poking, needle bills.

The wide Pacific flares in sunset.
Somewhere over there was once your home.
You study the things which start from scratch.

Nicely like a pearl is a poem
begun with an accidental speck
from the ocean of the actual.

A grain, a grit, which once admitted
irritates the mantle of thought
and coats itself in lacquers of the mind.

(1982)

Mau Than

A Poem at Tet for To Lai Chanh

1

Friend, the Old Man that was last year
has had his teeth kicked in; in tears
he spat back blood and bone, and died.
Pielike, the moon has carved the skies
a year's worth to the eve. It is Tet
as I sit musing at your doorstep,
as the yellowed leaves scratch and clutter.
The garden you dug and plotted
before they drafted you, is now
stony, dry, and wanting a trowel.
"For my wife," you said, taking a plum,
but the day never came nor will it come
to bring your bride from Saigon.
Still the boats fetch stone, painted eyes on

their prows, plowing the banana-green river;
and neighbor children splash and shiver
where junks wait to unload their rock.
But shutters locked, the door of your house is locked.

2

A year it was of barbarities
each heaped on the other like stones
on a man stoned to death.
One counts the ears on the GI's belt.
Market meats come wrapped in wrappers
displaying Viet Cong disemboweled.
Cries come scattering like shot.
You heard them and I heard them.
The blessed unmaimed may have too.
So many go stumping about.
The night you left I turned off Hoa Binh
and saw a mined jeep, the charred family.
A Vietnamese cop minded the wreckage;
his gold buck teeth were shining
in a smile like a bright brass whistle.
Can you tell me how the Americans,
officers and men, on the night of
the mortaring, in the retching hospital,
could snap flash photos of the girl whose
vagina was gouged out by mortar fragments?
One day we followed in a cortege
of mourners, among the mourners, slowing walking,
hearing the clop of the monk's knocking stick.

3

If there were peace, this river would be
a peaceful place. Here at your door
thoughts arrive like rainwater, dotting,
overspreading a dry, porous rock.
In a feathery drizzle, a man and wife
are fishing the river. The sidling waves
slap at her oar as she ladles the water

and fixes the boat with bored precision.
His taut wrists fling whirring weights;
the flying net swallows a circle of fish.
His ear wears a raindrop like a jewel.
Here at evening one might be as quiet
as the rain blowing faintly off
the eaves of a rice boat sliding home.
Coming to this evening
after a rain, I found a buff bird
perched in the silvery-green branches
of a water-shedding spruce. It was
perched like a peaceful thought. Then
I thought of the Book of Luke and, indeed,
of the nobleman who began a sojourn
to find a kingdom and return.

4

Out of the night, wounded
with the gibberings of dogs,
wheezing with the squeaks of rats,
out of the night, its belly split
by jet whine and mortar blast,
scissored by the claws of children,
street sleepers, ripping their way free
from cocoons of mosquito netting
to flee the rupturing bursts
and the air dancing with razors
—out, I came, to safe haven.
Nor looked, nor asked further.
Who would? What more? I said.
I said: Feed and bathe me.
In Japan I climbed Mt. Hiei in midwinter.
The deer snuffled my mittens.
The monkeys came to beg.
I met Moses meeting God in the clouds.
The cold wind cleared my soul.
The mountain was hidden in mist. Friend,
I am back to gather the blood in a cup.

                                    (1974)

JAN BARRY

Born in upstate New York in 1943, Jan Barry enlisted for an intended career in the U.S. Army in 1962. By the end of that year he found himself stationed at Nha Trang, Vietnam, where he spent almost a year as a radio technician in the army's Eighteenth Aviation Company. As he has written about these early stages (in Al Santoli's Everything We Had*), it took many months to realize "we were supporting a police state" and "that* we *were the war": "If we wanted to go out and chase people around and shoot at them and get them to shoot back at us, we had a war going on. If we didn't do that, they left us alone."*

Barry was ordered back to the United States because he had been appointed a cadet at West Point. In 1964 he resigned his appointment to West Point, and in 1967 he became one of the cofounders of Vietnam Veterans Against the War.

Together with Larry Rottmann and Basil Paquet, Barry collected the anthology Winning Hearts and Minds: War Poems by Vietnam Veterans. *Unable to find a commercial publisher, the three veterans formed their own publisher, 1st Casualty Press, which issued that seminal volume in 1972. Within six months they had sold out their first printing of ten thousand copies, and eventually were able to have McGraw-Hill reissue the book.* Winning Hearts and Minds *sold a total of forty-five thousand copies, an almost unheard of figure for a volume of poetry. Along with W. D. Ehrhart, Barry coedited the successor volume,* Demilitarized Zones: Veterans after Vietnam *(1976), and he later edited* Peace Is Our Profession: Poems of War Protest *(1981).*

Barry's subsequent books of his own poems include Veterans Day *(1982),* War Baby *(1983),* Morning in Moscow *(1987), and* Cold War Blues *(1988). He now lives in Montclair, New Jersey, where he has been working as a journalist.*

In the Footsteps of Genghis Khan

There, where a French legionnaire
once walked patrol
around the flightline perimeter of the airfield
at Nha Trang,
ten years later I walked,

an American expeditionary forces
soldier on night guard duty
at Nha Trang,
occupied even earlier,
twenty years before
(a year more than my nineteen),
by the Japanese.

Unhaunted by the ghosts, living and dead
among us
in the red tile-roofed French barracks
or listening in on the old Japanese telephone line
to Saigon,
we went about our military duties,
setting up special forces headquarters
where once a French Foreign Legion post had been,
oblivious to the irony
of Americans walking in the footsteps
of Genghis Khan.

Unencumbered by history,
our own or that of 13th-century Mongol armies[1]
long since fled or buried
by the Vietnamese,
in Nha Trang, in 1962, we just did our jobs:
replacing kepis with berets, "Ah so!" with "Gawd!
Damn!"

(1972)

Thap Ba

The old Cham temple of Thap Ba,
the locals say it's a thousand years
old,
older than this stilted Anglo-
Saxon language I use

---

[1] Having conquered China and much of Europe, Mongol armies led by Kublai Khan were defeated in three massive attempts to invade Vietnam between 1257 and 1287. [Ed.]

Older they say than the use
of bullets, ballots, and the printing
press
older than the airplane and the bomb
older than napalm

was hit yesterday by a twenty-year-old
helicopter pilot
fresh from the states
Who found it more ecstatic than
the firing range
for testing his guns

(1972)

LADY BORTON

Lady Borton's service in Vietnam began in 1969 when the American Friends Service Committee assigned her to work in Quang Ngai. In the early 1980s she worked with Vietnamese boat people in Malaysia. During the late 1980s and early 1990s, she lived and labored with a family in a Vietnam village. Between 1993 and 1995, she served as field director for the American Friends Service Committee in Hanoi. She is the author of Sensing the Enemy: An American Woman Among the Boat People of Vietnam *(1984),* After Sorrow: An American Among the Vietnamese *(1995), and books for children including* Fat Chance! *(1993) and* Junk Pile *(1995).*

A Boom, A Billow

While waiting for a plane to DaNang
I watched American bombers a mile away.
The uninvolved objectivity with which I stared at the sleek jets,
their wings sloping back in fiercely powerful lines,
confused and disturbed me.
The jets swooped down,
then up quickly,
to circle and swoop once more.
A boom.
A billow of dark gray smoke.
Napalm.

That afternoon I met a boy at the Helgoland hospital ship.
He sought me out because I came from Quang Ngai,
his ancestral home.
He had no nose,
only two holes in the middle of his face.
His mouth was off to the side.
One eye was gone;
there was a hollow in his forehead above the other.
All his face was shiny red scar tissue.
Most of the rest of his body was the same.

One hand was partly usable,
the fingers of the other,
soldered to his wrist.
Napalm.

(1973)

RON CARTER

Born in 1941, Ron Carter was in the U.S. Navy from 1963 to 1967 and served as communications officer aboard the destroyer escort USS Bronstein *in the South China Sea in 1966. He now teaches English at Rappahannock Community College in Virginia.*

Vietnam Dream

Sometimes still   in my deepest sleep.
Someone orders "Turn"   and we turn.
The ship swings lazily   like a log
Caught in a current,   and
The guns point to something I cannot see.

Then someone orders "Fire"   and we fire,
The first shell spinning out of the barrel
Like a football   thrown for a gain.
Where it touches the earth
Smoke puffs   like popcorn.

And then   all is still.
I have been ready now for years,
Waiting the order that never came.
The sneer of cold command,
The Jews lined up at the bathhouse door.

I cannot see beyond that moment
Whether   shaking my head   I turn
Away   or whether   when someone
orders
"Kill"   I kill.

(1976)

HORACE COLEMAN

Born in 1943 in Dayton, Ohio, Horace Coleman as a paperboy in his African-American neighborhood went "down all those streets named after Civil War battles and into the park to talk to the WW I vets who were still coughing up their lungs from that distant war." With "all those experimental planes" from nearby Wright-Patterson Air Force Base flying overhead, it seemed natural to him to join Air Force ROTC at Bowling Green University. In 1965 he began his five years as an air force officer, where "they made me an intercept director/air traffic controller—a sky cop directing vehicles and death." During his year (1967–1968) at Saigon's Tan San Nhut, the base was attacked as part of the Tet Offensive.

After leaving the air force in 1970, Coleman received a master of fine arts degree in creative writing from Bowling Green and taught for seven years at Ohio University, which he calls "my 'penance' for Nam." Since then he has worked mainly as a technical writer, and he now lives in Huntington Beach, California.

Coleman published a volume of poetry, Between a Rock & a Hard Place, *in 1977. His poems have appeared in* American Poetry Review, Kansas Quarterly, New Letters, Viet Nam Generation, In These Times, *and such anthologies as* From A to Z: 200 Contemporary American Poets, Speak Easy, Speak Free, Demilitarized Zones, Peace Is Our Profession, Unaccustomed Mercy, Leaving the Bough: 50 American Poets for the 80s, *and* Carrying the Darkness, *which took its title from his most frequently reprinted poem, "OK Corral East / Brothers in the Nam." This is the first publication of "The Adrenaline Junkie and 'The Daily Emergency,'" the poem most immediately involved with his job in Vietnam.*

OK Corral East
Brothers in the Nam

Sgt. Christopher and I are
in Khanh Hoi　　　　down by the docks
in the Blues Bar where the women
are brown and there is no Saigon Tea
making our nightly HIT—'Hore Inspection Tour
watching the black　　　　digging night sights
　　　soul sounds　　　　getting tight

the grunts in the corner raise undisturbed hell
the timid white MP has his freckles pale
as he walks past the high dude
in the doorway in his lavender jump-suit
to remind the mama-san quietly of curfew
      he chokes on the weed smoke
      he sees nothing his color here
and he fingers his army rosary   his .45

but this is not Cleveland or Chicago
he can't cringe any one here and our
gazes like brown punji stakes impale him

we have all killed something recently
we know who owns the night
and carry darkness with us

                      (1977)

The Adrenaline Junkie
and "The Daily Emergency"

Once my heart actually stops as, loaded down with air traffic at Tan
    Son Nhut
(the world's busiest airport then where a radar screen looks like
bagless pop corn puffing up behind a microwave's glass door),
I just happen to see a phosphorous dot streaking toward one that's four
    F4Cs
so I snap out the flight leader's call sign saying "Traffic, 12
    o'clock, 5 miles,
closing fast!" and the pilot is scared because I hear him say
"Pull up, fast!" and grunt as he pulls Gs and I wait to see
if you can hear a midair crash through a closed mike but I only hear
    "Thanks"
so I know it's close and how could sixteen airborne eyes
and four airborne radars (with a maximum range of 200 miles)
miss that stuff. And then there's monsoon when it rains sideways and
the VC love to play and some ding bat calls up complaining (bragging)
    about

he's "Bingo Fuel!" and requests an immediate hand-off to RAPCON
with a straight-in approach (meaning he's going to flame out
and crash *his* flight within five minutes)
and I say, coolly—because that's the only way to deal with it—
"Roger, understand, you're third" and he officiously says
"No, *you* don't understand, Paris Control, *Bingo* Fuel!" So I tell him
"Squawk flash" and "Radar contact, you're *third*"! adding
(so he knows what the score is) "The flight in front of you has three
     minutes
and the flight in front of *it* has two" meaning "Don't bug me with the
     small stuff—
you're two minutes fat, back off and let me work."
Or, it could be the perfect rescue when I've got top cover
over the crash site and choppers on the way but
the guy was so low when he ejected that his chute doesn't open fully
and it's body bag time or the jet jockey who gets shot down and
I'm trying to get a fix on him so I can tell the chopper where to go—
I *know* where the chopper can go—and I say "Look, stay in one place
so I can steer these guys in" and he breathlessly says
"They're chasing me" and I give him a 'zipper'
(two mike clicks in acknowledgment) because there's nothing to say.
And a pilot from Thailand, late for an awards ceremony at the O Club
(The TOOM—Tan Son Nhut Officers Open Mess),
can't wait for me to work him through the traffic so
he leaves my frequency to crack up close to Bien Hoa.
Winning a new piece of tin for his tomb and they want to court
martial
me because if there's a dead pilot and a live controller
guess who's guilty?—until the tapes save me—
or how about the guy pinned under the skid of a Huey
with a dead engine and I can't find a Chinook to get the damn thing off
     him
before he's pushed face down into the mud so Hueys keep landing
and they and their crews muscle the thing off him—wonder if he made
     it?—   .
and *another* F102 has *another* AC/DC power failure
and some guy comes back with his instruments out and the canopy blown
and every piece of dirt and paper that ever was in that bird is
     blinding him,

swirling around the cockpit at Mach .5, as I try to make an intercept
     with a chase
plane so it can match speeds and get him on the ground, mostly in one
     piece,
And B52s are going to drop some fresh-from-Guam bombs
on an Army field headquarters and SAC doesn't talk to peons
and I've seen two out of three kids born—a real rush—
and sex is nice too, booze, going too fast and some drugs (so I hear)
but there's nothing like trying to get a chopper load of guns and ammo
to the American Embassy during Tet when the VC are downstairs
     blowing doors
and grunts are throwing hand guns through the windows
to staff racing to the roof and I'm giving directions
to a chopper from the boonies with an old street map, assisted by
a Saigonese sergeant (who only speaks broken English and my
Vietnamese isn't too tough), and I can't even see the bird on radar
he's so close and so low but he finally finds the place—and gets shot
     down
and I wonder "Who's got the guns now? Who's hurt or hit?"
and say to myself "Well, this is *another* fine mess you've gotten us
     into."

(1995)

FRANK A. CROSS, JR.

Frank A. Cross, Jr., was born in 1945 in Lancaster, California. Drafted into the army, he served in 1969–1970 as sergeant and radioman in a recon platoon of the Americal Division in Quang Ngai province, Vietnam, where he received a Bronze Star, Army Commendation Medal, and Combat Infantryman's Badge. He now farms cotton, corn, and wheat near Chowchilla, California, in the San Joaquin Valley.

Gliding Baskets

"Eight Six Foxtrot—Eight Six Foxtrot.
This is One One Zulu. Over."

> The woman in blue
> Carried the weight swiftly, with grace,
> Her face hidden by her
> Conical rice straw hat.

"One One Zulu—this is Eight Six Foxtrot. Go."
"Roger Eight Six. I have Fire Mission.
Dink in the open, Grid: Bravo Sierra,
Five Six Niner, Four Six Five, Range:
Three thousand, Proximity: Eight hundred. Over"

> The two heavy baskets
> Balanced on tips
> Of the springing Chogi stick
> Glided close to the hard smooth path.

"Read back, One One Zulu."
"Roger Copy, Eight Six."
"Shot, on the way, wait."
"Shot out, Eight Six."

> A sighing 105 mm round slides through its
>   parabola
> Then the explosive tearing at the steel which
>   surrounds it,

247

And the shrapnel catches the gliding baskets,
And they crumple with the woman in blue.

near An Trang
August 14, 1969
(1972)

Rice Will Grow Again

We were walking
On the dikes
Like damn fools—
Steppin over dud rounds.

Mitch was steppin light
When he saw the farmer.
    The farmer:
    With black shirt
    And shorts.
    Up to his knees
    In the muck
    Rice shoots in one hand,
    The other darting
    Under the water
    And into the muck
    To plant new life.

Mitch saw the farmer's hand
Going down again
With another
        Shoot
          But the hand
          Never came up
          Again—
After Mitch
Ripped the farmer up the middle
With a burst of sixteen.
We passed the farmer,
As we walked
Along the dike, and
I saw rice shoots

Still clutched in one hand.
He bubbled strange words
Through the blood
In his mouth.
Bong, the scout,
Told us the farmer
Said:
> "Damn you
> The rice will
> Grow again!"

Sometimes,
On dark nights
In Kansas,
The farmer comes to
> Mitch's bed:
And plants rice shoots
> all around.
>> (1976)

W. D. EHRHART

Born in rural Pennsylvania, W. D. Ehrhart enlisted in the U.S. Marines right out of high school at the age of seventeen in 1966. He served in the marines until 1969, including a year (1967–1968) in Vietnam, where as a sergeant in combat intelligence he was wounded in the battle to retake the city of Hue during the Tet Offensive.

Ehrhart is one of the foremost figures in the literature of the Vietnam War. He ranks among the three or four most distinguished American poets to emerge from the war, steadily winning more followers with the regular appearance of new chapbooks and collections since 1975. He is surely the preeminent anthologist of Vietnam War poetry; beginning as coeditor of Demilitarized Zones: Veterans after Vietnam *(1976), he has since largely defined the canon of Vietnam War poetry in his widely adopted* Carrying the Darkness *(1985, 1989) and* Unaccustomed Mercy: Soldier-Poets of the Vietnam War *(1989). His nonfiction includes* In the Shadow of Vietnam: Essays, 1977–1991 *(1991) and a series of autobiographical memoirs unsurpassed among veterans' prose writings in their combination of personal experience and historical understanding:* Vietnam-Perkasie: A Combat Marine Memoir *(1983);* Passing Time: Memoir of a Vietnam Veteran Against the War *(1986, 1989);* Going Back: An Ex-Marine Returns to Vietnam *(1987); and* Busted: A Vietnam Veteran in Nixon's America *(1995).*

Ehrhart is now a full-time writer and lecturer. He lives in Philadelphia with his wife, Leela, and their daughter, Anne.

Guerrilla War

It's practically impossible
to tell civilians
from the Vietcong.

Nobody wears uniforms.
They all talk
the same language,
(and you couldn't understand them
even if they didn't).

They tape grenades
inside their clothes,

and carry satchel charges
in their market baskets.

Even their women fight
and young boys,
and girls.

It's practically impossible
to tell civilians
from the Vietcong;

after a while,
you quit trying.

(1975)

Making the Children Behave

Do they think of me now
in those strange Asian villages
where nothing ever seemed
quite human
but myself
and my few grim friends
moving through them
hunched
in lines?

When they tell stories to their children
of the evil
that awaits misbehavior,
is it me they conjure?

(1975)

To Those Who Have Gone Home Tired

After the streets fall silent
After the bruises and the tear-gassed eyes are healed
After the consensus has returned
After the memories of Kent and My Lai and Hiroshima

lose their power
and their connections with each other
and the sweaters labeled Made In Taiwan
After the last American dies in Canada
and the last Korean in prison
and the last Indian at Pine Ridge
After the last whale is emptied from the sea
and the last leopard emptied from its skin
and the last drop of blood refined by Exxon
After the last iron door clangs shut
behind the last conscience
and the last loaf of bread is hammered into bullets
and the bullets
scattered among the hungry

What answers will you find
What armor will protect you
when your children ask you
Why?

(1976)

The Invasion of Grenada

I didn't want a monument,
not even one as sober as that
vast black wall of broken lives.
I didn't want a postage stamp.
I didn't want a road beside the Delaware
River with a sign proclaiming:
"Vietnam Veterans Memorial Highway."

What I wanted was a simple recognition
of the limits of our power as a nation
to inflict our will on others.
What I wanted was an understanding
that the world is neither black-and-white
nor ours.
What I wanted was an end to monuments.
But no one
ever asked me what I wanted.

(1984)

For Mrs. Na

Cu Chi District
December 1985

I always told myself,
if I ever got the chance to go back,
I'd never say "I'm sorry"
to anyone. Christ,

those guys I saw on television once:
sitting in Hanoi, the cameras rolling,
crying, blubbering
all over the place. Sure,

I'm sorry. I never meant
to do the things I did.
But that was nearly twenty years ago:
enough's enough.

If I ever go back
I always told myself,
I'll hold my head steady
and look them in the eye.

But here I am at last—
and here you are.
And you lost five sons in the war.
And you haven't any left.

And I'm staring at my hands
and eating tears,
trying to think of something else to say
besides "I'm sorry."

(1990)

Guns

Again we pass that field
green artillery piece squatting
by the Legion Post on Chelten Avenue,
its ugly little pointed snout
ranged against my daughter's school.

"Did you ever use a gun
like that?" my daughter asks,
and I say, "No, but others did.
I used a smaller gun. A rifle."
She knows I've been to war.

"That's dumb," she says,
and I say, "Yes," and nod
because it was, and nod again
because she doesn't know.
How do you tell a four-year-old

what steel can do to flesh?
How vivid do you dare to get?
How to explain a world where men
kill other men deliberately
and call it love of country?

Just eighteen, I killed
a ten-year-old. I didn't know.
He spins across the marketplace
all shattered chest, all eyes and arms.
Do I tell her that? Not yet,

though one day I will have
no choice except to tell her
or to send her into the world
wide-eyed and ignorant.
The boy spins across the years

till he lands in a heap
in another war in another place
where yet another generation
is rudely about to discover
what their fathers never told them.

                                          (1993)

JOAN A. FUREY

Joan A. Furey was born in Brooklyn in 1947. From 1969 to 1970, she served with the Army Nurse Corps in the Intensive Care Unit of the Seventy-first Evacuation Hospital in Pleiku in the central highlands of Vietnam near the Cambodian border. She wrote her first poem in Vietnam after the death of one of her patients. Furey was coeditor of the groundbreaking anthology Visions of War, Dreams of Peace: Writings of Women in the Vietnam War, *and is currently director of the Center for Women Veterans of the Department of Veterans Affairs.*

Camouflage

The green fatigues seem to be everywhere.
Half watching the evening news
I notice,
every story seems to contain men
and even
an occasional woman
In green fatigues or camouflage,
jungle garb
designed for war.
And then, I remember
the children.
The children,
I've seen them so often
at the malls and in the halls
and most recently
at the Wall.
In their green fatigues and camouflage shorts
with matching shirts and hats and socks.
And I think,
I wore green fatigues once.
Bloused over boots and hats and badges
a uniform of war
soiled by blood and mud
and dirt and death.
Unable to be washed clean of

the lingering reminders,
one piece remains
hanging in my closet
near the back.
I can no longer don it
and parade
Nor can I discard it.

So it remains in my closet,
near the back
for me a last reminder
of the devastation
encountered by a youthful mind
who now shuns
thoughts of war
and dreams of peace;
haunted
by the children
playing innocently and walking
by the Wall.
The irony of my vision
stated by tears
for the young men and women
whose last statement
is engraved
in brilliant black granite reflecting
the children
walking by in camouflage sunsuits
smiling.
Unknowingly and unaware
little boys and girls
playing.
While I shudder
at thoughts
of lessons left unlearned.

                                        (1991)

SHARON GRANT

Sharon Grant graduated from the College of Nursing, University of South-western Louisiana, in 1969. She served with the Army Nurse Corps in Vietnam from 1970 to 1971, working in the Emergency Room at the Seventy-first Evacuation Hospital in Pleiku and on postsurgical floors at the Sixty-seventh Evacuation Hospital in Qui Nhon. She currently lives in Calgary, Alberta, Canada.

The Best Act in Pleiku,
No One Under 18 Admitted

I kissed a Negro, trying to breathe life into him.
When I was a child—back in the world—
the drinking fountains said, "White Only."
His cold mouth tasted of dirt and marijuana.
He died and I put away the things of a child.

Once upon a time there was a handsome, blond soldier.
I grabbed at flesh
combing out bits of shrapnel and bits of bone
with bare fingers.

A virgin undressed men,
touched them in public.
By the time I bedded a man
who didn't smell like mud and burned flesh
He made love and I made jokes.

(1985)

STEVE HASSETT

Born in 1946, Steve Hassett dropped out of college in his sophomore year in early 1966 to enlist as a paratrooper. He spent a year in Vietnam as a machine gunner and squad leader with the First Air Cavalry and then a year in Korea as an intelligence analyst. He was a founding member of the Buffalo chapter of Vietnam Veterans Against the War in 1970 and testified at the first war crimes hearings in Washington that December. After working a variety of blue-collar and white-collar jobs, he went to law school in 1977 and became a legal services attorney specializing in family and veterans law. He is currently an assistant attorney general for the State of Washington doing child protection cases. He is married and has an adult daughter.

And What Would You Do, Ma

And what would you do, ma,
if eight of your sons step
out of the TV and begin
killing chickens and burning
hooches in the living room,
stepping on booby traps
and dying in the kitchen,
beating your husband and
taking him and shooting
skag and forgetting in
the bathroom?

would you lock up your daughter?

would you stash the apple pie?

would you change channels?

(1976)

Christmas

The Hessian in his last letter home
said in part
"they are all rebels here

258

who will not stand to fight
but each time fade before us
as water into sand . . .

the children beg in their rude hamlets

the women stare with hate

the men flee into the barrens at our approach
to lay in ambush

some talk of desertion . . .
were it not for the hatred
they bear us, more would do so

There is no glory here.
Tell Hals he must evade the Prince's levy
through exile or deformity

Winter is hard upon us. On the morrow we enter
Trenton. There we rest till the New Year. . . ."

(1976)

JUNE JORDAN

Born in Harlem, New York, in 1936, June Jordan has published twenty volumes of poetry and prose, has written plays and song lyrics, and received, among many other awards, the 1970 Prix de Rome for Environmental Design. Her writings have been translated into six languages.

All of Jordan's work, from her much admired poetry and essays to her lectures and black-consciousness children's books, is distinguished by a remarkably unified synthesis of personal experience, passionate commitment to social justice, and the highest aesthetic standards. She is currently professor of Afro-American studies and women's studies at the University of California, Berkeley.

To My Sister, Ethel Ennis, Who Sang "The Star-Spangled Banner" at the Second Inauguration of Richard Milhous Nixon, January 20, 1973

gave proof through the night
that our flag was still there

on his 47th inauguration of the killer king
my sister
what is this song
you have chosen to sing?

and the rockets' red glare
the bombs bursting in air
my sister
what is your song to a flag?

to the twelve days of Christmas
bombing when the homicidal holiday shit tore forth
pouring from the b-52 bowels loose over Hanoi and the skin
and the agonized the blown limbs the blinded eyes the
silence of the children dead on the street and the
incinerated homes and Bach Mai Hospital blasted and
drowned by the military the American shit vomit
dropping down death and burying the lives the people

of the new burial ground
under the flag

for the second coronation of the killer king
what is this song
you have chosen to sing?

my sister
when will it come finally clear
in the rockets' red glare
my sister
after the ceremonial guns salute the ceremonial rifles
saluting the ceremonial cannons that burst forth a choking
smoke to celebrate murder
will it be clear
in that red that bloody red glare
my sister
that glare of murder and atrocity/atrocities
of power
strangling every program
to protect and feed and educate and heal and house
the people

(talking about *us*/you and me talking
about *us*)

when will it be clear to you

which night will curse out the stars with the blood
of the flag
for you
for enough of us

by the rockets' red glare
when will it be clear
that the flag that this flag is still there is still
here and will smother you smother your songs

can you see
my sister
is the night
and the red glaring blood clear at last
say

can you see
my sister

say you can see
my sister

and sing no more of war
                    (1973)

PENNY KETTLEWELL

Born in Midland, Texas, Penny Kettlewell served two tours as a U.S. Army nurse in Vietnam, the first at the Sixty-seventh Evacuation Hospital in Qui Nhon from September 1967 to September 1968, the second at the Twenty-fourth Evacuation Hospital in Long Binh from May 1970 to May 1971. She has left nursing and now lives "in the wilds of northern Minnesota."

The Coffee Room Soldier

I walked into the coffee room for a cup of brew.
The push was over and I needed energy to re-group
for the next assault on our forces
and on my senses.

I initially stepped casually over his shattered body
laid out, unbagged, on the coffee room floor
out of the way
thinking, where would I find them next:
in my bed?

I turned with cup in hand and ascertained the damage.
His chest wall blown away, exposing his internal organs
An anatomical drawing.
Dispassionately I assessed his wounds
and sipped from my cup.

I then saw his face
that of a child in terror
and only hours ago
alive as I
or maybe I was dead as he,
because with another sip, a cigarette and a detached analysis
I knew I could no longer even feel.

I stepped out and grabbed a mop and pail
so we would stop slipping in the blood on the R&E floor
bagged the extra body pieces and the coffee room soldier
re-stocked supplies, then went outside to watch the sunrise,
alone and destitute of tears.

(1991)

263

YUSEF KOMUNYAKAA

When Yusef Komunyakaa won the 1994 Kingsley Tufts Award of $50,000 for Neon Vernacular, *his 1993 book of new and selected poems, the news seemed not worth printing in any major newspaper. A month later when the same book won the 1994 Pulitzer Prize for Poetry, there was a hasty scramble to answer the question, Who is Yusef Komunyakaa? His identity, however, was no mystery to those familiar with the literature of the Vietnam War.*

Born in 1947 in Bogalusa, Louisiana, where he was educated in still-segregated black schools, Komunyakaa spent the years from 1968 to 1971 in the U.S. Army. In 1969–1970 he served as editor and war correspondent for the army newspaper The Southern Cross *in Vietnam, where he was awarded a Bronze Star. He graduated from the University of Colorado in 1975 and received a master of fine arts in creative writing at the University of California, Irvine, in 1980. Since 1986 he has been a professor of English at Indiana University, Bloomington.*

Komunyakaa's first books of poems, Dedications and Other Dark-horses *(1977),* Lost in the Bonewheel Factory *(1979), and* Copacetic *(1983), do not deal explicitly with the Vietnam experience. It was not until 1983 that he wrote "Somewhere Near Phu Bai," his first poem about the war. "It took me fourteen years actually to approach that topic," he told an interviewer. "I had written very systematically around the Vietnam War." Even in his 1986 volume,* I Apologize for the Eyes in My Head, *the war is still not in the foreground. But in 1988 came* Dien Cai Dau, *his stunning book of poems about Vietnam. His next collection,* Magic City *(1992), was about Bogalusa, the other place that Komunyakaa has said he has had to recover from: "I've been through a healing process from the two places."*

Prisoners

> Usually at the helipad
> I see them stumble-dance
> across the hot asphalt
> with crokersacks over their heads,
> moving toward the interrogation huts,
> thin-framed as box kites
> of sticks & black silk
> > anticipating a hard wind
> > that'll tug & snatch them

out into space. I think
some must be laughing
under their dust-colored hoods,
knowing rockets are aimed
at Chu Lai—that the water's
evaporating & soon the nail
will make contact with metal.
How can anyone anywhere love
these half-broken figures
bent under the sky's brightness?
The weight they carry
is the soil we tread night & day.
Who can cry for them?
I've heard the old ones
are the hardest to break.
An arm twist, a combat boot
against the skull, a .45
jabbed into the mouth, nothing
works. When they start talking
with ancestors faint as camphor
smoke in pagodas, you know
you'll have to kill them
to get an answer.
Sunlight throws
scythes against the afternoon.
Everything's a heat mirage; a river
tugs at their slow feet.
I stand alone & amazed,
with a pill-happy door gunner
signaling for me to board the Cobra.
I remember how one day
I almost bowed to such figures
walking toward me, under
a corporal's ironclad stare.
I can't say why.
From a half-mile away
trees huddle together,
& the prisoners look like
marionettes hooked to strings of light.

                              (1988)

The Dead at Quang Tri

This is harder than counting stones
along paths going nowhere, the way
a tiger circles & backtracks by
smelling his blood on the ground.
The one kneeling beside the pagoda,
remember him? Captain, we won't
talk about that. The Buddhist boy
at the gate with the shaven head
we rubbed for luck
glides by like a white moon.
He won't stay dead, dammit!
Blades aim for the family jewels;
the grass we walk on
won't stay down.

(1988)

DENISE LEVERTOV

In the four decades since her first book of poems was published in 1946, Denise Levertov has authored, edited, or translated over three dozen volumes of poems and essays. She is now generally acknowledged to be one of the preeminent American poets of the second half of the twentieth century.

Born in 1923 in England, Levertov spent the years from 1943 to 1945 as a nurse in a London hospital working with casualties of World War II. Married to American soldier and writer Mitchell Goodman in 1947, she emigrated in 1948 to the United States. By 1964 she was widely admired and anthologized as a major American poet, with eight published volumes. Then the Vietnam War became more and more intermingled with her life and work. Levertov participated in many antiwar demonstrations, was arrested in one in the nation's capital, cofounded Writers and Artists Protest Against the War, and traveled to Hanoi in late 1972. The war became a central theme in her poems.

When Denise Levertov became a prominent antiwar activist and as her poetry transformed because of the war, many of her earlier admirers became embarrassed or defensive, for she was now violating the dicta against "politicizing" literature. (As Michael Bibby has pointed out, some anthologies pointedly omit every Levertov poem written between 1964 and 1978.) Since the mid-1960s, her work has become a focus of debate about relations between literature and social engagement, a debate in which she has continued to participate as poet, essayist, and activist for peace and justice.

From Staying Alive:
Prologue: An Interim (i & ii)

i

While the war drags on, always worse,
the soul dwindles sometimes to an ant
rapid upon a cracked surface;

lightly, grimly, incessantly
it skims the unfathomed clefts where despair
seethes hot and black.

ii

Children in the laundromat
waiting while their mothers fold sheets.
A five-year-old boy addresses
a four-year-old girl. 'When I say,
Do you want some gum? say *yes.*'
'Yes . . .' 'Wait!—Now:
Do you want some gum?'
'Yes!' 'Well yes means no,
so you can't have any.'
He chews. He pops a big, delicate bubble at her.

O language, virtue
of man, touchstone
worn down by what
gross friction . . .

              And,
'"It became necessary
to destroy the town to save it,"
a United States major said today.
He was talking about the decision
by allied commanders to bomb and shell the town
regardless of civilian casualties,
to rout the Vietcong.'

O language, mother of thought,
are you rejecting us as we reject you?

Language, coral island
accrued from human comprehensions,
human dreams,

you are eroded as war erodes us.
                               (1971)

The Pilots[1]

Because they were prisoners,
because they were polite and friendly and lonesome and homesick,
because they said Yes, they knew
        the names of the bombs they dropped
    but didn't say whether they understood what these bombs

---

[1]Levertov visited U.S. POWs in Hanoi in late 1972. [Ed.]

are designed to do
to human flesh, and because
I didn't ask them, being unable to decide
whether to ask would serve
any purpose other than cruelty, and
because since then I met Mrs. Brown, the mother of one of
their fellow prisoners,
and loved her, for she has the same lovingkindness in her
that I saw in Vietnamese women (and men too)
and because my hostility left the room and wasn't there
when I thought I needed it
while I was drinking tea with the POW's,

because of all these reasons I hope
they were truly as ignorant,
as unawakened,
as they seemed,
I hope their chances in life up to this point
have been poor,
I hope they can truly be considered
victims of the middle America they come from,
their American Legionnaire fathers, their macho high schools
their dull skimped Freshman English courses,

for if they did understand precisely
what they were doing, and did it anyway, and would do it again,

then I must learn to distrust
my own preference for trusting people,

then I must learn to question
my own preference for liking people,

then I must learn to keep
my hostility chained to me
so it won't leave me when I need it.

And if it is proved to me
that these men understood their acts,

how shall I ever again
be able to meet the eyes of Mrs. Brown?

(1975)

Fragrance of Life,
Odor of Death

All the while among
the rubble even, and in
the hospitals, among the wounded,
            not only beneath
            lofty clouds

                in temples
            by the shores of lotus-dreaming
            lakes

a fragrance:
flowers, incense, the earth-mist rising
of mild daybreak in the delta—good smell
of life.

It's in America
where no bombs ever
have screamed down smashing
the buildings, shredding the people's bodies,
tossing the fields of Kansas or Vermont or Maryland into
                                            the air
to land wrong way up, a gash of earth-guts . . .
it's in America, everywhere, a faint seepage,
I smell death.

                                    Hanoi-Boston-Maine
                                    November 1972
                                    (1975)

A Poem at Christmas, 1972,
during the Terror-Bombing
of North Vietnam

Now I have lain awake imagining murder.
At first my pockets were loaded with rocks, with knives,
wherever I ran windows smashed, but I was swift
                                    and unseen,

    I was saving the knives until I reached
certain men . . .
      Yes, Kissinger's smile faded,
he clutched his belly, he reeled . . .
But as the night
wore on, what I held
hidden—under a napkin perhaps,
    I as a waitress at the inaugural dinner—
was a container of napalm:
and as I threw it in Nixon's face
and his crowd leapt back from the flames with crude
              yells of horror,
and some came rushing to seize me:
    quick as thought I had ready
a round of those small bombs designed
to explode at the pressure of a small child's weight,
and these instantly
dealt with the feet of Nixon's friends and henchmen,
who fell in their own blood
while the foul smoke of his body-oils
blackened the hellish room . . .
It was of no interest
to imagine further. Instead,
the scene recommenced.
Each time around, fresh details,
variations of place and weapon.
All night imagining murder.
O, to kill
the killers!

It is
to this extremity

the infection of their evil

thrusts us . . .

               (1975)

GERALD McCARTHY

Born in Endicott, New York, in 1947, Gerald McCarthy served in the U.S. Marine Corps from 1965 to 1968, including a 1966–1967 tour in Vietnam. Then he deserted and spent time in military prison. After his discharge, he worked as a stonecutter and concrete finisher before attending the Writers Workshop at the University of Iowa. His poems have appeared in numerous magazines and anthologies, and he has published three volumes of poetry: War Story *(1977),* Shoetown *(1992), and* Throwing the Headlines *(1994). He has taught writing in Attica Prison and migrant labor camps and is currently an associate professor of English at St. Thomas Aquinas College. He lives with his wife and two sons in Nyack, New York.*

From War Story

1

They brought the dead
in helicopters and trucks
and tried to piece the bodies
back together,
shoved them in plastic bags
to be sent home.
Sometimes there was an arm or leg
leftover,
it lay around until the next shipment;
they made it fit in somewhere.

8

The night the crackers
burned a cross
in front of Doc Brown's tent,
Turner and I pulled
the late guard.
We watched the fire
rise out of the compound,
and I could sense his anger
across the close dark

of our sandbagged hole,
when he sighed—
I knew they'd get around to this.
Staring through the starlight scope,
I thought I saw that burning cross
spread its flames beyond
the headlands, reddening the sky—
until the dawn took me by surprise,
the raw daylight settling around us
like a wound.

9

We found him
his chest torn open,
shirt sticky with black blood.
A corporal with a K bar
cut off his ears
and kicked the body
in passing.

11

Wading through streams
rifles overhead,
they photograph us for LOOK
and some idiot smiles.

12

Hot sun
Mai looks up at me from the cot,
her eyes like the dark petals
of the night flowers.
She smiles as I stare,
her small hands clutch
the folded money.
Sweat sticks to my fatigues
and I turn away.
Outside the tin-roofed hut,
another GI waits his turn.

16

Going home
khakis creased with dirt,
I stand in the bus station
hoping someone
will notice the ribbons
pinned above the pocket
of my shirt.

19

John Bradt said: It'll be all right
when he gets home.

The farmers in Hale Valley
are waiting for the sun to rise.
The train winds slowly
through the mountains.
A voice of strangers
knocking politely on doors.
The soldiers are coming home,
they carry the sadness with them
like others carry groceries
or clothes in from the line.
There is no music in the parade;
the sound of their coming
waits at the bottoms of rivers,
stones rubbing against each other
in the current.

                              (1977, 1994)

Finding the Way Back

Morning.
Two sparrows sit on the tin roof
puffing themselves up
like old men in a park.
The longest war of this century
refuses to be ended.

I watch them signing their peace
with twelve different pens
live on t.v.

I remember the ocean
the breeze off the water
sunlight through the curtains of rain.
The young men running
darkness falling around their shoulders.
The children gone
their hearts in open throats.

The faces
the last columns of smoke
tearing the pages from my eyes.

There was never anything to come back to.
Aubrey knew it at Binh San
under the afternoon sun
staring into death.
My brother
I went on living.
There was nothing else
I could do.

(1977)

The Sound of Guns

1

The sparrow hawk drops to the cornfield
and in the same motion rises.
December's cold tightens around me,
a spider's web frozen white against the glass.

All day the sky is bleak with the coming snow,
the hours seem to pause like the bird
caught in an uplift of wind.
Out back the hay lies in rolls
the cows huddled together near the water troughs.

The highway runs past the brown fields
all the way west to Omaha, and just keeps going.
At the university in town
tight-lipped men tell me the war in Vietnam is over,
that my poems should deal with other things:
earth, fire, water, air.

2

A friend told me once
that ours was a generation of love;
and I know he meant that this was a generation
that took too much, that turned from one death
to another.

I don't know what it is that's kept me going.
At nineteen I stood at night and watched
an airfield mortared. A plane that was to take
me home, burning; men running out of the flames.

Seven winters have slipped away,
the war still follows me.
Never in anything have I found
a way to throw off the dead.

                                                        (1977)

MARILYN M. McMAHON

Marilyn McMahon was born in 1944 in Seattle, where she attended Catholic schools from first grade through college. She served as a U.S. Navy nurse from 1967 through 1972, including almost two years working with Marine Corps war casualties in Philadelphia and a 1969–1970 stint at Da Nang Naval Hospital. She began writing in 1985 by taking a college course in journal writing, and has published two chapbooks of her poetry, some of which has begun to be reprinted in anthologies and journals.

In This Land

In this land of lush jungle and squalid
refugee camps, the beach and the patio form
a haven. A beach for play: smooth sand,
gentle waves. The patio for sitting, talking,
drinking: grey concrete, kept clean by mama-
sans with hose and broom; dotted with small
tables, each with its brightly striped umbrella.

She sits in a lawn chair, aluminum with yellow
webbing, exactly like those in Mom's backyard.
He sits in another, green.

The tropical sun is warm, quiet, serene.

Last night's explosions are over—forgotten—
as a bad dream is forgotten in the morning.
The breeze from the north is cooling, salt
laden as it moves from the Pacific across
the harbor to where they sit.

The noises of war: helicopters, jets, boat
engines; tanks, APC's, jeeps, Hondas are
ignored. Not heard. Only his deep voice,
sharing items of interest to colonels, and
her soft voice, responding to his rank and
masculinity. Her dress is sleeveless, short,
sunflower yellow, allowing her to bask in
the sun. It is not important that her role

is that of listener—admirer—the assigned
role of her sex for hundreds of years. It
is only important to feel warm, treasured,
wanted; safe for the moment. She squints
her eyes, idly scans the sun-glittered waves,
sips her gin and tonic, and listens with the
part of her brain not otherwise engaged.

He speaks of his days: how it is to be a
lawyer in a war zone, of a problem the Marines
are having with the Army. He speaks of
helicopter crashes, and botched rescues,
and negligence. She listens and nods, sunbathes
and daydreams. She gazes at the water, today
so similar to her own beloved Pacific, thousands
of miles away.

She notes that something new has appeared
on the waves. Idly she wonders that she had
not seen it before. She considers where it
might have come from and what it might be.
She watches, and sunbathes.

Her stomach begins to chill. She knows.
She asks: look, what is it? She is afraid
to say what she knows.

He cannot see it—continues to speak of what
is important to him. She is silent. The sun
glares, no longer warms. The ocean is foreign,
alien, violent. The object—she cannot
say its name yet—floats closer on the tide.

Finally others see it—but now there are
two—they launch a boat, row out to retrieve
the body. Another body. A third.
In flight suits, swollen with three days
submersion. White. Blue. Black. Khaki.

She remains silent. Ice cold. Unable to
see the white of the sun or the blue of the
waves, only the black of the shadows.

He becomes still.

The beach remains, sun-drenched, wave-washed.
The patio is clean, flat. Empty.

(1988)

Wounds of War

I

He walks off the chopper
bleeding.
In his relief at being out of the fire zone
    he has forgotten that he hurts
    or that he was in terror.

II

The shell fragment is too large
it has invaded his heart
    his lungs, his liver, his spleen.
He will not survive the night.

III

In order that another,
    who has a better chance,
    might survive,
she must remove this patient from life
    support equipment.
Her professional smile calms the other patients,
    hides the anguished murderer inside.

IV

Each wound receives the surgeon's scrutiny:
    this we will close, this we will drain,
    this entire area must be removed.
The eye surgeon, the chest surgeon,
    the orthopedist.
Each focuses on his own plot
forgetting for a time
    their common ground.

V

Infection sets in.
The wound becomes a greenhouse
for exotic parasitic growths.

VI

Wounds heal from the bottom up
    and from the outside in.
Each must be kept open,
    must be probed
    and exposed to light.
Must be inspected
    and known.

VII

She sits at the side of the road
offering to sell stolen oranges
    to the jeep riders passing by.
She does not name herself wounded.
Two rockets blew away her home
and rice paddy.
        Her husband is dead.
        Her son has been drafted.
        Her baby will never cry again.

VIII

He wheels his custom chair
    through the crowded bookstore.
He focuses on narrow aisles and tall shelves
    avoiding images
        of jungle trails and buried mines
        of leaving in the mud
            his legs
            and his left hand.

IX

In rage he shatters another window with his fist.

The glass shards never cut deeply enough
    to cleanse the guilt.

X

She is afraid to trust again.
Her days are haunted
    by the texture of blood
    the odor of burns
    the face of senseless death;
friends known and loved
    vanished
    abandoned.
She sits alone in the darkened room
    scotch her only hope.

XI

He stares at the gun he saved,
turning it over and over in his tired hands.
He is desperate to stop the sounds
    and the pictures.

XII

Wounds must be inspected
    and known.
Must be kept open
    and probed
    and exposed to light.
Healing is from the bottom up
    and from the outside in.

               (1988)

July 20, 1969
. . . an Introduction in 3 Voices

In Seattle, almost 9:00 PM
after bedtime
for little girls
not quite fully dark.

                              In DaNang, noon
                              the next day.

On the moon . . .
day.

                    In Seattle, Mom and Dad
                    watched on their TV
                    4-year-old Shelley,
                    pleased at the chance
                    to stay up late,
                    snug in Mom's lap.
                    Janice, bored with waiting
                    read her book.
                    Front and back doors
                    propped open to catch
                    the breeze
                    off Salmon bay.

                                        In DaNang, 8
                                        guerrillas crept
                                        quietly to a make
                                        shift platform near
                                        Marble Mountain
                                        and aimed their
                                        launcher at the air
                                        base for a foolhardy
                                        daylight
                                        attack on the
                                        expected in-bound
                                        plane.

On the moon, one man
stepped from a small
metal craft
bounced lightly on the
ladder, and out onto
the dusty ground.

                    Later, as Dad carried
                    his sleeping daughter
                    up to bed
                    as Mom closed the doors

and made a pitcher
of iced tea,
as Janice returned
to her book,

as the man on the moon
returned to his lander
for rest, water, food,

                              a squad of Marines
                              found the guerillas
                              foolish enough to
                              fire rockets in
                              daylight and shot
                              them all.

A Continental Airlines 707
which had been circling
for 2 hours
above the airstrip
waiting for the shelling
to stop,
landed.
163 American servicemen,
Commander Betsy Jackson
and I filed
down the ladder.

                                                  (1990)

Dying with Grace

Did that eight-year-old boy,
racing gleefully into the playground,
black eyes shining with the joy
of kicking a soccer ball
ahead of him,
and met by two bullets
from an automatic machine gun,
did he die with grace?

Or his grandmother?
Who was rail-thin at 35
from too little food
and too many babies
and too much defoliant
and too few hopes,
who fell asleep in the refugee camp
and never woke up,
did she die with grace?

The white man in the suit and tie
on television
tells me that if I believe
in jesus
and in heaven
and jesus' love for me,
I can die with grace.

Could that be true?

The other white man
on television
tells us that this young man
once from Brooklyn
who fired his weapon
while struggling through the mud
on Hamburger Hill
or at Salerno
or deep in the Mekong jungle,
killing 12 of the enemy
before he was felled by a grenade,
that he died with grace.
The man calls it honor
and announces that his country
is proud of him.

An old man
once awarded the Silver Star
and Purple Hearts
and rank upon ranks
of honors and medals

dies of the cold in a park
across the street from the White House.
His death is not called graceful,
it is judged shameful
and it is named alcoholism.

And the woman
who wrote to the *San Francisco Examiner*
that finally, at the Vet Center,
she had found a way out
of nightmares
of choppers full of wounded
and dead
and flashbacks of nights torn
with mortars and rockets;
then could not live with her memories
and jumped from the Golden Gate Bridge.
Who is there to say that she died with grace
or did not?

(1990)

Confession

Day before First Friday
we file from our classroom to the church
at our assigned time.
"Bless me, Father,
for I have sinned.
It has been one month
since my last confession:
I was angry with my little sister
I was jealous of her new doll.
I was selfish, and did not share
my roller skates.
I was proud, and I boasted."
In that dark cozy place,
my eyes are tightly closed.
Father does not know

who I am.
A blessing, the Sign of the Cross.
I march to the altar rail,
gaze bent to the floor.
I kneel, hiding my eyes in my knuckles.
Three Hail Marys, and the Act of Contrition.
I am forgiven.
My soul is pure white.
Tomorrow, I may receive Holy Communion.

Sunday morning Mass
after ten hour night shift
admissions, transfers, two deaths.
Armpits still chilled from warming
frozen plasma.
Fingernail stained orange-
Betadine prep for an emergency trach.
We sit wearily in metal folding chairs.
Bright, sun-filled quonset hut:
the Chapel of Saint Luke.
Slowly we stand as the priest
and his attendants file in.
We bow our heads,
one sign of the cross
sketched in the air.
My silent catalogue:
Bless me Father, for . . .
I was enraged, wanted to hurt another.
I committed adultery two, no, three times.
I was proud, would not pray.
Thirty others forgiven at the same time.
Our souls are purified
we may receive Communion.

Night
the black hour
when sleep has fled again.
Poison gas in Iran and Iraq.
In El Salvador, disembowelled priests
and two women.
Star Wars

and Minutemen.
Martinis and handshakes in Beijing
across one thousand bodies.
Blockades create starvation
and democracy.
Arms shipments.
I am enraged
and frightened of my rage.
I am appalled
and made helpless.
I am guilty of fear
helplessness
failure to believe or hope
having believed and having
asked no questions.
Where is forgiveness
and purification of soul?
Where is communion? and when?

The dark, private cubicle is empty
door closed tight.
The sun-filled chapel
was blown up by those
who believed in a different god.
Knuckles can no longer provide
a safe dark.
I will not pray.

(1990)

Knowing

*("Recent research indicates Dioxin
is the most potent toxin ever studied."
—news report, September 1987)*

I watched the helicopters
flying slowly north and south
along the DaNang river valley,
trailing a grey mist

which scattered the sun
in murky rainbows.
I never wondered if I knew
all I ought to know
about what they were doing.

I knew that it was called
defoliation,
that the spray would destroy
the hiding places of snipers
and ambushing guerrillas.
I did not know to ask:
at what price?

Every evening,
the sunset choppers arrived
filled with soldiers burning
from jungle fevers:
malaria, dengue, dysentery.
We took them directly
to the cooling showers,
stripped their wet
dirt encrusted uniforms
as we lowered their temperatures
and prepared them for bed.
I did not ask where they had been,
whether they or the uniforms I held
had been caught in the mist,
whether defoliation
had saved their lives.
I did not know to ask.

I knew part of the price
when nine other women
who had watched the helicopters
and seen the mist
talked of their children:
Jason's heart defects, and
Amy's and Rachel's and Timothy's.
Mary's eye problems.
The multiple operations

to make and repair digestive organs
for John and Kathleen and little John.
How lucky they felt
when one child was born healthy
whole.
How they grieved
about the miscarriages
Their pain, their helplessness,
their rage when
Marianne died of leukemia at 2,
and Michelle died of cancer at $2\frac{1}{2}$.
Their fear of what might yet happen.

I knew more
when I watched my parents
celebrate their fortieth
wedding anniversary,
four children, three grandchildren
sitting in the pews.
I knew what I would never know,
what the poisons and my fears
have removed forever from my knowing.
The conceiving, the carrying of a child,
the stretching of my womb, my breasts.
The pain of labor.
The bringing forth from my body a new life.

I choose not to know
if my eggs are
misshapen and withered
as the trees along the river.
If snipers are hidden
in the coils of my DNA.

(1988)

JANICE MIRIKITANI

Born in 1942, Janice Mirikitani spent her first few years in the Rohwer, Arkansas, concentration camp because her parents were second-generation Americans of Japanese descent. She is the author of two volumes of poetry and prose, Awake in the River *(1978, 1982, 1984) and* Shedding Silence *(1987); coauthor of* Breaking Free: A Glide Songbook *(1989); and editor of numerous books, including* Time to Greez!: Incantations from the Third World, Third World Women Anthology, Ayumi—Four Generations of Japanese in America, *and* Making Waves. *Her poetry has been published in many anthologies and journals in the United States and in Japan. Her latest book is* Watch Out, We're Talking, *an anthology of work by survivors of incest and abuse.*

Mirikitani lives with her husband, the Reverend Cecil Williams, in San Francisco, where she is president of the Glide Foundation and executive director of programs for Glide Church/Urban Center, a multicultural, multiservice agency.

Loving from Vietnam to Zimbabwe

Here, in this crimson
room,
with silk skimming our skin,
I shape into thought
these strange burnings
starting in my fingertips
as they lick your nipples,
hairs standing to the touch.

> You are marching in
> the delta
> the river water
> at your boots
> sucking through the leather.
> Sand has caked your color yellow.

Your chest moves
to the rhythm of my heart,
warm skin singing.

You plod, weighted by
days of marching
nights of terror
holding this patch of ground
shaped like a crotch.

My teeth on your
shoulder
hungry to enter your flesh
as you call me strange names.

Water/water
sinking sand.
They are coming
as you raise the blade
of your bayonet,
clean it with
your sweat.

My mouth driven
to your thighs
the sweet inside
just below the swinging
songs of your life.

Deeper into
the Mekong,
The grass has eyes
the wind has flesh
and you feel the trigger
pressed back for release.

Your thighs tremble
your long fingers like marsh grass
in my hair
as I reach down
onto Mt. Inyangani.[1]

You have seen them
hanging in the trees
after american troops

---

[1]The highest peak in Zimbabwe. [Ed.]

had finished.
Slanted eyes bugging,
crooked necks,
genitals swinging from
their mouths.

Sweat from your neck
I think they are tears
as I move
into the grassy plain
of your chest.

You never saw them alive
but knew they looked like me
And you got sick a lot
wondering what color
their blood.

As I hold
your skin between my
teeth
I can feel the blood
pulsing
on my tongue
springing like the
beginning
of Zambezi River.[2]

You turned in your rage
knowing how they have used you.
Not the invisible ones
whose soil you were sent to seize
but those behind you,
pushing you,
pulling
     pulling
your trigger.

And I massage
your back

---

[2]One of the great rivers of southern Africa. [Ed.]

large/black like the shadowed
belly of a leaf
as you in
your stillness
hold me
like a bird.

They stripped you.
Held you down
in the sand
took the bayonet off your gun
and began to slice . . .
lopped off your head
and expected you to die.

I, in the heavy
hot air
between us,
in the crimson room
that begins to blur
feel you enter
my harbor/kiss
the lips of my soul.
Call me my Strange Names

My Lai
Bach Mai
Haiphong[3]

Loving in this world
is the sliver splinting
edge
is the dare
in the teeth of the tiger
the pain of jungle rot
the horror of flesh unsealed
the madness of surviving.

(1978)

---

[3]My Lai is a village in South Vietnam where U.S. troops raped dozens of women and murdered hundreds of civilians. The Bach Mai hospital in Hanoi and Hanoi's port of Haiphong were devastated by U.S. aerial bombing in December 1972. [Ed.]

RICHARD M. MISHLER

Born in 1947, Richard Mishler served in the U.S. Army from 1967 to 1970, including more than two years (1968–1970) in Vietnam with the Eleventh Armored Cavalry Regiment. His Vietnam era poetry has appeared in more than a dozen reviews and journals, as well as in several anthologies.

Ceremony

The 'copter lays flat the rice stalks
as it first hovers and then rises over the water
with the pilot pulling back on the stick.
The abducted, a fulvous skinned farmer, watches
his hamlet shrink into a tear.

Another Vietnamese aboard, hands bound
behind his back, with the rope looped tight
around his neck, stares with suspicion.

Both wear black, worn shiny, silk pajamas.
The bound one has no shirt over his scarred,
emaciated chest, while the farmer wears a buttonless
US Army jungle shirt, with one sergeant stripe hanging
on the left sleeve. It is permanently sweat-stained.

The 'copter flies lazily 2,000 feet above the paddies.
Through an interpreter, the American Lt.
asks the farmer three quick questions.
He replies with the same quickness. He doesn't know.
He is only a farmer, a poor man with half a crop
and half a family. A poor farmer who knows nothing,
nothing. Two more questions are asked of him, knowing
he is only a farmer and cannot know. And nothing.
One more, with the threat of him being dropped
from the 'copter. Tears of fear and resignation fall.

Without ceremony, he is shoved over the side.
He seems to glide. His scream floats up to the ears
of the bound VC, whose muscles tighten against the ropes.

The water buffalo jumps at the splash, and the
sucking mud swallows the crumpled body, buries him
in the ground of his ancestors. The sun burns
in the sky - incensed.

Even before the questions are asked of the VC,
the Lt. knows he will talk. And the VC knows he
will not, because he knows the sun also burns for
him; his ancestors are also below. Already
the cricket's chirp fills his marrow.

(1981)

BASIL T. PAQUET

Born in 1944 in Hartford, Connecticut, Basil T. Paquet was drafted in 1966 as a conscientious objector and served in the U.S. Army as a medic until 1968, including a year (1967–1968) with the Twenty-fourth Evacuation Hospital in Long Binh, Vietnam. Together with Jan Barry and Larry Rottmann, Paquet coedited Winning Hearts and Minds: War Poems by Vietnam Veterans *and formed 1st Casualty Press, to publish that seminal anthology in 1972 (see page 237). The following year he coedited with Wayne Karlin* Free Fire Zone: Short Stories by Vietnam Veterans, *also published by 1st Casualty Press.*

Paquet's own poems have been printed in a wide variety of anthologies and other publications, including the New York Review of Books, Freedomways, WIN Magazine, *and* New Times, *and he is the winner of the Wallace Stevens Award for Poetry.*

Morning—A Death

Turn—Character 1

I've blown up your chest for thirty minutes
And crushed it down an equal time,
And still you won't warm to my kisses.
I've sucked and puffed on your
Metal No. 8 throat for so long.
And twice you've moaned under my thrusts
On your breastbone. I've worn off
Those sparse hairs you counted noble on your chest,
And twice you defibrillated,
And twice blew back my breath.
I've scanned the rhythms of your living,
Forced half-rhymes in your silent pulse,
Sprung brief spondees in your lungs,
And the caesura's called mid-line, half-time,
Incomplete, but with a certain finality.
The bullet barks apocalyptic
And you don't unzip your sepulchral
Canvas bag in three days.
No rearticulation of nucleics, no phoenix,

No novae, just an arbitrary of one-way bangs
Flowing out to interstitial calms.
The required canonical wait for demotion
To lower order, and you wash out pure chemical.
You are dead just as finally
As your mucosity dries on my lips
In this morning sun.
I have thumped and blown into your kind too often,
I grow tired of kissing the dead.

Counterturn — Character 2

I'd sooner be a fallen pine cone this winter
In a cradle of cold New England rock,
Less hurt in it than nineteen years.
What an exit! Stage left, fronds waving,
Cut down running my ass off at a tree line.
I'm thinking, as I hear my chest
Sucking air through its brand new nipple,
I bought the ticket, I hope I drown fast,
The pain is all in living.

Stand — Character 1

I grow so tired of jostled litters
Filling the racks, and taking off
Your tags and rings, pulling out
Your metal throats and washing
Your spittle down with warm beer at night,
So tired of tucking you all in,
And smelling you all on me for hours.
I'd sooner be in New England this winter
With pine pitch on my hands than your blood,
Lightly fondling breasts and kissing
Women's warm mouths than thumping
Your shattered chests and huffing
In your broken lips or aluminum windpipes,
Sooner lift a straying hair from her wet mouth
Than a tear of elephant grass from your slack lips.
I'd so much rather be making children,
Than tucking so many in.

                                                           (1969)

PEDRO PIETRI

Poet and playwright Pedro Pietri has been a leading figure in the Nuyorican movement ever since it first emerged as the vibrant literary voice of Puerto Ricans in New York. Born in Ponce, Puerto Rico, in 1943, Pietri has lived in New York State since 1945. His 1971 satiric epic Puerto Rican Obituary, *title poem of his 1973 collection, quickly became a classic expression of the nightmare experienced by those who fled from poverty on the island to urban hells in the northeastern United States.*

Pietri served in the U.S. Army from 1966 to 1968. In poems such as "Para la Madre de Angel Luna" and "The B-52 Blew," he encapsulated much of the meaning of the Vietnam War for the Puerto Rican people and the Nuyorican movement.

Later volumes of Pietri's poems include Invisible Poetry *(1979),* Uptown Train *(1980), and* Traffic Violations *(1983); his plays appear in* The Masses Are Asses *(1984) and* Illusions of a Revolving Door *(1992). Along with many older and newer artists, Pietri still reads his poems in what has become one of New York City's great cultural institutions, the Nuyorican cafe in Manhattan's East Village.*

Para la Madre de Angel Luna

El hijo tuyo
queria irse A.W.O.L.
la noche antes
de salir para Vietnam
con su nombre Boricua
adentro de ese
uniforme norteamericana
fabricado en wallstreet
por esos inhumanos
que quieren conquistar
al mundo entero

El hijo tuyo
comprendia quien era
el enemigo verdadero
queria irse A.W.O.L.

la noche antes
de salir para Vietnam
pero no se fue
porque no queria
hacer a su madre sufrir
cuando la policia militar
fuera a su hogar
en el south bronx
para encarcelarlo

La noche antes
de salir para Vietnam
lo ultimo que
El hijo tuyo
le dijo a sus
compañeros Boricua
fue: So no regreso vivo
diganle a mi madre querida
que me entierren en
la tierra de Borinken

(1971)

For the Mother of Angel Luna[1]

Your son
wanted to go A.W.O.L.
the night before
leaving for Vietnam
with his Puerto Rican name
inside that
northamerican uniform
made in wallstreet
by those inhumans
who wish to conquer
the entire world
Your son
knowing who was

---

[1]English translation by H. Bruce Franklin.

the true enemy
wanted to go A.W.O.L.
the night before
leaving for Vietnam
but he did not go
because he didn't want
to make his mother suffer
when the military police
came to his home
in the south bronx
to imprison him

The night before
leaving for Vietnam
the last thing
your son
said to his
Puerto Rican friends
was: If I don't come back alive
tell my dear mother
they should bury me in
the land of Puerto Rico

STAN PLATKE

Stan Platke, a rifleman in the Fourth Infantry Division in Vietnam from 1968 to 1969, received the Army Commendation Medal and Combat Infantryman's Badge. Some of his poems were published in Winning Hearts and Minds *and* Demilitarized Zones. *He currently lives in St. Louis.*

Bury the Body, Bury the Thought

In Nam there are helicopters
That pick up
Parts and pieces of bodies
Placed neatly in a body bag
So that bodies get back
To the world
So parents can decide
Whether to open the casket
And see what used to be
Their son

Bury the body
Bury the thought

So some parents can say
I'm so proud he's here
Instead of Canada

(1976)

DALE RITTERBUSCH

Born in 1946, Dale Ritterbusch served in the U.S. Army from April 1966 to September 1969, mainly as an operations and intelligence specialist, including a year (1968–1969) in Vietnam and Thailand. As a liaison officer he was responsible for coordinating shipments of antipersonnel mines used along the Ho Chi Minh trail and other infiltration routes. He is the author of Lessons Learned *(1995), a collection of more than seventy poems on the Vietnam War and its aftermath written between 1966 and 1994.*

Ritterbusch has undergraduate and graduate degrees from the University of Pennsylvania and a fine arts degree from Bowling Green State University. Currently he teaches writing and literature in the Department of Modern Languages and Literatures at the University of Wisconsin, Whitewater.

Search and Destroy

They came out of the hootch
with their hands up—surrendered—
and we found all that rice
and a couple of weapons. They
were tagged and it all seemed so easy—
too easy, and someone started to torch
the hootch and I stopped him—something
was funny. We checked the hootch
a couple times more; I had them probe it
like we were searching for mines and
a lucky poke with a knife
got us the entrance to a tunnel.
We didn't wait for any damn
tunnel rats—we threw down
CS and smoke and maybe two hundred
yards to our right two gooks popped up
and we got 'em running across the field,
nailed 'em before they hit the trees.
We went to the other hole and popped more
gas and smoke and a fragmentation grenade
and three gooks came out coughing, tears
and red smoke pouring out of their eyes and

nose. We thought there were more
so we threw in another grenade and one of the
dinks brought down his arms, maybe he started
to sneeze with all that crap running out of his face,
maybe he had a weapon concealed, I didn't know,
so I greased him. Wasn't much else I could do.
A sudden move like that.

(1985)

At the Crash Site of a B-52: January 1994

for H. Bruce Franklin

When the Americans come back
they search for artifacts
the way Europeans once excavated the ruins
of Tra-kiêu or Mi-so'n or Tham Khuyen.
They sift earth still black
from the fires of war: jet fuel
and ammunition that burned
all day, all night, so long ago—
sift through a fine screen
until they find a Seiko watch,
its world-time dial unable
to tell the time anywhere
in any city in this world.
They find a major's insignia,
a piece of velcro, some metal pitted,
corroded, burned beyond recognition
and a few slivers of bone.
They dig deeper, screen more bone,
but the bones of a child:
the mother remembers, knows the major,
the captain, the sergeant are all buried with her son—
she recognizes the bones of her son
the way she imagines the major's
mother would recognize hers, if she let go,
if she let her son sink into the earth

that is beginning again to smell like soil
that will grow things, the way it did before,
if she'd just let go, if she'd only learn
that war is not something you come back from
whether you died or not, that the resurrection
is only a story for the gods—that a candle,
the perfume of burning incense, a flower
growing from the garden of this blackened earth
brings more than a lasting peace, more
than a mother can hope for.

(1995)

LARRY ROTTMANN

Larry Rottmann is the only author represented in this volume by both fiction and poetry. See his biography on page 18.

APO 96225[1]

A young man once went off to war in a far country,
and when he had time, he wrote home and said,
"Dear Mom, sure rains a lot here."

But his mother—reading between the lines as mothers
     always do—wrote back,
"We're quite concerned. Tell us what it's really like."

And the young man responded,
"Wow! You ought to see the funny monkeys."

To which the mother replied,
"Don't hold back. How is it there?"

And the young man wrote,
"The sunsets here are spectacular!"

In her next letter, the mother pleaded,
"Son, we want you to tell us everything. Everything!"

So the next time he wrote, the young man said,
"Today I killed a man. Yesterday, I helped drop napalm
     on women and children."

And the father wrote right back,
"Please don't write such depressing letters. You're
     upsetting your mother."

So, after a while,
the young man wrote,
"Dear Mom, sure rains here a lot."

(1972)

---

[1]*APO 96225, Army Post Office Number 96225 —Official address of the 25th Infantry Division in Vietnam*

For Cissy Shellabarger, R.N.,
Wherever You Are

Tet-stunned
and very nearly scalped
by a hundred razored fragments
from a Chicom 122mm rocket,
my unconscious carcass
was hastily carted to the Cu Chi hospital
and added to the long line
already there and awaiting attention.

An anguished and blood-sotted doctor
too weary and rushed and young
for what he'd already been conscripted to do,
glanced at my cranial lacerations,
shook his head sadly,
and went on to the next American teenager,
who obviously had a far better
"survival probability."

But an Army nurse (someone told me later)
just as weary and rushed and young
had already seen enough of death that night
and simply decided to buck the odds one time.
"Nobody croaks on Cissy!" she warned both me and God.

And she was right.
I didn't die.
In fact, I suspect the more grievous wounds were hers.

(1993)

What Kind of War?

What kind of war is this
where you can be pinned down
all day in a muddy rice paddy
while your buddies are being shot
and a close-support Phantom jet
which has been napalming the enemy

wraps itself around a tree and explodes
and you cheer inside?

(1972)

Thanks, Guys

In a firefight as mean as any wartime combat

six dozen hard-core Detroit cops
exchanged bullets with a lone gunman
cornered behind the counter of a downtown 7-11

A thousand rounds smashed every plate glass window
exploded shelf-after-shelf of canned goods
shattered the upright coolers of Coke and Pepsi and RC Cola
and littered the parking lot and street with hot, smoking shell
casings

And when the wary SWAT team—
many of them Vietnam vets
who'd been firing at the demons in their own eyes—
finally closed in on their quarry

All they found was the bullet-riddled body
of a skinny middle-aged black man
who had died with a smile on his face
a crumpled pink slip in his pocket

and a pair of green-taped dog tags[1] around his neck.

(1993)

---

[1]GI's in Vietnam frequently taped their dog tags to keep them from rattling.

The Bones of an American M.I.A. Speak to the Members of the Joint Casualty Resolution Team

Please, just leave me be.
I'm fine.
I'm not missing.
I know exactly where I am.
Two klicks northwest of My Tho.
Precisely where the U.S. Army left me.

I've now been resting here
for longer than I lived in Oklahoma.
My blood and flesh and organs and sinews have fused
    with the land.
Bombs and tanks and water buffaloes and wooden hoes
have kneaded me into the earth for over two decades,
until I have become the very soil which nurtures
    the rice and the people.

Please, just leave me be.
I've finally found peace
here in this quiet paddy.
The southeast Asian sun warms me.
Giant cumulus temples of perfect ivory float high overhead.
And the lazy Mekong bathes me regularly.

I am not alone.
Busy cranes stalk bugs and frogs here.
The great horse snake frequently slides by silently.
Happy children who never saw me in camo fatigues
often fish for the elusive *ca ro*[1] in the soft glow of dusk.
And at night, ten thousand crickets sing languid lullabies.

Please, just leave me be.
Don't scatter me all about, or scrounge up my bits and pieces
so some bored lab technician in Honolulu can grind me
    into unrecognizable dust,

---

[1] *ca ro*—tiny minnow-like fish that lives in flooded rice paddies.

or some bozo politician can use me—again.
And whatever you do,
don't sell me to H. Ross Perot!

Take the dog tags, if you must.
They belong to the government, but I do not.
You invested me in Vietnam
because you said it was worth my life.
I believed you then. I believe it even more now.
So please, just leave me be.

(1993)

LUIS OMAR SALINAS

Born in Texas in 1937, Luis Omar Salinas spent several childhood years in Mexico and then moved to California. Since the 1960s he has lived near Fresno, where he has been a prominent figure in the Chicano literary and social movements, which were powerfully influenced by the Vietnam War. One of the epicenters of the movement during the war was at Fresno State University, where in 1970 Salinas published Crazy Gypsy, *his first major collection of poetry, including "Death in Vietnam." Since 1969, Salinas's poems have been widely anthologized. In 1973 he coedited* From the Barrio, *an important anthology of Chicano literature. Since then Salinas has published four additional volumes of his own poetry, of which* Sadness of Days: New and Selected Poems *(1987) is the most representative collection.*

Death in Vietnam

> the ears of strangers
> listen
> fighting men tarnish the ground
> death has whispered
> tales to the young
> and now choir boys are ringing
> bells
> another sacrifice for America
> a Mexican
>
> comes home
> his beloved country
> gives homage
> and mothers sleep
> in cardboard houses
>
> let all anguish be futile
> tomorrow it will rain
> and the hills of Viet Nam
> resume
> the sacrifice is not over

(1970)

LYNDA VAN DEVANTER

Twenty-one years old and fresh out of nursing school, Lynda Van Devanter in 1968 was commissioned as a second lieutenant in the U.S. Army. In June 1969 she began a one-year tour in Vietnam, where she served as a nurse at the Seventy-first Evacuation Hospital in Pleiku and the Sixty-seventh Evacuation Hospital in Qui Nhon.

Nobody has done more than Lynda Van Devanter to focus public attention on the 265,000 American women, civilian and military, who served in Vietnam during the war. In 1980 the Vietnam Veterans of America Women's Project became, as she has written, "my entire life." Her best-selling memoir, Home Before Morning: The Story of an Army Nurse in Vietnam, *was published in 1983. In 1991 she coedited* Visions of War, Dreams of Peace, *the first collection of poetry by women who served in Vietnam. She was one of the leaders in obtaining authorization and funding for the Vietnam Women's Memorial, which was dedicated on the grounds of the Vietnam Veterans Memorial in 1993.*

Van Devanter is currently an emergency room nurse in her home state of Virginia.

TV Wars—First Blood Part II

Beside the ship leaving port
For the hot, dry gulf
The white-haired woman says
I'm proud of my grandson
He has to go
To protect our interest.

Dear lady,
Your interest just left on that ship.

(1991)

For Molly

What did you do in the war, Mommy?
Hazel eyes shining brightly
Pony tails bobbing softly
One pierced earring and an orange juice mustache.

Where did that man's arm go, Mommy?
Plastic slinky bouncing wildly
Tie dye T-shirt hanging loosely
Looks at me so earnestly I have to touch her.

I wrote a story about a war Mommy.
Where nobody got guns or dead
This one was a good war
Don't you know?

Why do you have tears now, Mommy?
Little girl with dreams so peaceful
Alphabets and clowns and people
I don't want you growing up too soon.

(1991)

BRUCE WEIGL

Bruce Weigl is certainly one of the three or four most highly acclaimed American poets to emerge from the Vietnam War. His poetry, now widely anthologized, has won him many prestigious awards, including an Academy of American Poets Prize, two Pushcart Prizes, and three major writing fellowships.

Born in the industrial city of Lorain, Ohio, Weigl was inducted into the U.S. Army just after graduating from high school in 1967. Later that year and before his nineteenth birthday, he began a one-year tour with the First Air Cavalry in Vietnam, where he was awarded a Bronze Star. After leaving the army in 1970, he attended Oberlin College, the University of New Hampshire, and the University of Utah, where he received a Ph.D. in 1979. He has been teaching in college since 1975, and is currently a professor of English at Pennsylvania State University.

The Vietnam experience was rendered with increasing eloquence and complexity in Weigl's first five books: A Sack Full of Old Quarrels *(1976);* Executioner *(1976);* A Romance *(1979);* The Monkey Wars *(1985); and* Song of Napalm *(1988), which brings together many of the earlier and later Vietnam poems. In 1994, Weigl and Thanh T. Nguyen produced an astonishing volume,* Poems from Captured Documents: Selected and Translated from the Vietnamese, *which demonstrates the power and prevalence of poetry among the Vietnamese who were killing and being killed by men like many of the poets in this volume, including Weigl himself.*

Surrounding Blues on the Way Down

I was barely in country.
We slipped under rain black clouds
Opening around us like orchids.
He'd come to take me into the jungle
So I felt the loneliness
Though I did not yet hate the beautiful war.
Eighteen years old and a man
Was telling me how to stay alive
In the tropics he said would rot me—
Brothers of the heart he said and smiled

Until we came upon a mama san
Bent over from her stuffed sack of flowers.
We flew past her but he hit the brakes hard,
He spun the tires backwards in the mud.
He did not hate the war either,
Other reasons made him cry out to her
So she stopped,
She smiled her beetle black teeth at us.
In the air she raised her arms.

I have no excuse for myself.
I sat in that man's jeep in the rain
And watched him slam her to her knees,
The plastic butt of his M-16
Crashing down on her.
I was barely in country, the clouds
Hung like huge flowers, black
Like her teeth.

                                                                     (1984)

Burning Shit at An Khe

Into that pit
    I had to climb down
With a rake and matches; eventually,
    You had to do something
Because it just kept piling up
    And it wasn't our country, it wasn't
Our air thick with the sick smoke
    So another soldier and I
Lifted the shelter off its blocks
    To expose the home-made toilets:
Fifty-five gallon drums cut in half
    With crude wood seats that splintered.
We soaked the piles in fuel oil
    And lit the stuff
And tried to keep the fire burning.
To take my first turn
I paid some kid
    A care package of booze from home.

I'd walked past the burning once
    And gagged the whole heart of myself—
It smelled like the world
    Was on fire,
But when my turn came again
    There was no one
So I stuffed cotton up my nose
    And marched up that hill. We poured
And poured until it burned and black
    Smoke curdled
But the fire went out.
    Heavy artillery
Hammered the evening away in the distance,
    Vietnamese laundry women watched
From a safe place, laughing.
    I'd grunted out eight months
Of jungle and thought I had a grip on things
    But we flipped the coin and I lost
And climbed down into my fellow soldiers'
    Shit and began to sink and didn't stop
Until I was deep to my knees. Liftships
    Cut the air above me, the hacking
Blast of their blades
    Ripped dust in swirls so every time
I tried to light a match
    It died
And it all came down on me, the stink
    And the heat and the worthlessness
Until I slipped and climbed
    Out of that hole and ran
Past the olive drab
    Tents and trucks and clothes and everything
Green as far from the shit
    As the fading light allowed.
Only now I can't fly.
    I lay down in it
And finger paint the words of who I am
    Across my chest
Until I'm covered and there's only one smell,
    One word.

                           (1984)

Him, on the Bicycle

There was no light; there was no light at all . . .
                                                              –Roethke

In a liftship near Hue
the door gunner is in a trance.
He's that driver who falls
asleep at the wheel
between Pittsburgh and Cleveland
staring at the Ho Chi Minh trail.

Flares fall,
where the river leaps
I go stiff,
I have to think, tropical.

The door gunner sees movement,
the pilot makes small circles:
four men running, carrying rifles,
one man on a bicycle.

He pulls me out of the ship,
there's firing far away.
I'm on the back of the bike
holding his hips.
It's hard pumping for two,
I hop off and push the bike.

I'm brushing past trees,
the man on the bike stops pumping,
lifts his feet,
we don't waste a stroke.
His hat flies off,
I catch it behind my back,
put it on, I want to live forever!

Like a blaze
streaming down the trail.

                                                              (1979)

Song of Napalm

for my wife

After the storm, after the rain stopped pounding,
We stood in the doorway watching horses
Walk off lazily across the pasture's hill.
We stared through the black screen,
Our vision altered by the distance
So I thought I saw a mist
Kicked up around their hooves when they faded
Like cut-out horses
Away from us.
The grass was never more blue in that light, more
Scarlet; beyond the pasture
Trees scraped their voices into the wind, branches
Criss-crossed the sky like barbed wire
But you said they were only branches.

Okay. The storm stopped pounding.
I am trying to say this straight: for once
I was sane enough to pause and breathe
Outside my wild plans and after the hard rain
I turned my back on the old curses. I believed
They swung finally away from me . . .

But still the branches are wire
And thunder is the pounding mortar,
Still I close my eyes and see the girl
Running from her village, napalm
Stuck to her dress like jelly,
Her hands reaching for the no one
Who waits in waves of heat before her.
So I can keep on living,
So I can stay here beside you,
I try to imagine she runs down the road and wings
Beat inside her until she rises
Above the stinking jungle and her pain
Eases, and your pain, and mine.

But the lie swings back again.

The lie works only as long as it takes to speak
And the girl runs only as far
As the napalm allows
Until her burning tendons and crackling
Muscles draw her up
Into that final position
Burning bodies so perfectly assume. Nothing
Can change that; she is burned behind my eyes
And not your good love and not the rain-swept air
And not the jungle green
Pasture unfolding before us can deny it.

                                          (1984)

Snowy Egret

My neighbor's boy has lifted his father's shotgun and stolen
Down to the backwaters of the Elizabeth
And in the moon he's blasted a snowy egret
From the shallows it stalked for small fish.

Midnight. My wife wakes me. He's in the backyard
With a shovel so I go down half-drunk with pills
That let me sleep to see what I can see and if it's safe.
The boy doesn't hear me come across the dewy grass.
He says through tears he has to bury it,
He says his father will kill him
And he digs until the hole is deep enough and gathers
The egret carefully into his arms
As if not to harm the blood-splattered wings
Gleaming in the flashlight beam.

His man's muscled shoulders
Shake with the weight of what he can't set right no matter
        what,
But one last time he tries to stay a child, sobbing
Please don't tell . . .
He says he only meant to flush it from the shadows,
He only meant to watch it fly
But the shot spread too far

Ripping into the white wings
Spanned awkwardly for a moment
Until it glided into brackish death.

I want to grab his shoulders,
Shake the lies loose from his lips but he hurts enough,
He burns with shame for what he's done,
With fear for his hard father's
Fists I've seen crash down on him for so much less.
I don't know what to do but hold him.
If I let go he'll fly to pieces before me.
What a time we share, that can make a good boy steal away,
Wiping out from the blue face of the pond
What he hadn't even known he loved, blasting
Such beauty into nothing.

(1984)

Dialectical Materialism

Through dark tenements and fallen temples
we wander into Old Hanoi,
oil lamps glowing in small
storefronts and restaurants
where those, so long ago my enemy,
sit on low chairs and praise the simple evening.
On one block
the rich steam from pho,
their morning and evening soup, rises,
on another
brown smoked ducks are strung up in a row.
The people talk and smoke,
men hold each other's hands again in that old way
and children,
their black and white laughter all around us,
kick the weighted feather
with such grace into the air
because the bombs have stopped. And further

to the Long Bien bridge
where we meet a man

filling buckets
hung across his back's yoke
to bring cool water to his corn
in the moonlight.
When we ask our questions
he points to a stone and stick
house beyond the dikes
one thousand meters from the bridge
our great planes
could not finally knock down.
He doesn't say
how he must have huddled
those nights with his family,
how he must have spread himself
over them
until the village bell
called them back to their beds.
There are questions which
people who have everything
ask people who have nothing
and they do not understand.

Hanoi, December 1985
(1988)

Glossary

AK-47: Assault rifle used by NLF and DRV forces.
APC: Armored personnel carrier.
ARVN: Army of the Republic of Vietnam (Saigon government).
B-52: The largest U.S. Air Force bomber.
Charlie, Charles: Short for Victor Charlie; see VC.
Chicom: Chinese communist.
Chinook: The CH-47, a large cargo helicopter.
chopper: Helicopter.
Cobra: U.S. Army helicopter gunship.
CP: Command post.
DEROS: Date of expected return from overseas.
dink: Racist term for Vietnamese or other Asian.
DMZ: Demilitarized zone; established at the seventeenth parallel by the 1954 Geneva Conference to separate the forces of the French Union from those of the Democratic Republic of Vietnam. Later used by the United States to distinguish "North Vietnam" from "South Vietnam," a distinction recognized by no government in either Saigon or Hanoi.
DRV: Democratic Republic of Vietnam; government of Vietnam inaugurated in 1945, defeated the French in 1954, administered Vietnam north of the seventeenth parallel until 1975, all of Viet-

nam subsequently; referred to as North Vietnam by U.S. government and military.

F-105: U.S. Air Force jet fighter-bomber.

F-4: U.S. Air Force jet fighter-bomber; the "Phantom."

frag: To kill one's own officer, often with a fragmentation grenade.

Free Fire Zone: Area in which any person is considered hostile and U.S. forces are authorized to fire at will.

gook: Racist term for Vietnamese or other Asian.

greased: Killed.

grunt: U.S. foot soldier of low rank.

hooch: Peasant hut; by extension, any living quarters.

Huey: UH-1 combat helicopter.

KIA: Killed in action.

klick: Kilometer.

liftship: Helicopter.

LRRP (lurp): Long-range reconnaissance patrol.

LZ: Landing zone.

M-16: Standard assault rifle of U.S. forces.

MIA: Missing in action.

NLF: National Liberation Front of South Vietnam; formed in 1961 to organize armed revolution against the rule of Ngo Dinh Diem; called the "Viet Cong" by Diem government and United States.

NVA: "North Vietnamese Army"; U.S. term for armed forces of "North Vietnam" (the DRV), officially known as the People's Army of Viet Nam (PAVN). Incorrectly applied to insurgent south Vietnamese units trained and equipped in the north.

PAVN: People's Army of Viet Nam; the armed forces of the DRV.

Pentagon Papers: Top-secret Pentagon history of U.S. involvement in Vietnam, 1945-1967; leaked to the press in 1971.

PF: Popular Force; locally recruited auxiliaries for Saigon regime.

Phoenix: U.S. and Saigon government campaign designed to wipe out the NLF infrastructure through arrests, torture, and assassination.

PIO: Public information officer.

point: First man in line on patrol.

POW: Prisoner of war.

PRG: Provisional Revolutionary Government of South Viet Nam; successor to the NLF and one of the four parties to the 1973 Paris Peace Agreements.

PTSD: Post-traumatic stress disorder; severe psychological condition of many veterans.

punji stick: Sharpened stick, often dipped in human excrement, used in booby traps by the NLF.

R & R: Rest and relaxation.

RVN: Republic of Viet Nam; government in Saigon from 1954 to 1975 which claimed to be the legitimate ruler of all Vietnam.

SAC: Strategic Air Command.

SAM: Surface to air missile.

skag: Heroin.

slope: Racist term for Vietnamese or other Asian.

Tet Offensive: Massive offensive launched January 31, 1968, by the NLF and PAVN during Tet, the lunar New Year holiday.

VC: Short for Viet Cong; also Victor Charlie or Charlie.

Viet Cong: Derogatory term used by the Ngo Dinh Diem government in Saigon to denote those who had fought against French colonial rule; later used to denote the combatants of the National Liberation Front of South Vietnam.

the World: Anyplace but Vietnam, specifically the United States.

Bibliographies and Secondary Sources on Vietnam War Literature

As the vast literature about the Vietnam War grows and grows, bibliographies cannot keep pace. *Vietnam War Literature: An Annotated Bibliography of Imaginative Works about Americans Fighting in Vietnam*, 2nd edition (Metuchen, NJ: Scarecrow Press, 1988), by John Newman, is based primarily on the Vietnam War Literature Collection at Colorado State University in Fort Collins, a preeminent archival collection of fiction and poetry; its 752 listings (compared with the 226 items in the 1982 1st edition) are organized chronologically and by genre. Considerably more extensive, with 1,749 items, but still by no means comprehensive, is Sandra M. Wittman's *Writing about Vietnam: A Bibliography of the Literature of the Vietnam Conflict* (Boston: G. K. Hall, 1989); because many of its listings are based on databases, indexes, and other bibliographies rather than the original works, this volume contains quite a few errors, and of course a great deal of literature has appeared since it was compiled. A number of works not listed by Wittman appear in the far less ambitious but useful brief compilation by Deborah A. Butler, *American Women Writers on Vietnam: Unheard Voices: A Selected Annotated Bibliography* (New York: Garland, 1990). The most comprehensive bibliography of the literature is *Willson's Bibliography: War in Southeast Asia*, 3rd edition, by David A. Willson (Auburn, WA:

private printing, 1991), available from Willson at Green River Community College, Auburn, WA 98002. An excellent guide to the immense and expanding criticism is Philip K. Jason, *The Vietnam War in Literature: An Annotated Bibliography of Criticism* (Pasadena, CA, and Englewood Cliffs, NJ: Salem Press, 1992).

Besides the hundreds of novels and volumes of poetry and stories by individual authors, there are many notable collections of American Vietnam War literature. *Where Is Vietnam? American Poets Respond*, edited by Walter Lowenfels (Garden City, NY: Anchor Books, 1967), is a historic anthology of antiwar poems by eighty-seven contributors, including many of the most distinguished American poets. The two collections that introduced the achievement of the poet-veterans were *Winning Hearts and Minds: War Poems by Vietnam Veterans*, edited by Larry Rottmann, Jan Barry, and Basil T. Paquet (New York: 1st Casualty Press, 1972) and *Demilitarized Zones: Veterans after Vietnam*, edited by Jan Barry and W. D. Ehrhart (Perkasie, PA: East River Anthology, 1976). What these two volumes did for poetry was done for fiction by *Free Fire Zone: Short Stories by Vietnam Veterans*, edited by Wayne Karlin, Basil T. Paquet, and Larry Rottmann (Coventry, CT: 1st Casualty Press, 1973). Another distinguished early collection of fiction is *Writing Under Fire: Stories of the Vietnam War*, edited by Jerome Klinkowitz and John Somer (New York: Dell Publishing, 1978). W. D. Ehrhart's *Carrying the Darkness: The Poetry of the Vietnam War* (Lubbock, TX: Texas Tech University Press, 1989) has been the defining contemporary poetry anthology since its original publication in 1985. Its major shortcoming is remedied by *Visions of War, Dreams of Peace: Writings of Women in the Vietnam War*, edited by Lynda Van Devanter and Joan A. Furey (New York: Warner Books, 1991). Among specialized collections, one of the most important is *Vietnam and Black America: An Anthology of Protest and Resistance*, edited by Clyde Taylor (Garden City, NY: Anchor Books, 1973). *In the Field of Fire*, edited by Jeanne Van Buren Dann and Jack Dann (New York: Tor, 1987), is a well-selected anthology of science fiction and fantasy stories about the war. *The Vietnam Songbook*, compiled and edited by Barbara Dane and Irwin Silber (New York: The Guardian, 1969), collects more than one hundred American and international songs about the war, including seven from Vietnam. The most valuable ongoing source for literature and criticism is Viet Nam Generation in Woodbridge, CT, whose fine collections include

Swords Into Ploughshares: A "Home Front" Anthology, edited by Sandra Gurvis (1991) and *Nobody Gets Off the Bus: The Viet Nam Generation Big Book* (1994).

The most incisive book-length studies of American literature about the war include Philip Beidler's *American Literature and the Experience of Vietnam* (Athens, GA: University of Georgia Press, 1982) and *Re-Writing America: Vietnam Authors in Their Generation* (Athens, GA: University of Georgia Press, 1991); John Hellmann, *American Myth and the Legacy of Vietnam* (New York: Columbia University Press, 1986); Donald Ringnalda, *Fighting and Writing the Vietnam War* (Jackson, MS: University Press of Mississippi, 1994); and the following three important collections of essays: *Search and Clear: Critical Responses to Selected Literature and Films of the Vietnam War*, edited by William J. Searle (Bowling Green, OH: Bowling Green State University Popular Press, 1988); *America Rediscovered: Critical Essays on Literature and Film of the Vietnam War*, edited by Owen Gilman, Jr., and Lorrie Smith (New York: Garland, 1990); and *Fourteen Landing Zones: Approaches to Vietnam Literature*, edited by Philip K. Jason (Iowa City: University of Iowa Press, 1991). Excellent books focusing specifically on the poetry are James Mersmann's *Out of the Vietnam Vortex: A Study of Poets and Poetry Against the War* (Lawrence, KS: University of Kansas Press, 1974), which mainly explores the work of established poets before the veteran poets became recognized; and Vince Gotera, *Radical Visions: Poetry by Vietnam Veterans* (Athens, GA: University of Georgia Press, 1994), likely to remain the definitive work on its subject. Two important collections about visual representations are Linda Dittmar and Gene Michaud, *From Hanoi to Hollywood: The Vietnam War in American Film* (New Brunswick, NJ: Rutgers University Press, 1990), and *Inventing Vietnam: The War in Film and Television*, edited by Michael Anderegg (Philadelphia: Temple University Press, 1991). For wider discussions of the war in American culture, see Susan Jeffords, *The Remasculinization of America: Gender and the Vietnam War* (Bloomington, IN: Indiana University Press, 1989); *The Vietnam Era: Media and Popular Culture in the US and Vietnam*, edited by Michael Klein (London: Pluto Press; and Winchester, MA: Unwin Hyman, 1990); *The Vietnam War and American Culture*, edited by John Carlos Rowe and Rick Berg (New York: Columbia University Press, 1991); H. Bruce Franklin, *M.I.A. Or Mythmaking in America* (New Brunswick: Rutgers

University Press, 1993); and Elliott Gruner, *Prisoners of Culture: Representing the Vietnam POW* (New Brunswick: Rutgers University Press, 1993).

Chronology

208 B.C.   The kingdom of Nam-Viet is founded.

111 B.C.   Nam-Viet is incorporated into the Chinese empire, where it remains for more than a thousand years despite frequent rebellions.

A.D. 40–43   The Trung sisters lead an insurrection against China that is successful for three years.

544–791   Insurrections take place but fail to oust the Chinese.

939   Vietnamese take advantage of the fall of the Tang dynasty in China to end direct Chinese rule.

1010   Hanoi (then Thanglang) becomes capital of the country.

1257   The first invasion of Vietnam by the Mongolian armies of Kublai Khan, who had conquered China and much of Europe. The invaders reach the capital but are driven out.

1284   Kublai Khan launches half a million men against Vietnam, but the invasion is defeated.

1287–1288   A new Mongolian invasion is defeated by the Vietnamese.

1407–1427   Invasion and occupation by China.

1418–1427   Chinese driven out in war led by Le Loi.

1771–1802   The Tay Son movement overthrows the regimes of feudal lords and reunifies the country, driving out the Chinese.

1804   The name Viet Nam is officially adopted.

1850   The French navy attacks Da Nang, beginning the colonial conquest of Vietnam.

1883   France declares "the name of Vietnam" extinct and divides the country into Cochin China (southern), Annam (central), and Tonkin (northern).

1890   Ho Chi Minh is born. He leaves Vietnam in 1911 as a cabin boy on a merchant vessel.

1917   Russian Revolution.

1919   During the Versailles conference ending World War I, Ho Chi Minh appeals to Wilson administration for aid in securing legal and political rights.

1920   At the French Socialist Party congress, Ho Chi Minh votes with the majority that splits to form the French Communist Party.

1930   Formation of Indochinese Communist Party (ICP). Major uprisings in Tonkin and Annam.

1932   French install Bao Dai as emperor.

1940   France falls to Germany. The Japanese invade Indochina. France's pro-Nazi Vichy government turns French Indochina over to Japan but continues colonial administration in collaboration with the Japanese until 1945. Two million Vietnamese are starved to death as their rice is used to supply Japanese armies throughout Southeast Asia.

June 1941   Founding of the Revolutionary League for the Independence of Vietnam (known as the Viet Minh), which leads the fight against the French colonialists and the Japanese occupiers.

March 1945   With the Viet Minh gaining strength, Japan unilaterally ends French rule in Indochina and establishes "independent" Vietnam under Emperor Bao Dai.

July–August 1945 At the Potsdam Conference, the U.S., Britain, and the Soviet Union decide that Britain will occupy Vietnam and disarm Japanese troops south of the sixteenth parallel and China will do the same north of the sixteenth parallel.

August 15, 1945 Japan surrenders.

August 18–28, 1945 Viet Minh lead "August revolution," uprisings throughout Vietnam.

August 30, 1945 Bao Dai abdicates to the Viet Minh government.

September 2, 1945 Proclamation of independence. Founding of the Democratic Republic of Vietnam (DRV). In mid-September, British General Douglas Gracey lands, rearms Japanese and French colonial forces, and begins restoring French control south of the sixteenth parallel.

September 22, 1945 French troops arrive in Saigon; struggle in south begins.

October 1945 Ho Chi Minh appeals to President Harry Truman to support Vietnamese independence.

January 1946 DRV holds elections for the first National Assembly.

March 6, 1946 French sign agreement with Ho Chi Minh recognizing his government and semi-independence of Vietnam as a "Free State" in the French Union. DRV's purpose: to dislodge Chinese forces. Ho Chi Minh explains: "It is better to sniff French dung for a while than eat China's all our lives."

November 1946 The French, using U.S. ships, bombard Haiphong, killing 6,000 civilians, and invade Haiphong and Hanoi.

December 19, 1946 Viet Minh attack French forces. The war between France and the DRV has begun.

1948 Truman administration begins funding the French war.

1949 The Élysée Agreement between France and "the State of Vietnam" in March declares Vietnam's "independence" as an "associated state" within the French Union. In April, the French reinstall Bao Dai as head of state.

October 1949 The Chinese Communists proclaim the establishment of the People's Republic of China.

1950   China and the Soviet Union recognize the Democratic Republic of Vietnam headed by Ho Chi Minh. The U.S. recognizes the Bao Dai regime. Both Vietnamese governments claim sovereignty over all of Vietnam. The U.S. Military Assistance Advisory Group (MAAG) is sent to Vietnam by the Truman administration. U.S. advisers and eventually some 250 U.S. pilots participate with the French forces in the fighting, and U.S. ends up providing 80 percent of the financing of the French war.

1954

March 13   Battle of Dien Bien Phu begins.

April 16   Vice President Richard Nixon publicly proposes sending U.S. troops to Vietnam.

May 7   Fall of Dien Bien Phu to DRV army.

May 8-July 21   Geneva Conference. Ends with agreement that all foreign forces will be withdrawn from Vietnam; seventeenth parallel set as temporary demarcation line between forces of the French Union and those of the DRV; Vietnam to hold internationally supervised elections in 1956 to choose government of the entire country.

June 1   Colonel Edward Lansdale arrives in Saigon to set up the Saigon Military Mission and coordinate covert attacks on DRV.

June 16   Bao Dai, as head of the State of Vietnam, appoints Ngo Dinh Diem as his premier.

July 1   Ngo Dinh Diem arrives in Saigon.

September 8   U.S. arranges the creation of the Southeast Asia Treaty Organization (SEATO), consisting of the U.S., Britain, France, Australia, New Zealand, Pakistan, Thailand, and the Philippines, and mandating the "collective defense" of Laos, Cambodia, and the "State of Vietnam."

October 23   President Eisenhower pledges to Ngo Dinh Diem that U.S. will support his regime as "the Government of Vietnam" (the entire country).

1955-1956   Ngo Dinh Diem gains control over Saigon, rejects national elections guaranteed by the Geneva Accords, defeats Bao Dai in a rigged election in the south, proclaims the Republic of Vietnam with himself as president, and begins repression of those who had fought with the Viet Minh. U.S. finances his government and trains and equips his security police and the Army of the Republic of Vietnam (ARVN).

1956–1959   Terror campaign extends Saigon's rule over the countryside. Creation of "agrovilles" or "strategic hamlets."

1959   Diem's Law 10/59 legitimizes massive repression. Scattered resistance breaks out.

December 1960   Formation of the National Liberation Front of South Vietnam (NLF), which Saigon and Washington call the "Viet Cong." NLF begins full-scale revolution against Diem regime.

1961   President John F. Kennedy approves secret military plan for Vietnam and Laos, including covert war against North Vietnam, and Special Forces covert operations in Laos and South Vietnam. U.S. begins chemical defoliation in South Vietnam ("Operation Hades," later "Operation Ranch Hand"). U.S. military personnel increased to more than 3,000.

1962   Establishment of U.S. Military Assistance Command, Vietnam (MACV). U.S. military personnel increased to more than 11,000.

1963

> *May–August*   Buddhist demonstrations violently repressed by Saigon government.

> *August–October*   U.S. ambassador Henry Cabot Lodge plans with Washington and ARVN generals to overthrow Ngo Dinh Diem.

> *November 1–2*   Generals stage coup, assassinating Diem and his brother Ngo Dinh Nhu, head of the secret police.

> *November 22*   President Kennedy is assassinated; Lyndon B. Johnson becomes president.

> *November 26*   President Johnson issues NSAM 273, secret plan for a full-scale U.S. war in Vietnam.

> U.S. military personnel now between 16,000 and 19,000.

1964

> *February 1*   U.S. Operations Plan 34A (Oplan 34-A) is imple-

mented, including raids by mercenaries and Saigon comman-
dos on North Vietnamese coastal installations.

June General William Westmoreland becomes head of MACV;
General Maxwell Taylor replaces Lodge as ambassador.

August 2 U.S. destroyer *Maddox* fires on North Vietnamese PT
boats responding to an Oplan 34-A raid on coastal islands.

August 4 U.S. claims, despite lack of evidence, that the destroy-
ers *Maddox* and *C. Turner Joy* were attacked on the high seas
for four hours by North Vietnamese PT boats. President
Johnson orders "retaliatory" aerial bombing of North Vietnam.

August 7 Congress passes—with only two dissenting votes—the
Gulf of Tonkin Resolution, giving the president virtually un-
limited power to conduct war in Southeast Asia.

September–November President Johnson, successfully campaigning to be elected president, repeatedly promises that he will
never send "American boys" to fight in Vietnam.

December U.S. military personnel number more than 23,000.

1965

February 7 NLF attack U.S. forces at Pleiku.

February 8 "Retaliatory" bombing of North Vietnam.

February 27 U.S. White Paper alleges that war in South Vietnam
is not indigenous, but a North Vietnam campaign of aggression.

March 2 Operation Rolling Thunder, the sustained U.S. bombing of North Vietnam, begins; continues until October 31,
1968.

March 8 U.S. Marines, the first officially acknowledged combat
units, go ashore at Da Nang to join the 24,000 U.S. military
personnel already in Vietnam.

March–June Antiwar teach-ins on many U.S. campuses.

April 17 Twenty-five thousand people march in Washington
against the war.

June The eighth military government since the overthrow of
Diem comes to power in Saigon, headed by Air Vice Marshal
Nguyen Cao Ky and General Nguyen Van Thieu.

October–November   Large antiwar demonstrations in Washington and forty other U.S. cities.

December   U.S. military personnel number more than 184,000.

1966   By year end, General Westmoreland commands over one million troops, including 385,000 Americans. During 1966, more than 5,000 Americans are killed and more than 30,000 wounded.

1967   Huge antiwar demonstrations take place throughout the year. More than 9,000 Americans are killed in Vietnam and close to 100,000 are wounded. By the fall, U.S. troop strength is close to half a million, and the forces under U.S. command number more than 1.3 million.

> *April 4*   Martin Luther King, Jr., denounces the war and calls the U.S. government "the greatest purveyor of violence in the world today."

> *November 21*   General Westmoreland, called back home to do public relations, tells the nation that "the enemy's hopes are bankrupt," his forces are "declining at a steady rate," and soon the South Vietnamese army will "take charge of the final mopping up of the Vietcong."

1968

> *January 30–February 24*   The Tet Offensive: NLF and PAVN launch simultaneous attacks on all U.S. military bases in Vietnam and 110 cities and towns in South Vietnam.

> *March 1*   Frenzied buying of gold, which breaks through the $35-an-ounce price held since 1934.

> *March 12*   Antiwar senator Eugene McCarthy comes close to beating President Johnson in the New Hampshire Democratic primary.

> *March 16*   Antiwar senator Robert Kennedy enters presidential race.

> *March 16*   U.S. soldiers massacre hundreds of villagers in My Lai.

> *March 22*   Announcement that General Westmoreland is being relieved of his command.

> *March 31*   President Johnson announces a partial halt of the bombing of North Vietnam and withdraws from the presidential race.

April 4   Martin Luther King, Jr., is assassinated.

April 4–11   Riots and rebellions in 125 U.S. cities; Army reserves called up.

May 10   Peace talks between U.S. and DRV open in Paris.

June 4–5   Robert Kennedy wins Democratic primary in California, with 88 percent of the votes going to him and rival antiwar candidate McCarthy. That night Kennedy is assassinated in Los Angeles.

July 5   U.S. Marines, proclaiming a major victory, withdraw under fire from the formerly besieged base of Khe Sanh.

August 5–8   Republican convention in Miami Beach nominates Richard Nixon, who pledges that he will end the Vietnam War as soon as he takes office. A line of tanks has sealed off Miami Beach from the riots taking place in Miami.

August 26–29   Democratic convention in Chicago nominates Vice President Hubert Humphrey, although he has won only 2.2 percent of the delegates in the state primaries, which were swept by McCarthy and Kennedy. Outside, police battle antiwar demonstrators.

November 5   Richard Nixon is elected president.

1969

January   NLF and Saigon government join the peace talks.

January–June   President Nixon and H. Ross Perot secretly plan a massive POW/MIA campaign to build support for continuing the war.

February   U.S. troops attack in Laos (Operation Dewey Canyon I).

March   U.S. forces in Vietnam peak at 541,000.

May 8   The NLF puts forward its ten-point position at the Paris negotiations.

May 14   In a televised speech, President Nixon presents his eight-point negotiating position and announces the withdrawal of 25,000 U.S. troops.

June 25   The Provisional Revolutionary Government of South Vietnam (PRG) is announced.

September 2   Ho Chi Minh dies.

October 15   Millions of Americans participate in the antiwar Moratorium.

November 15   During the antiwar Mobilization, one million protesters march in Washington and San Francisco while many GIs in Vietnam, including entire units, stage antiwar demonstrations.

1970

February   Henry Kissinger and Le Duc Tho begin secret peace talks in Paris.

April 29   U.S. and ARVN troops invade eastern Cambodia.

May   Nationwide protest demonstrations erupt, during which demonstrators are shot to death by soldiers at Kent State University and by police at Jackson State College.

June 24   Senate repeals Gulf of Tonkin Resolution.

December   Congress bans U.S. combat troops from Laos and Cambodia.

1971

February–March   Dewey Canyon II: invasion of Laos by ARVN troops with U.S. air support turns into debacle.

April   As part of a massive antiwar demonstration in Washington, Vietnam veterans stage Dewey Canyon III, during which several hundred throw their medals and ribbons at the Capitol.

June   *New York Times* begins serial publication of the *Pentagon Papers*, the top-secret Pentagon history of the Vietnam War.

October   Nguyen Van Thieu, running unopposed, is elected president of South Vietnam.

1972

February   President Nixon visits China.

March–May   Major offensive by insurgent forces in South Vietnam.

May   Nixon orders mining of Haiphong harbor.

June   Nixon's "plumbers" are apprehended during burglary of Democratic headquarters in the Watergate hotel.

October   Kissinger and Le Duc Tho reach agreement on peace terms; Nixon announces peace is at hand; Thieu rejects terms.

November   Nixon wins reelection in landslide.

December 13   Peace talks break down when Le Duc Tho rejects changes in agreement demanded by Thieu.

December 18–31   Operation Linebacker II: the massive "Christmas bombing" of Hanoi and Haiphong during which many B-52s and other planes are shot down.

December 26   Peace talks resume, leading essentially to reinstatement of October agreement.

1973

January 27   Peace agreement, signed by U.S., DRV, RVN, and PRG, implements almost the entire 1969 NLF ten-point position.

February 1   In a secret letter to Hanoi's Prime Minister Pham Van Dong, Nixon pledges over $4 billion of U.S. aid to North Vietnam.

March   The last U.S. combat troops are withdrawn from Vietnam. The last U.S. POWs are released; they are made the heroes of the war in the Nixon administration's Operation Homecoming. U.S. draft ends.

July   Congress bans funds for U.S. combat in Indochina.

November   Congress passes War Powers Act over presidential veto.

1974

January–May   Cease-fire breaks down; Saigon launches major offensive.

May   House Judiciary Committee begins impeachment hearings.

August–September   Nixon resigns. He is replaced by Gerald Ford, whom he had appointed vice president after Vice President Spiro Agnew resigned in 1973 while being indicted for several felonies for which he was later convicted. Ford pardons Nixon for any and all crimes he may have committed while president.

1975

January–April   Major offensive by NLF and PAVN. Saigon's army collapses. Thieu resigns.

April 30   Saigon surrenders to the revolutionary forces. Last U.S. personnel leave in emergency helicopter airlift from the roof of the U.S. embassy.

May 16   U.S. imposes trade embargo on Vietnam.

1976   Vietnam is unified as the Socialist Republic of Vietnam (SRV) with Hanoi as capital. After fifteen months of hearings and investigations, the House Select Committee on Missing Persons in Southeast Asia reports that there is no credible evidence that any U.S. POWs are being held against their will in Vietnam.

1977   Khmer Rouge, now rulers of Cambodia, launch attacks on Vietnamese villages in Tay Ninh province. SRV admitted to the United Nations.

1978   Vietnam signs friendship pact with USSR in November. In December, President Jimmy Carter normalizes relations with China, while Vietnam, allied with dissident Khmer Rouge forces, invades Cambodia.

1979   In January, Vietnamese forces defeat Khmer Rouge and help install a friendly government in Cambodia. China invades northern Vietnam in February but is defeated by mid-March.

1981   President Ronald Reagan's administration begins covert operations in Laos, Thailand, and the U.S. to promote the POW/MIA issue.

1982   Vietnam War Memorial is unveiled in Washington. President Reagan sets up the POW/MIA Interagency Group with leading POW/MIA activists in key positions.

1983   On January 23, President Reagan declares that from now on the POW/MIA issue will be the "highest national priority."

1989   After eight years of fomenting the POW/MIA issue, the Reagan administration's final report on the question admits that it has found no reliable evidence of any U.S. POWs alive in Southeast Asia. Last Vietnamese troops are withdrawn from Cambodia.

1991

April 9   President George Bush announces a "road map" for full normalization of relations with Vietnam in two years.

July   Phony pictures of alleged U.S. POWs in Vietnam unleash POW/MIA media blitz.

August 2   Creation of Senate Committee on POW/MIA Affairs, which begins eighteen months of hearings.

1993

January   Senate Committee on POW/MIA Affairs releases an inconclusive final report.

July   President Bill Clinton's administration announces that it will no longer block IMF loans to Vietnam.

September   Clinton administration maintains the U.S. trade embargo against Vietnam that has been in effect since 1975 but allows U.S. companies to begin bidding on future contracts for projects in Vietnam funded by international development agencies.

1994   On February 3, President Clinton announces that he is lifting the trade embargo on Vietnam to get more "answers" about MIAs and states that "any decisions about our relationships with Vietnam should be guided by one factor and one factor only—gaining the fullest possible accounting for our prisoners of war and our missing in action."

(continued from page iv)

Balaban, John, "Along the Mekong" and "Mau Than." Copyright © 1974 by John Balaban. "In Celebration of Spring," "News Update," "For Mrs. Cam," and "After Our War" appeared in *Blue Mountain* (Unicorn Press, 1982). All poems reprinted by permission of the author.

Barry, Jan, "In the Footsteps of Genghis Khan" and "Thap Ba" from *Winning Hearts and Minds: War Poems by Vietnam Veterans*, edited by Larry Rottmann, Jan Barry, and Basil T. Paquet. Copyright © 1972 by 1st Casualty Press. Reprinted by permission of the author.

Borton, Lady, "A Boom, A Billow." Copyright © 1991 by Lady Borton. Reprinted by permission of the author.

Butler, Robert Olen, "A Good Scent from a Strange Mountain" from *A Good Scent from a Strange Mountain* by Robert Olen Butler. Copyright © 1991 by Robert Olen Butler. Reprinted by permission of Henry Holt and Company, Inc.

Carter, Ron, "Vietnam Dream" first appeared in *Four Quarters*, Spring 1976. Copyright © 1976 by Ron Carter. Reprinted by permission of the author.

Coleman, Horace, "OK Corral East / Brothers in the Nam" from *Four Black Poets* (BkMk Press, 1977). "The Adrenaline Junkie and 'The Daily Emergency.'" Copyright © 1994 by Horace Coleman. Both poems reprinted by permission of the author.

Cross, Frank A., Jr., "Gliding Baskets" from *Winning Hearts and Minds*, edited by Larry Rottmann, Jan Barry, and Basil T. Paquet. Copyright © 1972 by 1st Casualty Press. "Rice Will Grow Again" from *Demilitarized Zones: Veterans after Vietnam*, edited by Jan Barry and W. D. Ehrhart, East River Anthology, 1976. Both poems reprinted by permission of the author.

Cross, Ronald Anthony, "The Heavenly Blue Answer." Copyright © 1987 by Jeanne Van Buren Dann and Jack Dann. First published in *In the Field of Fire* (Tor Books, Tom Doherty Associates, Inc.). Reprinted by permission of the author.

Davis, George. "Ben" appeared in *Free Fire Zone: Short Stories by Vietnam Veterans*, edited by Wayne Karlin, Basil T. Paquet, and Larry Rottmann (Coventry, CT, 1st Casualty Press, 1973). Copyright © 1971 by George Davis. Reprinted by permission of the author.

Ehrhart, W. D., "Guerrilla War," "Making the Children Behave," "To Those Who Have Gone Home Tired," and "The Invasion of Grenada" reprinted from *To Those Who Have Gone Home Tired* by W. D. Ehrhart, Thunder's Mouth Press, 1984. "For Mrs. Na" reprinted from *Just for Laughs* by W. D. Ehrhart, Viet Nam Generation, Inc., & Burning Cities Press, 1990. "Guns" reprinted from *The Distance We Travel* by W. D. Ehrhart, Adastra Press, 1993. All poems reprinted by permission of the author.

Fogerty, John C., "Fortunate Son." Copyright © 1969 Jondora Music, BMI. Used by permission of Fantasy, Inc.

Fowler, Karen Joy, "The Lake Was Full of Artificial Things" appeared in *Isaac Asimov's Science Fiction Magazine*, October 1985. Reprinted by permission of the author.

Furey, Joan A., "Camouflage" reprinted from Lynda Van Devanter and Joan A. Furey, *Visions of War, Dreams of Peace* (Warner Books, 1991). Copyright © 1991 by Joan A. Furey. Reprinted by permission of the author.

Grant, Sharon, "The Best Act in Pleiku, No One Under 18 Admitted." Copyright © 1985 by Sharon (Grant) Wildwind. Reprinted by permission of the author.

Hassett, Steve, "And what would you do, ma" and "Christmas" first appeared in *Demilitarized Zones: Veterans after Vietnam*, edited by Jan Barry and W. D. Ehrhart, East River Anthology, 1976. Copyright © 1976 by Steve Hassett. Both poems reprinted by permission of the author.

Hazzard, Mary, excerpt from *Idle and Disorderly Persons* (Madrona Publishers). Copyright © 1981 by Mary Hazzard. Reprinted by permission of the author.

Huddle, David, "The Interrogation of the Prisoner Bung by Mister Hawkins and Sergeant Tree" first appeared in *Esquire*, January 1971. Copyright © 1971 by David Huddle. Reprinted by permission of the author.

Jordan, June, "To My Sister, Ethel Ennis, Who Sang 'The Star-Spangled Banner' at the Second Inauguration of Richard Milhous Nixon." Copyright © 1973 by June Jordan. Reprinted by permission of the author.

Just, Ward, "The Congressman Who Loved Flaubert" first appeared in the *Atlantic Monthly*, October, 1972. Copyright © 1972 by Ward Just. Reprinted by permission of the author.

Karlin, Wayne, "Moratorium" first published in *Swords Into Ploughshares* (Vietnam Generation/Burning Cities Press, 1991). Copyright © 1991 by Wayne Karlin. Reprinted by permission of the author. "The Last VC." Copyright © 1992, 1994 by Wayne Karlin. This first publication of this version of the story is by permission of the author.

Kettlewell, Penny, "The Coffee Room Soldier." Copyright © 1991 by Penny Kettlewell. Reprinted by permission of the author.

Komunyakaa, Yusef, "Prisoners" and "The Dead at Quang Tri" from *Dien Cai Dau*, Wesleyan University Press, 1988. Reprinted by permission of the author.

Levertov, Denise, "Prologue: An Interim" (sections i & ii) from Denise Levertov, *To Stay Alive* (New Directions Books, 1971). Copyright © 1971 by Denise Levertov Goodman. "The Pilots," "Fragrance of Life, Odor of Death," and "A Poem at Christmas, 1972, during the Terror-Bombing of North Vietnam" from Denise Levertov, *The Freeing of the Dust* (New Directions, 1975). Copyright © 1975 by Denise Levertov. All poems reprinted by permission of New Directions Publishing Corp.

Mayer, Tom, "Kafka for President" from *The Weary Falcon* by Tom Mayer. Copyright © 1967, 1971 by Tom Mayer. Reprinted by permission of Houghton Mifflin Co. and the author. All rights reserved.

McCarthy, Gerald, "War Story" 1, 8, 9, 11, 12, 16, 19, "Finding the Way Back," and "The Sound of Guns" from *Throwing the Headlines* (Vietnam Generation/Burning Cities Press, 1994). All poems reprinted by permission of the author.

McCusker, Michael Paul, "The Old Man" first appeared in *Free Fire Zone: Short Stories by Vietnam Veterans*, edited by Wayne Karlin, Basil T. Paquet, and Larry Rottmann (Coventry, CT, 1st Casualty Press, 1973). Copyright © 1973 by Michael Paul McCusker. Reprinted by permission of the author.

McDonald, Joe, "I-Feel-Like-I'm-Fixin'-to-Die Rag." Copyright © 1965, renewed 1993 by Alkatraz Corner Music/BMI. Works and music by Joe McDonald. Used by permission.

McMahon, Marilyn M., "In This Land," "Wounds of War," and "Knowing" from *Works in Progress* by Marilyn McMahon, 1988. Copyright © 1988 by Marilyn McMahon. "July 20, 1969," "Dying with Grace," and "Confession" from *Works in Progress II* by Marilyn McMahon, 1990. Copyright © 1990 by Marilyn McMahon. All poems reprinted by permission of the author.

Mirikitani, Janice, "Loving from Vietnam to Zimbabwe" reprinted from *Awake in the River, Poetry and Prose by Janice Mirikitani*, Isthmus Press, San Francisco, 1978. Reprinted by permission of the author.

Mishler, Richard M., "Ceremony" first appeared in the *Beloit Poetry Journal*, Summer 1981. Copyright © 1981 by Richard M. Mishler. Reprinted by permission of the author.

O'Brien, Tim, "The Man I Killed" from the *Things They Carried* by Tim O'Brien. Copyright © 1990 by Tim O'Brien. Reprinted by permission of Houghton Mifflin Co. / Seymour Lawrence. All rights reserved.

Paquet, Basil T., "Morning — A Death" first appeared in the *New York Review of Books*, December 18, 1969. Copyright © 1969 by Basil T. Paquet. Reprinted by permission of the author.

Pietri, Pedro, "Para la Madre de Angel Luna." Copyright © 1973 by Pedro Pietri. Reprinted by permission of Monthly Review Foundation.

Platke, Stan, "Bury the Body, Bury the Thought" first appeared in *Demilitarized Zones: Veterans after Vietnam*, edited by Jan Barry and W. D. Ehrhart, East River Anthology, 1976. Copyright © 1976 by Stan Platke. Reprinted by permission of the author.

Ritterbusch, Dale, "Search and Destroy" first appeared in *Carrying the Darkness*, edited by W. D. Ehrhart (Avon Books, 1985). Copyright © 1985 by Dale Ritterbusch. "At the Crash Site of a B-52," copyright © 1994 by Dale Ritterbusch, is to appear in *Lessons Learned*, Burning Cities Press, 1995. Both poems reprinted by permission of the author.

Rottmann, Larry, "Thi Bong Dzu" first appeared in *Free Fire Zone: Short Stories by Vietnam Veterans*, edited by Wayne Karlin, Basil T. Paquet, and Larry Rottmann (Coventry, CT, 1st Casualty Press, 1973) and is reprinted courtesy of the author. "APO 96225" and "What Kind of War?" first appeared in *Winning Hearts and Minds*, edited by Larry Rottmann, Jan Barry, and Basil T. Paquet (1t Casualty Press, 1972). "For Cissy Shellabarger, R.N., Wherever You Are," "Thanks, Guys," "A Porter on the Trail," and "The Bones of an American M.I.A." first appeared in *Voices from the Ho Chi Minh Trail: Poetry of America and Vietnam, 1965–1993* by Larry Rottmann (Event Horizon Press, 1993). All poems reprinted by courtesy of the author.

Sadler, Barry, and Robin Moore, "The Ballad of the Green Berets."